# Transformative Education
# in Contemporary Ireland

# Transformative Education in Contemporary Ireland

## Leadership • Justice • Service

## Edited by Thomas G. Grenham

PETER LANG

Oxford • Bern • Berlin • Bruxelles • New York • Wien

Bibliographic information published by Die Deutsche Nationalbibliothek.
Die Deutsche Nationalbibliothek lists this publication in the Deutsche National-
bibliografie; detailed bibliographic data is available on the Internet at
http://dnb.d-nb.de.

A catalogue record for this book is available from the British Library.

Library of Congress Control Number: 2017945166

Cover image: iStock by Getty Images.

Cover design by Peter Lang Ltd.

ISBN 978-3-0343-1949-2 (print)  •  ISBN 978-1-78707-635-8 (ePDF)
ISBN 978-1-78707-636-5 (ePub)  •  ISBN 978-1-78707-637-2 (mobi)

© Peter Lang AG, International Academic Publishers, Bern 2018
Wabernstrasse 40, CH-3007 Bern, Switzerland
info@peterlang.com, www.peterlang.com, www.peterlang.net

This publication has been peer reviewed.

Printed in Germany

*In loving memory and appreciation of
Michael Joe Grenham and Teresa Scully, née Grenham,
and deep gratitude to Maureen for her enduring, kind presence.*

# Contents

viii

# Acknowledgements

This collection aims to commemorate and celebrate the educational values and ethos of All Hallows College, which was originally founded in 1842 as a missionary college by Fr John Hand. By the 1990s, the college had opened its doors to lay members of the public and it was established as an institution of higher education in 1998, later becoming a linked college of Dublin City University in 2008. At undergraduate level, students completed degree programmes in theology, philosophy, psychology and English literature and undertook postgraduate programmes in non-profit management, leadership and pastoral care, social justice, spirituality and ecology and religion, as well as research degree options. The college also established an innovative Adult Learning BA for Personal and Professional Development aimed at encouraging adults to return to education. By the time of its closure in 2016, over 3,400 students had graduated from its BA, MA and PhD programmes.

The editor is grateful for the support, encouragement and expertise of the faculty in All Hallows College, Dublin City University and all the adjunct faculty and staff associated with All Hallows College. In particular, the editor is grateful to the senior management team, the president of All Hallows Rev. Dr Patrick McDevitt, the vice-president for operations, Mary McPhillips, the bursar John Keaveney, and the Dean of Faculty Dr Andrew O'Regan. Special thanks and appreciation to Dr Sheena Hyland, who offered wise comments and helpful advice on the manuscript. The editor is grateful for the financial support for this project from the All Hallows Trust, which was set up after the closure of All Hallows College in 2016. This trust continues the legacy of the All Hallows College. This publication is part of that long legacy of transformative education and research since the founding of All Hallows in 1842. Special acknowledgement to my colleagues in the School of Human Development, Institute of Education at DCU for their continued encouragement and support.

Finally, the editor would like to thank Peter Lang and Christabel Scaife, commissioning editor, for her invaluable professional support and detailed editorial work throughout this project. All manuscripts need the care and attention of a copy-editor for the finer detail and helpful suggestions, great gratitude goes to Michael Garvey for his wonderful work with this volume.

ANNE LOONEY

# Foreword

Michael D. Higgins, President of Ireland, is much given to referencing the exhortation of Raymond Williams that, in times of change, we should endeavour to be the arrow rather than the target. From addresses to groups of young people, to letters to children to gatherings of international media, he has drawn again and again on this powerful call to act rather than be acted upon.

This collection of essays and reflections is for and by those who have chosen to be arrows rather than targets. All Hallows College in Dublin was founded by Fr John Hand in 1842, in the spirit of the archer, to send Irish men to the world as Catholic priests, to go, to do and to teach across the world. In its more recent work, the college espoused the three core values of leadership, justice and service and these essays reflect those values as they found expression in the educational work of All Hallows during its final years as a higher education institution before its closure on 30 November 2016.

The essays document a range of educational transformations, from the interpersonal to the structural, from a wide range of perspectives. As is the case with most contemporary analyses of how Ireland is attempting to come to terms with a new way of being itself, to draw on the words of the introduction by the editor, there is no neat conclusion. The comfort of coherence is not offered; the challenge of contradiction and contestation is. Thus the collection also shows that leadership, justice, and service are not easy platitudes; rather, they are demanding concepts that require interrogation and reconceptualization for a new and more complex Ireland.

A number of the authors draw comparisons between the values of leadership, justice and service and what they see as the economic imperatives driving contemporary education reform, particularly in the higher education sector. For many of those working and studying in All Hallows, the college represented an alternative to this imperative, providing quality higher education programmes with explicit reference to leadership, justice and service and a strong tradition of work placement in the informal and voluntary sector for students and graduates. Dublin City University (DCU), which awarded the All Hallows degrees, including the innovative ALBA programme discussed in one of the chapters, now occupies the site of the All Hallows campus. Is that occupation simply a matter of real estate? Can the spirit of All Hallows 'occupy' a globally ranked higher education institution (HEI)? As a relatively new appointee to DCU, I'd like to think that, of all the HEIs in Ireland, DCU is the best hope to continue what was begun in All Hallows. DCU aspires to a vision of higher education that is transformative not just of economies but of people and communities. These goals are not mutually exclusive. Reconciling them is the challenge, and the struggle for all who believe that higher education is a critical site for the interrogation and reconceptualization of leadership, justice and service for our changing country and a changing world. These essays are part of that project.

All education systems are future-focused; those who work in education prepare current and subsequent generations for what is to come. Transformations are underway. We live in a maelstrom of arrows and targets. As educators, we choose to be arrows, committing not just to agency, but to the 'wisdom, openness and creative innovation' proposed by President Higgins in his address to the Pontifical Irish College on 22 May 2017 in Rome:

> Let us recognize the new realities – demographic, cultural, environmental – that will shape our future and respond to them with wisdom, openness, creative innovation, and with confidence exploring the connections of science, technology and yes, ethics and philosophy too. The simplistic solutions put forward by the voices of fear and cultural entrenchment are ones that are not fit for a world that requires more, not less, understanding of complexity, more, not less, cooperation, and more, not less, concerted action on the common issues that concern all those who dwell on this Earth.

THOMAS G. GRENHAM

# Introduction
# Education as Transformative and the Future of Irish Society

## Vision

Ireland's education system is changing rapidly. We are moving towards a genuinely pluralistic society, one that embraces human diversity and which offers both an opportunity and a challenge for transformative education. Ireland is undergoing a radical transformation in terms of its sense of itself as a nation as traditional narratives that shaped its past identity come under intense scrutiny. Identification with Irish nationalism and the Catholic Church no longer possess the same influence over what it means to be Irish. Today, in the post-Celtic Tiger era (from 2008 onwards), Ireland is attempting to come to terms with a new way of being itself.

This book explores transformative education in the context of a different Ireland, and the role of these forms of education on Irish culture, society, politics, religion and the economy. While education for the knowledge or 'smart' economy has been prioritized across funding agendas, the authors in this volume are interested in exploring education as a transformative enterprise, one which supports the personal and intellectual development of people.

This edited collection brings together diverse perspectives on the significance and role of transformative education in the areas of leadership, social justice and service. Challenging the current prioritization of education that primarily serves the interests of the economy, the contributors explore the social, political and personal value and nature of transformative education. This is an invaluable collection for teachers and learners, as well as the general public, interested in effective transformative education in Ireland and beyond. It brings together theoretical, reflective process and academic research with insights on the everyday professional experiences of those working in transformative educational contexts. The publication of such a volume contributes greatly therefore to research-led and practice-led teaching and learning across the spectrum of education generally. Though most of the chapters deal with third-level education, there are some chapters that deal with other, specific areas of education, such as primary-school education and adult education in a Christian faith community setting.

## Education That Is Transformative

Transformative learning involves exploring critically cultural, religious, political and economic assumptions. Exploring destructive prejudices against ourselves, others and the world around us can be a helpful way of uncovering any irrational perceptions of ourselves, others and the environment, especially irrational perceptions of those who are perceived to be 'different'. Transformative learning is inclusive of all. Such inclusion means not only learners from diverse cultures and backgrounds, but includes also all learners of various learning styles and learning challenges. The danger is that education could become commodified and fail to pay attention to the development of the human person and the value of a society as socially caring and compassionate in order to flourish with plurality and diversity. Education can be manipulated by large funding agencies and the corporate marketplace in order to acquire particular skills for the labour force, ignoring learning for its own sake. In order to provide a skilled labour force, important as it is, little attention may be given to how the person in the marketplace functions as an integral person. Education can become instrumentalized instead of addressing all aspects of being human and the potential of all learners to grow and be transformed in their lives.

This book deals with teaching and learning that is transformative in a postmodern Ireland. Postmodernism involves the critique and suspicion of 'grand' narratives of any kind that seem to impinge upon individual freedom and choice. Ireland is wrestling to understand its own evolving sense of self as a nation in a world of fragmentation and disenchantment with traditional, 'grand' narratives of education. This is of particular significance when we consider that these narratives shaped its previous identity; for example, rote learning, selection of curriculum and learning strategies, standardization of exams and assessment, and so on. Even the ethos of a school has a particular, standard narrative, be that religious or secular. There is a need for interdisciplinary and comprehensive research that facilitates teaching and learning in a changing Irish cultural and social context. This single volume does not try to do everything. It presents current research on contemporary Irish education, focusing mainly on transformative learning and education within the diverse disciplines of philosophy of education, teaching and learning methods and strategies, policy in education, history, psychology, theology, religion, philosophy, ethics and spirituality, among others. The project surveys the educational terrain in order to critique new policy and praxis and identify key challenges and opportunities in providing innovative, imaginative and cutting-edge teaching and learning for contemporary Irish society.

In the context of a holistic education that is transformative for both the individual and the community, the focus of teaching and learning is the growth and potential of every person, cognitively, affectively, aesthetically, spiritually and physically. This research will enable teachers and learners to understand and integrate into their learning and practice key themes emerging from current Irish educational research that straddles educational policy and practice and explores issues of cultural diversity and religious inclusion. The book challenges traditional assumptions of the teaching and learning community by exploring in an interdisciplinary manner how education is perceived and practised in various disciplines.

The book brings something fresh to the Irish educational debate. In its pages, qualified third-level educational specialists are collaboratively engaged in interdisciplinary reflection on their own teaching and learning, thereby making relevant and integrated research accessible to facilitate the learning and understanding of every learner. This research will be of great value to teachers and learners everywhere, especially in the context of outlining a holistic and effective education for our time. This type of education involves providing transformative leadership. Transformative education is justice-driven in the access and delivery of programmes of learning. Meeting the needs of society in providing services for human flourishing that are responsible, accountable and transparent is very important and is at the core of transformative teaching and learning. These areas (leadership, justice, service) were particular attributes of All Hallows College, Dublin, which served the community in education for many years. The chapters of this collection are a reflection of the great work carried out at the college since 1842.

The book will benefit not only the general public interested in a relevant and transformative education, but also students and teachers who wish to improve their educational vision, as well as exploring some teaching strategies, particularly the process of mentoring, to enhance their learning objectives in a changing educational environment.


## Organization of Content


In keeping with the title of the book, the content celebrates and analyses a plurality of voices and opinions on a range of issues relating to education that can transform both individuals and society. It presents interdisciplinary and multivalent perspectives. It includes a multiplicity of narratives, viewpoints and analyses within the discipline of transformative education. Religious and humanistic perspectives are included to give a flavour of different approaches to holistic education and to reflect a vision of educational pluralism that respects different voices and worldviews on the issue of education as transformative of minds and hearts and that is action-orientated for positive change.

The research is organized into related and interconnected chapters. Each chapter can be read independently. A brief introduction and summary facilitates this. The book attempts to reflect an interdisciplinary approach to transformative education, and the various contributions offer the reader a dynamic and broad perspective on the reality of education that aims to transform minds and hearts to create better citizens for the common good of all. The publication of such a volume contributes, therefore, to research-led and practice-led teaching and learning in education in Ireland and beyond.

The book is organized into three parts. Each part covers a particular issue or concern relevant to transformative education. Part I explores transformation itself and its role in leadership. Chapter 1 explores in great depth the theory of transformation, making reference to the writings of Jack Mezirow and others. Eileen Houlahan outlines Jack Mezirow's theory of transformative learning, critically reflecting on the strengths and weaknesses of the theory. She offers helpful insights into the vision of this type of learning, especially for adults.

In Chapter 2, Denis Robinson discusses the key qualities of effective leadership from a spiritual perspective. He suggests that contemporary leaders are 'charismatic and are differentiated from others' by a combination of particular personal characteristics. One such characteristic of leaders is that they should 'be willing to take risks and be prepared to engage in self-sacrifice in pursuit of the goals and aims of the group or organization'. Robinson proposes an ideal image of a leader, which is significant as good leaders should aspire to the ideal in their roles.

Chapter 3 focuses on transformation and counselling psychology. Dee McKiernan presents a scholarly account of the notion of transformation that can occur within a counselling, therapeutic and supervisory context. Great leadership can come from those who have a capacity to know the depths of themselves. Learning in the counselling and supervision context is a way to achieve powerful insights into effective leadership. The chapter concludes by stating that 'this understanding of self and increased self-awareness also links in with the notion of vocation, specifically as it pertains to the service of others'. Citing Conroy (1995a), McKiernan suggests that it is 'the privilege of companioning others' in leadership, justice and service that is important in the transformation of the individual and community. Transformative learning necessitates a mutual professional relationship in order to allow for the development of emotional intelligence.

Transformation and leadership in the Irish voluntary sector is the theme of Chapter 4. Andrew O'Regan observes that 'over the past twenty-five years or so there has been considerable growth in the number and range of educational programmes at third-level institutions aimed at the education of managers and leaders of organizations in the third, or non-profit, sector'. He takes the following approach in discussing the significance of this type of transformation and leadership: 'findings from research with individuals with experience of leading third-sector organizations are presented, then, these findings are considered in the light of particular ideas in philosophy, sociology, and leadership studies, and, finally, the implications for the provision of third-sector or non-profit management and leadership education are considered'. O'Regan concludes with the question, 'how is it possible to separate the knowledge of the practice of management from the social paradigm it has developed and upholds?' Answering this question is challenging as it involves offering appropriate postgraduate programmes that engage with the dilemma. O'Regan proposes that resolving such a question and other such dilemmas within the constraints of a postgraduate offering may not always be possible or feasible.

To conclude this section on transformation and leadership, in Chapter 5 Catherine Breathnach explores a case study in order to understand the effects of a programme of transformational learning that changes people's lives. Such a programme creates a space for learners to discover their gifts and talents for authentic leadership in the society in which they live. Breathnach 'explores the experience of the adult learning BA (ALBA) programme at All Hallows College as a case study of transformational learning in the Irish higher education context, and the challenges it experienced'. She offers a practical example of how adults can access education at a later stage in their careers and be dramatically changed by the experience and discover fresh insights and possibilities for their own personal lives and for the communities in which they live and work.

Part II deals with the issue of justice in education and the transformation that needs to occur for both the individual and society. Accessing a good education is a challenge in the contemporary world. Chapters in this section explore how education impacts on learners and their ability to transform their lives and the environment around them. In addition, these chapters consider how we come to have and use knowledge, which is essential for the creation of a just and equitable society.

Sheena Hyland, in Chapter 6, observes that 'Higher education is increasingly globalized, corporatized and entrepreneurial, and focused on employability and economics'. She discusses 'the experience of teaching in a learning environment that is rapidly vanishing from today's higher education landscape'. Hyland posits that, 'It is the "perceived needs of the economy", rather than academic or social imaginaries, which is crucial in driving change in higher education.' She concludes from her ten years of teaching experience that, 'Learning does not have to be a solitary or competitive exercise but can be re-imagined as a collaborative, novice "community of practice"'. She goes on to suggest that smaller-group learning is of critical importance and should replace large lectures of 400 or 500 students, who feel themselves to be at a great distance from the lecturer or the 'sage on the stage'. More resources will be needed in order to implement smaller learning groups that can feasibly interact with the teacher or lecturer at third level.

In Chapter 7, Ciarán Ó Mathúna examines in great detail adult learners returning to higher education and what this means for educational providers, arguing that access to education for adults is a justice issue. Ó Mathúna argues that 'such provision should therefore be founded on the principles of an adult methodological approach: andragogy, rather than pedagogy'. The chapter concludes by stating that, 'The experience of adult learners captured through the research tells us exactly the issues that helped and hindered their progression and learning. It is essential that we encourage greater debate concerning adult learners in higher education.' Ó Mathúna advocates for particular teaching strategies and learning methods in order to capture the imagination and make the most of the learning capacity of the adult in lifelong learning environments.

Chapter 8 addresses ethical education and the ability of teachers to assist learners to think for themselves, particularly in the primary-school sector. In relation to the contemporary debates about primary-school patronage and the call for ethics to be taught in schools, Gary Keogh argues that learners should not be taught what to think. Keogh suggests that, 'If we really wish to facilitate social progression, then we cannot teach in ethics classes what is or isn't right from our perspective, because that would hinder this progression. Teachers need to be careful not to allow their ethical views to seep through their practice.' The challenge illustrated here is the dilemma of teaching objectively, without the teacher's own subjective or personal views coming to the fore. This can be particularly difficult if a teacher is passionate about the subject being taught.

In Chapter 9, Mary Ivers outlines ways in which people can flourish in all sorts of situations and contexts, provided they have the necessary support systems. She states that 'my background in health and positive psychology and my experience both as a non-traditional student and as an educator in an institution that has placed great emphasis on the values of justice, leadership and service, have led to my increasing interest in the creation of the right atmosphere to support the possibility of flourishing'. She concludes by noting that 'education is central to the development of an inclusive, equal and fair society and has intrinsic and instrumental value'.

Chapter 10 describes a method of education developed by Bernard Lonergan which has a great impact on education strategies. Eugene Curran sets out to identify a model of education that uses Lonergan's methodology. That model was initiated by Maria Montessori, whose methods have been of great service to communities that have embraced the Montessori learning strategy and the transformation that it facilitates. Curran proposes 'that Maria Montessori provides a model for Lonergan's method of transformative education for personal and communal ethical responsibility'. Curran concludes that, 'The children in the Montessori room seem to be the living embodiment of Lonergan's third level of human interaction in society. Liberty, exercised through orientation or conversion and dependent on true personal relations, leads to terminal values. Activity and rest, interaction and independent work and skills involving different and combined aspects of the person are all integrated into the "work day".' Such a vision is a service to the development of a responsible and caring community or society. The methods and strategies proposed by both Lonergan and Montessori foster and sustain an ethical responsibility in the learning environment.

In Chapter 11, Gráinne Doherty observes that the highlighting of Catholic social teaching in various areas of human life and activity is a popular trend in literature on justice and transformation. Doherty explores aspects of Catholic social teaching in relation to education. She suggests that 'while the chapter will refer to some aspects of Freire's pedagogy, it will rather be to one of the great influences on his thought – the tradition of social teaching within the Catholic tradition – that it will turn in order to present one approach that could significantly help in the creating and flourishing of a value system needed for third-level education in Ireland today'. Doherty concludes that 'third-level education is in an unprecedented period of change – a change that is set only to increase in both form and pace as the *National Strategy* continues to be implemented'. The significance of Catholic social teaching is that it can be used by adherents to change themselves, others and the world for the better. It contributes another significant perspective on life-giving transformation.

Part III considers the role of transformative education in service of the community. It examines how education serves different needs of the individual and of the community. Education is not just for the individual to use for their own life and work. Learning involves moving from the self to the other. Questions are raised, such as: how does personal learning impact upon the other, who is also learning? How does individual learning serve the community? Can education serve the diverse needs of society socially as well as economically? Are educational programmes designed to serve the needs of the community? Or are postgraduate programmes particularly predominately prioritizing technical knowledge over human knowledge and insight in order to serve the ever-expanding technical, global and local marketplace?

Cora Lambert, in Chapter 12, uses a case study to explore the merits and challenges of community-based service learning at All Hallows College. The challenges and opportunities involved in integrating academic learning and community-based service are examined. Lambert suggests that, 'All Hallows College has attempted to build its programmes of study centred on developing three core values: social justice, leadership and service (All Hallows College Aisling Plan 2013–2017), with community-based service learning identified as a key learning strategy'. Lambert concludes that 'the challenge for the higher-education institute is to combine the constituent elements – academic knowledge, field placement, and theological reflection – into an embedded and transformative learning experience'. As the reader will discover, the transformative learning experience is dynamic and perhaps sometimes complex, in that it takes into consideration many of the influences being exerted on the learner.

Chapter 13 explores the transformative strategy of mentoring as a tool which is at the core of service in education. Marjorie Fitzpatrick 'addresses the importance of "mentoring" as a way of supporting transformative learning in the context of higher education. Theories of transformational learning are presented to illustrate that there are differences in how scholars view the transformation of individuals and communities.' Her conclusion is that, 'As a mentor in holistic education, there is an opportunity for the mentor to guide the learner through the interface of the mind, body and spirit, physical, emotional and spiritual dimensions'. Transformative learning occurs when effective mentoring is provided through a strategy of support grounded in a particular professional relational presence.

Thomas G. Grenham, in Chapter 14, deals with a significant aspect of transformation and service: he argues that tolerance, as a minimum, is a keystone for service in a pluralist society. Education is a service that can help transform learners of all ages to embrace acceptance and appreciation of others who are perceived to be 'different'. Grenham discusses a strategy for transformation from a religious perspective, grounded in the context of the Irish primary-school sector. The current debate about the role of religious education in Irish primary schools provides a backdrop for the development of inclusive strategies for fostering tolerance and mutual civil-mindedness in all learners. Grenham concludes with a strategy for transformation underpinned by a strategy for dialogue on the issues of religious pluralism and cultural diversity in the classroom, which is also relevant to Irish society more broadly.

Finally, in Chapter 15, Siobhán Larkin explores service in a faith-based community and the development of an adult faith. Larkin's vision of service is grounded in the Catholic tradition. She proposes that 'the major hypothesis underpinning this discourse is that the faith development of adults is fundamental to a renewed hope and dedication of members of the Church community, and has the potential to enable growth in people's own lives, and in their understanding of their mission as baptized Christians'. Critically surveying the educational theories of Thomas Groome and the psychological theories of James Fowler, Larkin offers interesting insights into how adults grow in faith and can become active members of a faith community dedicated to the service of all. Larkin concludes that adult faith development that is transformative ought to be underpinned by effective theoretical frameworks.

PART I

# Transformation and Leadership

EILEEN HOULAHAN

# 1   Transformative Learning and Jack Mezirow

## Introduction

It has been shown in scholarly research that there are many different and overlapping approaches to adult learning and education. One of the key developments and subjects of debate and research in adult education is the theory and practice of transformative learning. There is a burgeoning amount of literature being published on this subject. As a result of its increasing influence on educational theory, an understanding of transformative learning and education is essential for adult educators today. It is also a prerequisite for those who may be directors or planners of programmes for adults in the future. For the work of this chapter, it is an indispensable resource, because the implications of the transformative learning approach to adult education underpins much of its theory and research.

Transformative learning reflects a particular vision for adult education and a conceptual framework for understanding how adults learn and make meaning of their experience.[1] It is a vision of education which is much more than the communication of knowledge in that it can touch a person at intellectual, affective and spiritual levels so that their horizons, values, judgements and behaviour may be transformed into greater personal and social authenticity and commitment. It includes a process by which adults learn to think for themselves, and to question previously uncritically accepted

---

1   J. Dirkx, *Transformative Learning Theory in the Practice of Adult Education: An Overview* (1998). [Electronic Version], 1–7, 78, <http://www.coe.iup.edu/ace/PAACE%20Journal%20PDF/PDF1998/Dirkx1998.pdf>, accessed 13 November 2009.

viewpoints towards which they may have been predisposed as a result of upbringing, education, social conditioning, culture or religion. Patricia Cranton, in *Understanding and Promoting Transformative Learning: A Guide for Educators of Adults*, states that 'transformative learning has to do with making meaning out of experiences and questioning assumptions based on prior experience'.[2] She also notes how the theory has developed over more than three decades from a ten-step transition model into a complex and comprehensive description of how adult learners interpret, validate, and reformulate the meaning of their experience.[3]

There are, today, several different approaches and many developments in the field of transformative learning theory, providing a vast amount of literature on the subject. It is beyond the scope of this work to deal with all of them. I have chosen to focus on Jack Mezirow as a key theorist, because he is the seminal thinker in this area. His theory of perspective transformation is of particular interest to this research. Mezirow posits that 'a transformation theory of adult learning would have as its central focus understanding the nature of meaning perspectives and how they can be changed to allow exciting new possibilities'.[4] This concept of transformative learning is so pivotal that many of the other theorists in this field acknowledge Mezirow as one of their points of departure (Brookfield, 2000b; Cranton, 2006; Daloz, 1987, 2000; King, 2005; Merriam, Cafferella, and Baumgartner, 2007; Mezirow and Associates, 2000; Taylor, 2009).[5] One finds in the

2    P. Cranton, *Understanding and Promoting Transformative Learning: A Guide for Educators of Adults* (San Francisco, CA: Jossey-Bass, 1994, 2nd edn), 8.
3    Ibid. 35.
4    J. Mezirow, 'Preface', in J. Mezirow and Associates (eds), *Fostering Critical Reflection in Adulthood: A Guide to Transformative and Emancipatory Learning* (San Francisco, CA: Jossey-Bass, 1990c), xiii–xxi (xv).
5    See S. D. Brookfield, 'Transformative Learning as Ideology Critique', in J. Mezirow (ed.), *Learning as Transformation: Critical Perspectives on a Theory in Progress* (San Francisco, CA: Jossey-Bass, 2000b), 125–50; P. Cranton, *Understanding and Promoting Transformational Learning: A Guide for Educators of Adults* (San Francisco, CA: Jossey-Bass, 2006); L. A. Daloz, *Effective Teaching and Mentoring: Realizing the Transformational Power of Adult Learning Experience* (San Francisco, CA: Jossey-Bass, 1987); L. A. Daloz, 'Transformative Learning for the Common Good',

literature that the majority of theorists are either expanding on Mezirow, reiterating him or critiquing him. Cranton, for instance, acknowledges that she essentially follows Mezirow's definition of transformative learning:

> Essentially, I follow Mezirow's (2000, 2003a) definition of transformative learning as a process by which previously uncritically assimilated, beliefs, values and perspectives are questioned and thereby become more open, permeable, and better validated.[6]

Developments in the area of transformative learning are ongoing. It has been described as 'a theory in progress'[7] and it has become 'the dominant teaching paradigm discussed within the field of adult education'.[8] International conferences on transformative learning theory are held periodically.

## The Vision of Jack Mezirow

The ongoing development of transformative learning theory, particularly the transformative dimensions of adult learning, has been greatly influenced by, and owes much to, the research and writings of Jack Mezirow, an emeritus professor of adult and continuing education at Teachers College,

---

in J. Mezirow (ed.), *Learning as Transformation: Critical Prespectives on a Theory in Progress* (San Francisco, CA: Jossey-Bass, 2000), 103–24; K. P. King, *Bringing Transformative Learning to Life* (Malabar, FL: Krieger Publishing Company, 2005); S. B. Merriam, R. S. Cafferella and L. M. Baumgartner, 'Transformational Learning', in *Learning in Adulthood: A Comprehensive Guide* (San Francisco, CA: Jossey-Bass, 2007), 130–58; J. Mezirow and Associates, *Learning as Transformation: Critical Perspectives on a Theory in Progress* (San Francisco, CA: Jossey-Bass, 2000); E. W. Taylor, 'Fostering Transformative Learning', in J. Mezirow, E. W. Taylor and Associates (eds), *Transformative Learning in Practice: Insights from Community, Workplace, and Higher Education* (San Francisco, CA: Jossey-Bass, 2009), 3–17.

6    Cranton, *Understanding and Promoting Transformational Learning*, 2.
7    Mezirow and Associates, *Learning as Transformation*.
8    Mezirow and Taylor, *Transformative Learning in Practice*, xi.

Columbia University, USA.[9] The evolution of transformative learning can be traced from the seminal research introduced by Mezirow in 1978 in his article 'Perspective Transformation' in *Adult Education Quarterly*.[10] Since then, the notion of 'transformative learning' has continued to be a subject of research and of theory building in the area of adult education. Writing about the introduction of the concept of transformative learning into the sphere of adult education, Mezirow states:

> The concept of transformative learning was introduced in the field of adult educa-
> tion in 1978 in an article that I entitled 'Perspective Transformation', published in
> the American journal *Adult Education Quarterly*. The article urged the recognition
> of a critical dimension of learning in adulthood that enables us to recognize and reas-
> sess the structure of assumptions and expectations which frame our thinking, feeling
> and acting. These structures of meaning constitute a 'meaning perspective' or frame
> of reference ... The research base for the concept evolved out of a comprehensive
> national study of women returning to community colleges in the United States.[11]

Mezirow initially describes a learning cycle of ten stages or movements. He regards this movement along a maturity gradient as a form of eman-cipatory learning. He was influenced in the development of his thinking by the emancipatory paradigms in the writings of Jürgen Habermas[12] and Paulo Freire.[13] Acknowledging the influence of Habermas, Mezirow states:

> The work of Jürgen Habermas (1984) was a major influence on Transformation
> Theory ... In particular, Habermas's delineation of the concepts of communica-
> tive competence and instrumental learning as the major domains of learning; the

---

9   J. Mezirow, 'Perspective Transformation', *Adult Education Quarterly*. 28 (2) (1978),
    100–10; J. Mezirow, *Transformative Dimensions of Adult Learning* (San Francisco,
    CA: Jossey-Bass, 1991); Mezirow and Associates, *Learning as Transformation*;
    Mezirow, Taylor and Associates, *Transformative Learning in Practice*.

10  See Mezirow, 'Perspective Transformation'.

11  J. Mezirow, 'An Overview on Transformational Learning', in K. Illeris (ed.),
    *Contemporary Theories of Learning* (New York: Routledge, 2009a), 90.

12  See J. Habermas, *The Theory of Communicative Action: Reason and Rationalization
    of Society*, trans. T. McCarthy, vol. 1 (Boston, MA: Beacon Press, 1984).

13  P. Freire, *Pedagogy of the Oppressed*, trans. M. Bergman Ramos (London: Penguin,
    1996, new revised edn).

recognition of the central role of discourse in validating beliefs; the idea of reflection as a form of self-formation that emancipates as it dissolves the constraining spell of unexamined beliefs – all became building blocks for Transformation Theory.[14]

Of Freire's impact, Mezirow says that although the context was different, 'our understanding of transformative learning was influenced by that of 'concientization', as described by Paulo Freire in his influential *Pedagogy of the Oppressed* (1970).[15] It is Mezirow's opinion that 'Freire not only identifies the development of a critical consciousness as a prerequisite for liberating personal development and social action, but he casts adult education in the role of catalyst' for emancipatory learning.[16]

In 'Transformative Learning: Insights from Adult Education', in *Toward an Adult Church*, Jane Regan comments on Mezirow's view of emancipatory learning, expressing the opinion that:

> Emancipatory learning involves critical reflection through which we are able to recognise inherent distortions, limitations, and narrowness of vision. Emancipatory learning is at the heart of transformative learning and essential to the various expressions of genuinely adult education.[17]

Key notions from Mezirow's work are important for an understanding of transformative learning, and, as a consequence, important for supporting the thesis that education can be transformative. The following sections of this chapter will outline the central dynamic of transformative learning, as presented in Mezirow's ten phases of perspective transformation. These phases are the founding principles of transformative learning. To enhance the understanding of these phases, some of the main recurring terms and themes in Mezirow's theory will then be examined. Finally, I shall look at some of the critiques of Mezirow's approach in order to further support

---

14    Mezirow and Associates, *Learning as Transformation*, xiii.
15    Ibid.
16    Mezirow, 'Perspective Transformation', 103.
17    J. E. Regan, *Towards an Adult Church: A Vision of Faith Formation* (Chicago: Loyola Press, 2002a), 78.

the vision of transformative learning and to identify some areas for the
further development of Mezirow's theory.

## Mezirow's Ten Phases of Personal Perspective Transformation

As a consequence of his research into the study of women returning to college after an extended time gap, Mezirow identified a process of personal
perspective transformation that includes ten phases.[18] He found that, in
essence, perspective transformation often follows some variation of the
following ten phases:

1. A disorientating dilemma;
2. Self-examination with feelings of fear, anger, guilt or shame;
3. A critical assessment of assumptions;
4. Recognition that one's discontent and the process of transformation
   are shared;
5. Exploration of options for new roles, relationships and actions;
6. Planning a course of action;
7. Acquiring the knowledge and skills for implementing one's plans;
8. Provisional trying of new roles;
9. Building competence and self-confidence in new roles and relationships;
10. A reintegration into one's life on the basis of conditions dictated by
    one's new perspective.

Mezirow contends that these ten phases do not necessarily follow sequen-
tially, in this particular order, but indicate a pattern of development in
which meaning becomes clarified.[19] These ten phases, devised by him in
1978, are part of the process of transformative learning theory development that continues to this day. The elements of transformation have not

---

18    See Mezirow, *Transformative Dimensions of Adult Learning*, 167–9, and Mezirow
      and Associates, *Learning as Transformation*, 22.
19    Mezirow, *Transformative Dimensions of Adult Learning*, 192.

changed in Mezirow's theory and continue to be an enormous influence in all contexts of transformative learning for adults.

## *1. A Disorientating Dilemma*

The first phase is that of experiencing 'a disorientating dilemma' – an experience which does not fit a person's existing meaning structure:

> Perspective transformation occurs in response to an externally imposed disorientating dilemma – a divorce, death of a loved one, change in job status, retirement, or other. The disorientating dilemma may be evoked by an eye-opening discussion, book, poem, or painting or by one's efforts to understand a different culture that challenges one's presuppositions. Anomalies and dilemmas of which old ways of knowing cannot make sense become catalysts or 'trigger events' that precipitate critical reflection and transformations.[20]

Patricia Cranton, an associate of Mezirow, is of the opinion that the 'trigger' occurrence which acts as a catalyst for transformational learning may also be a cumulative set of events or experiences which, over a period of time, challenge the existing perspective of the learner.[21] Mezirow concurs with this, stating that, 'Transformations may be *epochal* – sudden major reorientations in habit of mind, often associated with significant life crises – or *cumulative*, a progressive sequence of insights resulting in changes of point of view leading to a transformation in habit of mind'.[22]

## *2. Self-Examination with Feelings of Fear, Anger, Guilt or Shame*

Experiences of disorientating dilemmas can be both challenging and painful. They normally have an affective dimension, which motivates the learner

---

20   J. Mezirow, 'How Critical Reflection Triggers Transformative Learning', in *Fostering Critical Reflection in Adulthood: A Guide to Transformative and Emancipatory Learning* (San Francisco, CA: Jossey-Bass, 1990b), 1–20 (13–14).

21   Cranton, *Understanding and Promoting Transformational Learning* (2006), 36.

22   Mezirow, 'An Overview on Transformational Learning', 95.

to engage in self-examination and the processing of their emotional reactions. Mezirow states: 'These challenges are painful; they often call into question deeply held personal values and threaten our very sense of self'.[23] The learner might feel a resistance to change, augmented by the fear of the consequences of letting go of long-held beliefs to accommodate a new perspective. Consequently, 'even when we suspect that something might be wrong with how we see ourselves or the world around us, it is hard to admit that, let alone bring it out into the open and turn it around and look at it from different angles'.[24] It is evident, then, that a supportive and encouraging learning environment is important during this phase.

## 3. A Critical Assessment of Assumptions

Self-examination by the learner leads to the third phase, during which previously held assumptions and presuppositions are questioned and critically assessed. This involves examining the assumptions that have bolstered the perspectives and understanding we have of ourselves and the world around us.[25] According to Mezirow, 'reflective learning becomes transformative whenever assumptions or premises are found to be distorting, inauthentic, or otherwise invalid'.[26] Undergoing this type of critical assessment can be difficult for the learner and Mezirow acknowledges this: 'making a critical appraisal of the assumptions underlying our roles, priorities and beliefs is usually tension producing and can be acutely threatening'.[27] He also notes that the process of transformation includes 'reflecting critically on the source, nature and consequences of relevant assumptions – our own and others'.[28] The critical theorist Stephen Brookfield concurs with Mezirow, stating that 'thinking critically – reflecting on the assumptions underlying ours and others' ideas and actions, and contemplating alternative ways of

---

23    Mezirow, *Transformative Dimensions of Adult Learning*, 168.
24    Cranton, *Understanding and Promoting Transformational Learning* (2006), 64.
25    J. Regan, 'Transformative Learning: Insights from Adult Education', in *Towards an Adult Church*, 89.
26    Mezirow, *Transformative Dimensions of Adult Learning*, 6.
27    Mezirow, 'Perspective Transformation', 105.
28    Mezirow, 'An Overview on Transformational Learning', 94.

thinking and living – is one of the important ways in which we become adults'.[29] This critical assessment of assumptions is not only an individual experience; it also has a communal aspect.

### 4. Recognition that One's Discontent and the Process of Transformation Are Shared

There is a social dimension to the process as the learner, through 'reflective discourse', begins to recognize that other learners have faced similar disorientating dilemmas and challenges to their assumptions, and have worked through them to achieve transformed perspectives:

> Transformative learning involves participation in constructive discourse to use the experience of others to assess reasons justifying these assumptions ... Transformative learning has both individual and social dimensions and implications. It demands that we be aware of how we come to our knowledge and as aware as we can be about the values that lead us to our perspectives.[30]

Engaging in dialogue, conversation and more formal reflective discourse is central to the process of transformation. We need to engage in conversation with others in order to consider alternative perspectives, other points of view and other worldviews. We also need to engage with others in order to test and validate emerging perspectives.[31] Critical thinking and the capacity to question assumptions is significant for learning. Learning to interpret and reinterpret information can result in new insights into lived experiences. Such a process can be very meaningful for the learner and can help the learner achieve a certain wisdom regarding their own experiences, as well as the world around them. Eventually, the learner may make changes to how they think, feel and act in their environments.

---

29  S. D. Brookfield, *Developing Critical Thinkers: Challenging Adults to Explore Alternative Ways of Thinking and Acting* (Milton Keyes, UK: Open University Press, 1987), x.

30  J. Mezirow, 'Learning to Think Like an Adult': Core Concepts of Transformation Theory', in J. Mezirow (ed.), *Learning as Transformation: Critical Perspectives on a Theory in Process* (San Francisco, CA: Jossey-Bass, 2000), 8.

31  Cranton, *Understanding and Promoting Transformative Learning* (2006), 36.

## 5. Exploration of Options for New Roles, Relationships, and Actions

Having become critically aware of how and why previously held assumptions may have become constraints to the way in which they perceive, understand and feel about their world, learners engage in exploring options 'to make possible a more inclusive, discriminating and integrative perspective'.[32] This could include considering a career change, an evaluation of the learner's lifestyle or reflection by the learner on their relationships with a view to change and future action.[33] The use of imagination by the learner can be a powerful learning tool during this phase, resulting in a variety of options to be explored and possibly pertinent action.

## 6. Planning a Course of Action

As evident in the previous phase, 'action is an integral and indispensable component of transformative learning'.[34] The learner now has the opportunity to reflect further and to begin planning what actions are needed to put the new perspective into practice. 'All transformative learning involves taking action to implement insights derived from critical reflection'.[35] Cranton is convinced that 'the educator has a role in supporting actions arising out of transformative experiences. One way of supporting actions is to help students learn to develop and implement action plans.'[36]

## 7. Acquiring the Knowledge and Skills for Implementing One's Plans

Ways must now be found to acquire the knowledge and skills necessary to implement the proposed action plans. Implementing 'reflective insights

---

32    Mezirow, *Transformative Dimensions of Adult Learning*, 167.
33    Mezirow, 'Perspective Transformation', 102.
34    Mezirow, *Transformative Dimensions of Adult Learning*, 209.
35    Ibid. 225.
36    Cranton, *Understanding and Promoting Transformative Learning* (2006), 171.

often involves overcoming situational, emotional, and informational constraints that may require new learning experiences in order to move forward.'[37] Together with academic knowledge, skills may also need to be learnt in the areas of communication, assertiveness, decision-making and interpersonal relationships.[38] A holistic, interdisciplinary approach to learning is important during this phase.

## 8. Provisional Trying of New Roles

In this phase, provision is made for experimentation since 'implementing needed action may require trials and role testing.'[39] New learning and changed perspectives can lead to new opportunities and a desire to try to fill new roles in society. During this phase, 'we "try on" the new lenses to see how they fit and how well we can see with them'.[40] Mature students may consider trying new career options as a result of their studies. Pastoral and job placements form part of some degree and training programmes. 'These programmes provide a protected staging area in which to gain confidence … as a needed first step towards assuming new career and interpersonal roles upon completion of the programme'.[41]

## 9. Building Competence and Self-Confidence in New Roles and Relationships

The 'self-confidence needed for perspective transformation is often gained through an increased sense of competency and through a supportive social climate in which provisional tries are encouraged with minimum risk'.[42]

---

37  Mezirow, 'Learning to Think Like an Adult', 24.
38  Mezirow, 'Perspective Transformation', 102.
39  Ibid. 105.
40  Regan, *Towards an Adult Church*, 93.
41  Mezirow, 'Perspective Transformation', 102.
42  Ibid. 107.

Competence and self-confidence in new roles grow as the learners share their new perspectives and practise new skills in lived situations, helped by one or more sustaining relationships. 'This sustaining relationship can be provided by others in a political party, a women's movement, a religion, a learning group or by a friend, therapist or educational mentor.'[43] Subsequent reflection on the trial experience, through reflective discourse with tutors and companion learners, can affirm the learner and further build self-confidence.

*10. A Reintegration into One's Life on the Basis of Conditions Dictated by One's New Perspective*

In this phase, the learner makes a decision to live what they have come to believe through their new perspective until they 'encounter new evidence, argument or a perspective that renders this orientation problematic and requires reassessment'.[44] This requires the learner to live authentically: 'The authenticity of a learner's interests is measured by their congruence with the learner's self-concept or concept of the good life'.[45] This may also require the learner to venture into previously unknown territories. Kathleen P. King observes:

> Some people describe the final step as standing at the edge of a cliff, then stepping away from the support of the cliffside, and entering the unknown. While having growing confidence in the new perspective, and having experienced the roles in other settings, individuals face many unknown repercussions when putting their decisions into action in their daily lives. For learners who take the risk it may be a time of great hesitation and also great courage.[46]

Mezirow's ten-phase approach to transformative learning can be summarized by a model that contains four main components: 'experience,

---

43    Ibid. 105.
44    Mezirow, 'An Overview on Transformational Learning', 94.
45    Mezirow, *Transformative Dimensions of Adult Learning*, 226.
46    King, *Bringing Transformative Learning to Life*, 15–16.

critical reflection, reflective discourse, and action'.[47] In *Transformative Dimensions of Adult Learning*, Mezirow elaborates on perspective transformation as:

> the process of becoming critically aware of how and why our assumptions have come to constrain the way we perceive, understand, and feel about our world; changing these structures of habitual expectation to make possible a more inclusive, discriminating, and integrative perspective; and, finally, making choices or otherwise acting upon these new understandings.[48]

For Mezirow, critical reflection, critical self-reflection, the revision of habits of mind and taking part in discourse with others are central to transformational learning:

> The two major elements of transformational learning are first, critical reflection or critical self-reflection on assumptions – critical assessment of the sources, nature and consequences of our habits of mind – and second, participating fully and freely in dialectical discourse to validate best reflective judgement.[49]

In order to more fully grasp the implications of Mezirow's ten phases, it is important to examine some of his recurring themes and terms.

## Some Key Themes in Mezirow

A number of key themes and terms emerge, recur and weave themselves through Mezirow's transformative learning theory and writings. These terms are interrelated and some are used interchangeably. As we shall see, each time Mezirow defines a term, he tends to articulate it in a slightly different or in a more nuanced way.

47  Merriam, Cafferella and Baumgartner, 'Transformational Learning', 137.
48  Mezirow, *Transformative Dimensions of Adult Learning*, 167.
49  Mezirow and Associates, *Learning as Transformation*.

In the following sections, I will outline some of the basic terms and themes that continually appear and constitute important elements of Mezirow's theory. In the first and second sections, I will explore meaning perspectives and meaning schemes. I will then consider assumptions, critical reflection and rational discourse. I chose to focus on these particular elements because they develop further aspects of Mezirow's ten phases of perspective transformation.

## Meaning Perspectives/Frames of Reference/Habits of Mind or Habits of Expectation/Points of View

It is particularly important for adult educators to be aware of what adults carry with them into any learning experience. Recognition of the fact that mature students bring with them, from their past experiences, what Mezirow refers to as already established 'meaning perspectives' is crucial. Mezirow suggests that 'meaning perspectives constitute our "boundary structures" for perceiving and comprehending new data'.[50] Regan, commenting on Mezirow, writes that a '*meaning perspective* refers to the broad framework, or worldview, that serves as a lens through which new experiences are perceived and understood'.[51] A concrete example of a meaning perspective could be 'patriarchy' when it is a person's worldview or broad frame of reference.

In his writings, Mezirow continually redefines and elaborates his understanding of meaning perspectives:

> Meaning perspectives, or generalized sets of habitual expectation, act as perceptual and conceptual codes to form, limit, and distort how we think, believe, and feel and how, what, when, and why we learn.[52]

He later elaborates on his understanding of meaning perspective:

---

50    Mezirow, *Transformative Dimensions of Adult Learning*, 4–5.
51    Regan, *Towards an Adult Church*, 8.
52    Mezirow, *Transformative Dimensions of Adult Learning*, 34.

A meaning perspective is a habitual set of expectations that constitutes an orientating frame of reference that we use in projecting our symbolic models and that serves as a (usually tacit) belief system for interpreting and evaluating the meaning of experience.[53]

For Mezirow, psychological and cultural influences are predisposing factors in the formation of meaning perspectives, which are 'broad sets of predispositions resulting from psychocultural assumptions which determine the horizons of our expectations'.[54] The transformation of a meaning perspective 'is likely to involve our sense of self and always involves critical reflection upon the distorted premises sustaining our structure of expectation'.[55]

Mezirow also draws specific attention to 'frames of reference', which he understands as the meaning perspectives a person holds which are based on their assumptions and perceptions. 'A frame of reference is composed of two dimensions, a habit of mind and resulting points of view'.[56] It is important to be aware of this because people often have expectations of others without being aware of the grounding assumptions that operate as habits of mind.[57] Mezirow elaborates upon this further: 'Frames of reference are the structures of culture and language through which we construe meaning by attributing coherence and significance to our experience'.[58]

In his writings, Mezirow attempts to remedy a noticeable oversight in adult learning theory, which has resulted from a failure to appreciate the central roles played by an individual's acquired frame of reference, through which meaning is interpreted and all learning occurs, and by the transformation of these habits of expectation during the learning process.[59]

---

53   Ibid. 43.
54   J. Mezirow, 'Understanding Transformation Theory', *Adult Education Quarterly* 44 (4) (1994), 223.
55   Mezirow, *Transformative Dimensions of Adult Learning*, 167.
56   Mezirow and Associates, *Learning as Transformation*, 17.
57   J. Finnegan, 'An Introduction to Transformative Theory for Supervisors' (Milltown Institute: unpublished notes, 2009), 2.
58   Mezirow, 'An Overview on Transformational Learning', 92.
59   Mezirow, *Transformative Dimensions of Adult Learning*, 4.

He also refers to habits of expectation as 'habits of mind'. He defines habits of mind as:

> broad, abstract, orienting, habitual ways of thinking, feeling and acting, influenced by assumptions ... An example of a habit of mind is ethnocentrism, the predisposition to regard others outside one's own group as inferior, untrustworthy or otherwise less acceptable.[60]

Habits of mind/expectation may be conservative or liberal, professional-related or theory-based; they may have to do with patterns of acting (victim, perfectionist, controller) or worldviews and beliefs.[61]

Consequently, frames of reference, habits of mind and habits of expectation reflect Mezirow's theory of meaning perspectives. This is the framework from which we make value judgements:

> Meaning perspectives provide us with criteria for judging or evaluating right and wrong, bad and good, beautiful and ugly, true and false, appropriate and inappropriate. They also determine our concept of personhood, our idealised self-image, and the way we feel about ourselves.[62]

The development of an awareness of this understanding of meaning perspectives for mature students, who will normally already have internalized, often unconsciously, a value system, is part of the work of consciousness-raising by the adult educator.

*Meaning Schemes*

Meaning perspectives are closely related to what Mezirow calls 'meaning schemes'. He has defined meaning perspectives as 'sets of meaning schemes' and meaning schemes are 'specific attitudes and beliefs'.[63] A number of different meaning schemes can be contained within a meaning perspective:

---

60  Mezirow, 'An Overview on Transformational Learning', 92–3.
61  Finnegan, 'An Introduction to Transformative Theory', 2.
62  Mezirow, *Transformative Dimensions of Adult Learning*, 44.
63  Ibid. xv–xvi.

> A meaning scheme is the particular knowledge, beliefs, value judgements, and feel-
> ings that become articulated in an interpretation. Meaning schemes are the concrete
> manifestations of our habitual orientation and expectations (meaning perspectives)
> and translate these general expectations into specific ones that guide our actions.[64]

For Mezirow, a meaning scheme is 'the constellation of concept, belief, judgement, and feelings which shapes a particular interpretation' that includes 'specific beliefs, attitudes and emotional reactions'.[65] So, for exam-ple, meaning schemes within the meaning perspective of patriarchy could manifest themselves in advocating for the rights of men over the rights of women or the lack of equal pay for equal work. Mezirow gives his own examples of different types of meaning schemes: 'we expect food to satisfy our hunger ... that the sun will rise in the east ... turning a knob and pushing on a door will open it.'[66] All meaning schemes and meaning perspectives are based on particular underlying assumptions.

Mezirow suggests that 'although the transformation of meaning schemes through reflection is an everyday occurrence, it does not neces-sarily involve self-reflection on assumptions. For example, acquiring new knowledge may simply mean adding to our body of knowledge, which may act as a corrective to our beliefs, attitudes and emotions without involving any significant engagement in self-reflection – it is just knowledge. We often merely correct our interpretation'[67] without transforming our assumptions.

## Assumptions

The recognition by the learner of the influence of their assumptions, particu-larly their distorted assumptions, plays a significant role in transformative

---

64    Mezirow, *Transformative Dimensions of Adult Learning*, 44.
65    Mezirow, 'Understanding Transformation Theory', 223.
66    J. Mezirow, 'How Critical Reflection Triggers Transformational Learning', in *Fostering Critical Reflection in Adulthood: A Guide to Transformative and Emancipatory Learning* (San Francisco, CA: Jossey-Bass, 1990b), 2.
67    Mezirow, *Transformative Dimensions of Adult Learning*, 167.

learning. Transformative learning is facilitated by the correction of 'distorted assumptions':

> A distorted assumption or premise is one that leads the learner to view reality in a way that arbitrarily limits what is included, impedes differentiation, lacks permeability or openness to other ways of seeing, or does not facilitate an integration of experience.[68]

It is imperative for adult educators to be aware of the influence that previous experience and previous learning may have had on the assumptions carried by their students into education programmes, and to be able to facilitate the unpacking and, where necessary, the correction of these assumptions:

> The educator helps the learner focus upon and examine the assumptions – epistemological, social and psychological – that underlie beliefs, feelings, and actions; assess the consequences of these assumptions; identify and explore alternative sets of assumptions; and test the validity of assumptions through effective participation in reflective dialogue.[69]

In the theory of transformative learning, the appreciation by the adult learner that assumptions, especially distorted ones, need to be recognized and then questioned, through a process of critical reflection, is crucial.

*Critical Reflection*

An essential step on the path to transformation in adult education is to generate the willingness to critically evaluate beliefs, premises, processes, patterns and assumptions. 'Reflection enables us to correct distortions in our beliefs ... Critical reflection involves a critique of the presuppositions on which our beliefs have been built'.[70] Mezirow suggests that a process of critical reflection has profound transformative potential since 'uncritically assimilated meaning perspectives, which determine what, how, and why

---

68    Ibid. 118.
69    Ibid. 224.
70    Mezirow, 'How Critical Reflection Triggers Transformational Learning', 1.

we learn, may be transformed. Reflection on one's own premises can lead to transformative learning.'[71]

Critical reflection involves 'the intentional reassessment of prior learning to re-establish its validity by identifying and correcting distortions in its content, process, or premises'. It includes 'a critique of the premises or presuppositions upon which habits of expectation are predicated'.[72] Critical reflection alone will not lead the adult learner to transformation in Mezirow's theory. It is through rational discourse and informed dialogue with other learners and with tutors that new understandings and new points of view need to have their validity tested.

## Rational Discourse

Mezirow emphasizes the place of dialogue and rational discourse in his theory. He contends that 'discourse in the context of Transformation Theory, is that specialised use of dialogue devoted to searching for common understanding and assessment of the justification of an interpretation or belief'.[73] In his evaluation of the importance of rational discourse in the transformative learning process, he acknowledges the influence of the communicative learning theory of Habermas:

> In the domain of communicative learning, as Habermas noted, validity cannot be determined through the empirical-analytic kind of enquiry used in instrumental learning. Rather, validity testing takes the form of consensus reached through rational discourse.[74]

To engage in rational discourse 'one must access and understand, intellectually and emphatically, the frame of reference of the other and seek common ground with the widest range of relevant experience and points of view

---

71  Ibid. 18.
72  Mezirow, *Transformative Dimensions of Adult Learning*, 15.
73  Mezirow, 'Learning to Think Like an Adult', 10–11.
74  Mezirow, *Transformative Dimensions of Adult Learning*, 76.

possible'.[75] Mezirow views the 'university seminar' as an institutionalized model of 'collaborative discourse'.[76] Providing opportunities for collaborative or rational discourse is an important element in adult education since the 'goal' of adult education is:

> to help adult learners become more critically reflective, participate more fully and freely in rational discourse and action, and advance developmentally by moving towards meaning perspectives that are more inclusive, discriminating, permeable, and integrative of experience ... The ideal conditions for participating in critical discourse also constitute the ideal conditions for adult learning.[77]

However, not all theorists in the field of transformative learning are in full agreement with every aspect of Mezirow's theory.

## Critiques of Mezirow

Commentators on Mezirow have critiqued him under a number of headings and he has responded to some of these criticisms in his writing, often not specifically answering a particular person, but addressing the issue. Patricia Cranton has noted that, in fact, 'Mezirow invited and encouraged critiques of his work, hoping that within the community of educators interested in transformative learning, the theory would continue to evolve'.[78]

The principal critiques which are relevant to this research are the following:

---

75   Mezirow, 'An Overview on Transformational Learning', 91.
76   J. Mezirow, 'Adult Education and Empowerment for Individual and Community Development', in B. Connolly, T. Fleming, D. McCormack and A. Ryan (eds), *Radical Learning for Liberation 2* (Dublin: Maynooth Adult and Community Education, 2007), 14.
77   Mezirow, *Transformative Dimensions of Adult Learning*, 224–5.
78   Cranton, *Understanding and Promoting Transformational Learning* (2006), 22.

1. The theory is overly cognitive.
2. The theory is too individualistic.
3. There are ethical issues regarding the role of the educator.
4. Critical reflection does not guarantee transformation.

## An Overly Cognitive Theory?

Some have critiqued Mezirow's theory as being overly cognitive and rational, without sufficient emphasis on the affective and imaginative dimensions of the transformative process. Valerie Garbov has described it as a process that is primarily 'rational, analytical and cognitive'.[79] Jane Regan points out that the rational 'provides only one angle on the process of transformation and transformative learning'. Regan further observes that 'there is also an affective, intuitive, creative and imaginative dimension'.[80] Edward Taylor states that some reviewers have 'concluded that critical reflection is granted too much importance in perspective transformation, a process too rationally driven'.[81] He argues for a more holistic orientation, which 'encourages engagement with other ways of knowing – the affective and relational'. A holistic approach to transformative learning would aim to engage 'the whole person' and include 'presentational as well as expressive ways of knowing such as music, art, dance, mime, drama and meditation'.[82]

Acknowledging the validity of some of the issues raised by his critics, Mezirow accepts 'the need for more clarification and emphasis on the role

79   V. Grabov, 'The Many Facets of Transformative Learning Theory and Practice', in P. Cranton (ed.), *Transformative Learning in Action: New Directions for Adult and Continuing Education*, vol. 74 (San Francisco, CA: Jossey-Bass, 1997), 90–1.

80   Regan, 'Transformative Learning', 96.

81   E. W. Taylor (ed.), *The Theory and Practice of Transformative Learning: A Critical Review* (Columbus: ERIC Clearinghouse on Adult Education, Centre on Education and Training for Employment, College of Education, Ohio State University, 1998), 33–4.

82   E. W. Taylor, 'Fostering Transformative Learning', in J. Mezirow, E. W. Taylor and Associates (eds), *Transformative Learning in Practice: Insights from Community, Workplace, and Higher Education* (San Francisco, CA: Jossey-Bass, 2009), 10–11.

played by emotions, intuition and imagination in the process of transformation'. He states:

> This criticism of the theory is justified ... Imagination of how things could be oth-
> erwise is central to the initiation of the transformative process. As the process of
> transformation is often a difficult highly emotional passage, a great deal of additional
> insight into the role of imagination is needed and overdue.[83]

Regarding his strong emphasis on the rational dimension of transformation, Mezirow makes no apology and argues that 'transformative learning
is essentially a metacognitive process of reassessing reasons supporting our
problematic meaning perspectives'.[84]

*An Overly Individualistic Theory?*

Others have critiqued what they see as 'a lack of any social dimension to
his theory', positing that 'he focuses on individual transformation rather
than on social transformation'.[85] 'The theory itself, locating perspective
transformation within the individual ... fails to explore the constitutive
relationship between individuals and sociocultural, political and historical
contexts in which they are situated'.[86] Regan contends that while Mezirow
'argues for the place of rational discourse in the process of critical reflection
and the validating of new meaning perspectives he gives no attention to the
sustaining role of the person's significant relationships, reference groups,
and community'.[87] Regan proposes that Mezirow's attention 'primarily
to personal transformation' and Freire's 'process of social transformation',
when taken together, are complementary and provide a corrective to the
deficiency in the social aspect of Mezirow's theory.[88]

---

83   Mezirow, 'An Overview on Transformational Learning', 95.
84   Ibid.
85   L. Boyle, *Educational Models: Learning and Learners* (Dublin: Milltown Institute,
     unpublished notes, 2006), 19.
86   M. Carolyn and A. L. Wilson Clarke, 'Context and Rationality in Mezirow's Theory
     of Transformational Learning', *Adult Education Quarterly* 41 (2) (1991), 90.
87   Regan, 'Transformative Learning'.
88   Ibid. 76.

Mezirow however, defends his theory against those who criticize it as de-emphasizing social action:

> Transformational theory also contends that adult education must be dedicated to effecting social change, to modifying oppressive practices, norms, institutions and socio-economic structures to allow everyone to participate more fully and freely in reflective discourse and to acquiring a critical disposition and reflective judgement. Transformative learning focuses on creating the foundation and insight and understanding essential for learning how to take effective social action in a democracy.[89]

Mezirow thus makes clear his stand on this issue, and has done so throughout his works, referring to the possibility of social action resulting from transformative learning.[90] He has stated that 'when adults learn to correct the distorted sociolinguistic assumptions that have constrained the adoption of more developmentally advanced meaning perspectives, learning to take social action – often collective social action – becomes an integral part of transformative learning'.[91] While the process of perspective transformation begins initially with the individual learner, the completion of the process depends on collaboration with others and can lead to social action.

## Ethical Issues Regarding the Role of the Educator

Another critique relates to 'ethical issues concerning the appropriate role of the adult educator' in promoting the transformation of the learner. Liam Boyle poses the question:

> If a person comes to you to learn a particular skill, do you have the right to aim for fundamental transformation? It seems intrusive and unethical. Though transformation may happen as a result of your input, you have no right to seek such an outcome.[92]

Regan contends that 'the power of the educator, which is always present in the educator–learner relationship whether desired or recognised by either

89   Mezirow, 'An Overview on Transformational Learning', 96.
90   Mezirow, 'Adult Education and Empowerment', 17.
91   Mezirow, *Transformative Dimensions of Adult Learning*, 208.
92   Boyle, 'Educational Models', 19.

party, is virtually ignored in Mezirow's work'.[93] However, with reference to the appropriate role of the educator in the transformational learning process, Mezirow has stated:

> Education becomes indoctrination only when educators try to influence specific actions as extensions of their will ... To show learners a new set of rules, tactics, and criteria that allows them to judge situations in which they must act is significantly different from trying to engineer learner consent to take action favoured by the educator.[94]

Mezirow thus makes a clear and adequate response to his critics on this issue.

### Critical Reflection Does Not Guarantee Transformation

Stephen Brookfield is a theorist who has shown a particular interest in transformational learning. He has written extensively on the subject of critical theory.[95] In Chapter 5 of *Learning as Transformation*, Brookfield 'presents a critique of Transformation Theory from a viewpoint compatible with current interpretations of Critical Theory'.[96] Brookfield contends that:

> although critical reflection is an ineradicable element of transformative learning, it is not a synonym for it ... critical reflection is a necessary but not sufficient condition of transformative learning. In other words, transformative learning cannot happen without critical reflection, but critical reflection can happen without an accompanying transformation in perspective or habit of mind.[97]

Mezirow himself would concur with this. As we have already seen, he believes that, together with critical reflection, rational discourse is an

---

93   Regan, *Towards an Adult Church*, 111.
94   Mezirow and Associates, *Fostering Critical Reflection in Adulthood*, 362.
95   See S. D. Brookfield, *Developing Critical Thinkers*. See also S. D. Brookfield, *Becoming a Critical Reflective Teacher* (San Francisco, CA: Jossey-Bass, 1995).
96   Mezirow and Associates, *Learning as Transformation*, xvi, 125–50.
97   Brookfield, 'Transformative Learning as Ideology Critique', 125.

essential element of the transformative process, and acting upon the emancipatory insights gained is also necessary.[98]

Finally, commenting on the ongoing research on transformative learning theory, Edward Taylor states:

> There is much to support in Mezirow's Theory, but at the same time there is need to reconceptualise the process of perspective transformation. The research reveals a learning process that needs to recognise to a greater degree the significant influence of context, the varying nature of the catalyst of the process, the interdependent relationship of critical reflection and affective ways of knowing, the relational nature of rational discourse, and an overall broadening of the definitional outcome of perspective transformation.[99]

The last word has not been written on transformative learning theory. There is much scope for ongoing research and development of the theory in the years ahead.

## Conclusion

This chapter has examined aspects of the theory of transformative learning, concentrating on perspective transformation within the field of adult education. The focus was on Mezirow, because he continues to be the seminal thinker in the area of transformative learning and his ten phases of perspective transformation serve as one of the primary research tools for exploring transformative education.

While there have been many developments in transformational learning theory since Mezirow first wrote his article on 'Perspective Transformation'

---

98   J. Mezirow, 'Conclusion: Toward Transformative Learning and Emancipatory Education', in J. Mezirow and Associates, *Fostering Critical Reflection in Adulthood*, 354–5.

99   E. W. Taylor, 'Analyzing Research on Transformative Learning', in J. Mezirow and Associates, *Learning as Transformation*, 322.

in 1978, it is still considered to be 'an evolving theory'.[100] The initial ten
phases of perspective transformation are foundational and remain key. It
is his stated belief that 'there is no higher priority for adult education than
to develop its potentialities for perspective transformation'.[101]

Arising from the exploration of Mezirow's approach to transformative learning theory, it can be posited that his ten phases of perspective
transformation, the development of the major relevant themes and the
contributions of his critics all offer significant criteria for the analysis of
transformative education. These criteria are:

1. In adult education, perspective transformation normally happens as
   the result of the learner experiencing a disorientating dilemma. A disorientating dilemma can be a sudden occurrence, a new insight gained,
   or it could be the result of a sequence of experiences or new learnings,
   over a period of time (Mezirow – Phase One).
2. Mature students entering such a study programme carry life experience
   and experiential knowledge with them. They come with an already
   established worldview or perspective. Previously established frames of
   reference, habits of mind, points of view and meaning schemes may
   all need to be re-evaluated in the light of new learnings (Mezirow –
   Phases Two and Three).
3. This re-evaluating and questioning of prior learning and experience can
   be an emotionally and intellectually difficult time for the adult learner.
   Thus, a supportive learning environment is important (Mezirow –
   Phases Two and Three).
4. In order to overcome these difficulties, critical self-reflection on
   assumptions by the learner is necessary, if the movement of personal
   and communal transformation is to progress (Mezirow – Phases Two
   and Three).

---

100   J. Mezirow, 'Transformative Learning Theory', in Mezirow, Taylor and Associates,
      *Transformative Learning in Practice*, 18.
101   Mezirow, 'Perspective Transformation', 109.

5. In adult study programmes, reflective group processes within the learning community can also form an important part of transformative learning (Mezirow – Phases Three and Four).

6. Support and encouragement for the adult learner are facilitated through such group processes. These help the adult participant to recognize that other learners are perhaps facing similar or different disorientating dilemmas, and are coping or have worked through them (Mezirow – Phase Four).

7. In order for the learner to gain confidence in his or her ability to work through the transformative process, engaging in rational discourse is an important stage. This enables the learner to share with other learners and with tutors the disorientating experience, to clarify meanings and to validate changed perspectives (Mezirow – Phases Four and Five).

8. Transformative learning may require the learner to use their imagination in discerning and planning a particular course of action As a result of new learnings and possible changed perspectives in an education programme, adult learners may feel the need to explore options relating to new roles in society, career changes or changes in their relationships with others (Mezirow – Phases Five and Six).

9. Participation in adult education programmes may involve the learner in study, training and practice in order to acquire the knowledge and skills needed for proposed new roles in preparation for the future. This may entail seeking opportunities for the provisional trying of these roles through group processes or supervised pastoral placements (Mezirow – Phases Five, Six, Seven and Eight).

10. Transformative learning in adult learning programmes includes: the implementation of the proposed action; building competence and self-confidence in new roles and relationships; and reintegration into the learner's life with a transformed perspective. These are important culminating aspects of the transformative process (Mezirow – Phases Nine and Ten).

11. In adult learning programmes, a holistic approach to transformative learning takes into account the affective as well as the cognitive dimensions of the learner.

12. In any adult faith-formation programme, the context – educational, social, cultural and religious – from which adult learners have come,

and within which transformative learning is fostered, is influential and needs to be recognized.

13. Transformation is never guaranteed through the transformative process, and cannot be coerced by adult educators. Learners, particularly in adult learning programmes, always have the right to choose for themselves how deeply they are prepared to personally engage in transformative learning.

14. Transformative learning is a vision of education which is more than the communication of knowledge in that it can touch a person on intellectual, affective and spiritual levels so that their horizons, values, judgements and behaviour may be modified, resulting in greater personal authenticity and social commitment.

## Bibliography

Boyle, L., 'Educational Models: Learning and Learners' (Milltown Institute: unpublished notes, 2006).

Brookfield, S. D., *Becoming a Critical Reflective Teacher* (San Francisco, CA: Jossey-Bass, 1995).

Brookfield, S. D., *Developing Critical Thinkers: Challenging Adults to Explore Alternative Ways of Thinking and Acting* (Milton Keyes, UK: Open University Press, 1987).

Brookfield, S. D., 'Transformative Learning as Ideology Critique', in J. Mezirow (ed.), *Learning as Transformation: Critical Perspectives on a Theory in Progress* (San Francisco, CA: Jossey-Bass, 2000), 125–50.

Carolyn, M., and Wilson Clarke, A. L., 'Context and Rationality in Mezirow's Theory of Transformational Learning', *Adult Education Quarterly* 41 (2) (1991), 75–91.

Cranton, P., *Understanding and Promoting Transformational Learning: A Guide for Educators of Adults* (San Francisco, CA: Jossey-Bass, 2006).

Cranton, P., *Understanding and Promoting Transformational Learning: A Guide for Educators of Adults* (San Francisco, CA: Jossey-Bass, 1994, 2nd edn).

Daloz, L. A., *Effective Teaching and Mentoring: Realizing the Transformational Power of Adult Learning Experience* (San Francisco, CA: Jossey-Bass, 1987).

Daloz, L. A., 'Transformative Learning for the Common Good', in J. Mezirow (ed.), *Learning as Transformation: Critical Perspectives on a Theory in Progress* (San Francisco, CA: Jossey-Bass, 2000), 103–24.

Dirkx, J., 'Transformative Learning Theory in the Practice of Adult Education: An Overview' [Electronic Version] (1998), 1–7, <http://www.coe.iup.edu/ace/PAACE%20Journal%20PDF/PDF1998/Dirkx1998.pdf>, accessed 13 November 2009.

Finnegan, J., 'An Introduction to Transformative Theory for Supervisors' (Milltown Institute: unpublished notes, 2009).

Freire, P., *Pedagogy of the Oppressed*, trans. M. Bergman Ramos (London: Penguin, 1996, new revised edn).

Grabov, V., 'The Many Facets of Transformative Learning Theory and Practice', in P. Cranton (ed.), *Transformative Learning in Action: New Directions for Adult and Continuing Education*, vol. 74 (San Francisco, CA: Jossey-Bass, 1997), 89–96.

Habermas, J., *The Theory of Communicative Action: Reason and Rationalization of Society*, trans. T. McCarthy, vol. 1 (Boston, MA: Beacon Press, 1984).

King, K. P., *Bringing Transformative Learning to Life* (Malabar, FL: Krieger Publishing Company, 2005).

Merriam, S. B., Cafferella, R. S., and Baumgartner, L. M., 'Transformational Learning', in *Learning in Adulthood: A Comprehensive Guide* (San Francisco, CA: Jossey-Bass, 2007), 130–58.

Mezirow, J., 'Adult Education and Empowerment for Individual and Community Development', in B. Connolly, T. Fleming, D. McCormack and A. Ryan (eds), *Radical Learning for Liberation 2* (Dublin: Maynooth Adult and Community Education, 2007), 9–18.

Mezirow, J., 'Conclusion: Toward Transformative Learning and Emancipatory Education', in J. Mezirow and Associates (eds), *Fostering Critical Reflection in Adulthood: A Guide to Transformative and Emancipatory Learning* (San Francisco, CA: Jossey-Bass, 1990a), 354–76.

Mezirow, J., 'How Critical Reflection Triggers Transformative Learning', in *Fostering Critical Reflection in Adulthood: A Guide to Transformative and Emancipatory Learning* (San Francisco, CA: Jossey-Bass, 1990b), 1–20.

Mezirow, J., 'Learning to Think Like an Adult: Core Concepts of Transformation Theory', in J. Mezirow (ed.), *Learning as Transformation: Critical Perspectives on a Theory in Process* (San Francisco, CA: Jossey-Bass, 2000), 1–33.

Mezirow, J., 'An Overview on Transformational Learning', in K. Illeris (ed.), *Contemporary Theories of Learning* (New York: Routledge, 2009a), 90–105.

Mezirow, J., 'Perspective Transformation', *Adult Education Quarterly* 28 (2) (1978), 100–10.

Mezirow, J., 'Preface', in J. Mezirow and Associates (eds), *Fostering Critical Reflection in Adulthood: A Guide to Transformative and Emancipatory Learning* (San Francisco, CA: Jossey-Bass, 1990c), pp. xiii–xxi.

Mezirow, J., *Transformative Dimensions of Adult Learning* (San Francisco, CA: Jossey-Bass, 1991).

Mezirow, J., 'Transformative Learning Theory', in J. Mezirow, E. W. Taylor and Associ-
    ates (eds), *Transformative Learning in Practice* (San Francisco, CA: Jossey-Bass,
    2009b), 18–32.
Mezirow, J., 'Understanding Transformation Theory', *Adult Education Quarterly* 44
    (4) (1994), 222–32.
Mezirow, J., and Associates, *Fostering Critical Reflection in Adulthood: A Guide to Trans-
    formative and Emancipatory Learning* (San Francisco, CA: Jossey-Bass, 1990).
Mezirow, J., and Associates, *Learning as Transformation: Critical Perspectives on a
    Theory in Progress* (San Francisco, CA: Jossey-Bass, 2000).
Mezirow, J., and Taylor, E. W., 'Preface', in J. Mezirow, E. W. Taylor and Associates
    (eds), *Transformative Learning in Practice: Insights from Community, Workplace,
    and Higher Education* (San Francisco, CA: Jossey-Bass, 2009), xi–xiv.
Regan, J. E., *Towards an Adult Church: A Vision of Faith Formation* (Chicago: Loyola
    Press, 2002a).
Regan, J. E., 'Transformative Learning: Insights from Adult Education', in *Towards
    an Adult Church: A Vision of Faith Formation* (Chicago: Loyola Press, 2002b),
    73–112.
Taylor, E. W., 'Analyzing Research on Transformative Learning', in J. Mezirow and
    Associates (eds), *Learning as Transformation: Critical Perspectives on a Theory
    in Progress* (San Francisco, CA: Jossey-Bass, 2000), 285–328.
Taylor, E. W., 'Fostering Transformative Learning', in J. Mezirow, E. W. Taylor and
    Associates (eds), *Transformative Learning in Practice: Insights from Community,
    Workplace, and Higher Education* (San Francisco, CA: Jossey-Bass, 2009), 3–17.
Taylor, E. W. (ed.), *The Theory and Practice of Transformative Learning: A Criti-
    cal Review* (Columbus: ERIC Clearinghouse on Adult Education, Centre on
    Education and Training for Employment, College of Education, the Ohio State
    University, 1998).

DENIS ROBINSON

# 2    Leadership and the Inner Life

## Introduction

In recent history, the failure of leadership, particularly in the Roman Catholic Church, our financial institutions and Irish political life has contributed immensely to suffering and social disruption, forcing us to question what constitutes good and trustworthy leadership as we move into the future. The US academic, Bill George, writes:

> In the past two decades, far too many leaders have been selected more for charisma than character, for style over substance, and for image rather than integrity. If charisma, style and image are the selection criteria, why are we surprised when leaders turn out to lack character, substance and integrity?[1]

We are faced with a serious dilemma: is it really possible for people to become advocates of ethical behaviour and exercise their leadership with integrity? Is there some way to find a competent and convincing alternative to leaders who have a tendency to operate primarily out of profit, ego, or self-interest rather than focus on the needs of people and organizations? Some researchers in leadership are adamant about the necessity for 'new standards of integrity and public accountability'.[2] They recognize the need

---

1    B. George, *Mindful Leadership: Compassion, Contemplation and Meditation Develop Effective Leaders* (2014), 2. <http://www.billgeorge.org>, accessed 6 June 2015.
2    L. Fry and J. Whittington, 'In Search of Authenticity: Spiritual Leadership Theory as a Source for Future Theory, Research, and Practice on Authentic Leadership', in W. Gardner, B. Avolio and F. Walumbwa (eds), *Authentic Leadership Theory and Practice: Origins, Effects, and Development. Monographs in Leadership and Management* (Greenwich, CT: JAI Press, 2005), 184.

for genuine, responsible leadership and campaign for a transparent, morally grounded accountability which offers hope to people who long for, and require, men and women who are skilled practitioners of authentic leadership and effective guides for these challenging times. There is no doubt that leadership is a complex human reality, and that the type and quality of leadership is determined by many variables, such as personality, context, gender, culture, organization, and numerous other factors. Nevertheless, over the past hundred years, the study of the theory and practice of leadership has made great strides in determining the fundamental characteristics of truly authentic and effective leadership.

## Can Anyone Be a Leader?

As research advances, the expectations about leadership, and leadership skills and qualities, have also evolved. Ideally, the expectations we have of contemporary leaders are that they be men and women who are charismatic and are differentiated from others by a combination of the following personal characteristics: they must be self-confident, realistic and down to earth; they must have a natural ability to influence and motivate others; possess a good self-image and strong convictions; must have high standards of ethical and moral behaviour, act as good role models; be articulate in presenting a vision for a group or organization; be good communicators; have high performance expectations; be willing to take risks and be prepared to engage in self-sacrifice in pursuit of the goals and aims of the group or organization. In other words, we are looking for leaders who can provide a sense of meaning and common purpose within a group or organization, can mobilize commitment, and also generate optimism and enthusiasm for the achievement of both individual and common goals.[3] Is it possible

---

3    W. Zhu et al., 'Revisiting the Mediating Role of Trust in Transformational Leadership Effects: Do Different Types of Trust Make a Difference?' *The Leadership Quarterly* (2013), 95–6.

to find people who have, or can cultivate, these necessary qualities and skills? No doubt, there are natural leaders who, because of their innate talents and abilities, will exercise leadership in some fashion within different organizations and spheres of influence. There are also many groups and corporations that require specific skill sets beyond the fundamental leadership talents. Regardless of the specific requirements, it is possible to determine what constitutes a good leader.

For example, when we look at the leadership style and global influence of people like Nelson Mandela and Aung San Suu Kyi, we, like many before us, are faced with the fascinating, and perennial question: can anyone be such a leader? Is it a question of nature or nurture, of opportunity or need? And how can we choose and encourage people with the potential for a similar quality of presence, natural ability, and skilled leadership style? Can we find such men and women for our time and circumstances? Whichever way one answers this question, there are essential traits and generic qualities which provide a practical description of what people need to be, and acquire, to become effective and authentic leaders.

What we find in Mandela and Suu Kyi are leaders who can attract interest and followers through the sheer power of their personality and charisma, rather than through any form of external power or authority. In them, we have discovered that personal integrity is the one value required of every authentic leader; without it, people quickly lose confidence in them. Such individuals are often shaped by difficult life experiences which inspire and define their personal values and beliefs. They possess the obvious ability to enthuse and motivate people to achieve extraordinary things and, in the process, allow groups to develop their own capacity to change what needs to be changed. Both Mandela and Suu Kyi, in their own unique ways, with guidance, support and commitment, challenged their nations to solve serious problems, to reform entrenched values and restructure longstanding beliefs. In situations of extreme diversity and lack of parity, they were not afraid to confront and oppose all forms of inequity, injustice and discrimination. Both had a vision of what people could become, and because of this they encouraged the gradual transformation of a people and the advance of a nation. In them, we see people who lead with the heart as well as the head, with passion and strategy. Leaders like Mandela and Suu Kyi know what they are about and where they are going; they are passionate individuals who have a deep-seated interest in genuine progress and have great conviction about their vision for a better world, and what is needed to accomplish this. They persistently expressed a genuine care for the well-being of others and were dedicated to the flourishing of groups and organizations.[4] Each, in their own way, reflects the kind of leadership qualities that are widely admired and indispensable for progress in society. They embody and personify what constitutes respect and trust; they accurately represent the power of honest appeal, natural ability, personal integrity and unfeigned authenticity. However, they also have weaknesses. They are not perfect. Both Mandela and Suu Kyi have their leadership questioned. During his earlier life as a revolutionary Mandela made some controversial decisions that may have caused the death of others. At one point Mandela suggested that violence would be necessary to end apartheid. Suu Kyi is currently embroiled in controversy over the situation of the Rohingya people in her own country. She is being accused of not speaking out in public about it. Given these controversies and possible transgressions are these leaders still worthy of our respect and admiration for all the life giving progress that has been achieved in both countries and beyond? It may seem that we want our leaders today to be heroes and heroines, who are impressive people with purpose, values, heart; who are both visionary and self-disciplined, and true to themselves and what they believe. However, it may be that there are a lot more heroes and heroines among us than we imagine. If we have a clear concept of what makes and constitutes a good leader, then it may be possible to identify and promote such authentic and effective leadership in others.

---

4    P. Northouse, *Leadership: Theory and Practice* (New Delhi: Sage Publication, 2013, 6th edn), 258.

## The Inner Life of a Leader

For so long, there has been a concentration on the techniques and practices of leadership, but research has begun to emphasize the inner life of the person as the most essential aspect of authentic and effective leadership.[5] For the first time in leadership studies, the inner life of a leader is identified as the essential source of good leadership. Some scholars argue that the inner life, and personal well-being, is more important than ability and dedication, or position and conviction. According to West-Burnham:

> For a host of culture and historical reasons we have tended to neglect the inner lives of leaders. It has always been seen as 'too personal' to make public but, I would argue, we continue to neglect it at our peril. The sustainability, resilience, effectiveness and well-being of leaders are directly related to the health of the 'inner-self'. Personal authenticity, moral confidence and professional courage are direct indicators of personal wholeness.[6]

This perspective stresses the increasingly acknowledged conviction that the real essence of leadership lies in the heart, in the core, in the human spirit of a leader. This new understanding emphasizes that one's inner life and personal values are crucial to good leadership. It draws attention to the interiority of a person because this is what shapes the way people perceive and determines how they will behave. Intentionally focusing on their inner selves helps leaders become more sensitive to their own needs and issues, and more in tune with how they can grow and develop as an individual to benefit themselves, their co-workers and organization. Such inner effort is seen as a means to develop, and perhaps even transform, leadership skills and qualities. However, a deliberate choice is required in order to seriously engage in this process. One has to aspire to be the best one can be, and be prepared to change in order to grow wiser, freer,

5    L. Fry and M. Kriger 'Towards a Theory of Being-Centered Leadership: Multiple Levels of Being as Context for Effective Leadership', *Human Relations* 62 (II) (2009).
6    J. West-Burnham, *Rethinking Educational Leadership: From Improvement to Transformation* (New York: Continuum, 2009), 82.

more genuinely autonomous, and more likely to discover authenticity and integrity in the service of our human ideals and the common good. This conscious 'going beyond one's self-interest' is understood as a core component for the development of effective and authentic leadership, as we see in the lives of Mandela and Suu Kyi.

Appreciating this movement from 'leadership based on having and doing, to leadership that rests on and evolves out of being'[7] helps us to understand that leadership is more than having the right traits, competencies, and behaviours; it is, rather, a question of being in touch with the source of meaning that inspires and guides us. Leaders cannot accompany and guide others into a new and better future unless their own lives have been changed and opened to new possibilities by delving into and growing their inner selves.[8] Researchers endorse this kind of personal work because in this process one cultivates 'a state of mind or consciousness that enables one to perceive deeper levels of experience, meaning, values, and purpose than can be perceived from a strictly material vantage point levels'.[9] Leading from this deeper level builds on and enhances one's natural abilities and skills, perhaps even to the point of transforming them.

Most leaders recognize that there is an inner dimension to their leadership. They know that their private and personal selves are not left at the door when they arrive at work. Such self-awareness is meant to promote and expand the understanding of personal values and feelings, and is intended to produce a more meaningful and creative mode of being, and a more genuine way of relating with others. Central to this is acknowledging the longing and need for deeper meaning in our lives. Leaders, no matter how good they are, are not the ultimate source of meaning, or the definitive

---

7    M. Kriger and Y. Seng, 'Leadership with Inner Meaning: A Contingency Theory of Leadership Based on the Worldviews of Five Religions', *The Leadership Quarterly* 16 (2005), 788.

8    W. Granberg-Michaelson, *Leadership from Inside Out: Spirituality and Organizational Change* (New York: Crossroad Publishing Company, 2004), 176.

9    S. Thompson, 'Spiritual Leadership – The Invisible Revolution', in P. Houston, A. Blankstein and R. Cole (eds), Spirituality in *Educational Leadership* (California: Corwin Press, 2008), 152.

measure of life, nor are they the total expression of human success. We need to acknowledge that there is a greater reality, a Higher Power, if you will, that is the ultimate ground of being, whether we call this being God, Allah, Buddha or some other name. It is well documented that Mandela and Suu Kyi have been hugely influenced by their own faith traditions, Christianity and Buddhism. We find in their personal lives and leadership practice that this relationship with the transcendent was the source of their essential vision of what it means to be a person, and the origin of the values that supported their desire for human flourishing and personal fulfilment for all, regardless of religion. Out of this vision, they were able to challenge conventional values, commit to change, generate hope, seek to serve, and stand humbly before others. This helps us appreciate the significance and influence of a leader's inner life, be it cultural, emotional, spiritual or psychological. A leader needs to tend to all aspects of the inner life to mature towards integrity and authenticity. Whatever method is used, a space for deep silence and reflection is needed to help leaders be more self-aware and consciously engage in their own interior and holistic development.[10] The quest for authentic leadership emphasizes being true to oneself, gaining self-knowledge and self-regulation, behaving consistently with one's values and internalized moral standards, in order to build trusting and transparent relationships. This interior growth, this leading from within, provides the opportunity to experience one's truest and deepest reality, and bring one's whole self to the challenges and demands that leaders must face in a complex world.[11]

Being equally concerned about the quality of one's interiority and leadership style are not incompatible; they are mutually beneficial. Growing as a person will influence the quality and style of leadership. This approach has the potential to create a new vision of leadership in which one is able to combine the everyday demands of an organization with one's individual inner progress. Having such a vision helps develop a deeper appreciation of the power and appeal of the inner life to promote ongoing personal and

10    L. Fry and M. Nisiewicz, *Maximizing the Triple Bottom Line through Spiritual Leadership* (California: Stanford University Press, 2013), 59.

11    Thompson, 'Spiritual Leadership – The Invisible Revolution', 152.

professional growth in that it can energize, provide added significance, inform commitment, and support the desire for excellence in all aspects of life. And, as we have seen in other leaders, it has the very real potential to mobilize high ideals, and motivate the desire for change for the benefit of all. Such leaders experience 'a sense of wholeness, harmony, and well-being produced through care, concern, and appreciation for both self and others'.[12]

People have lost faith in many things, including leadership, because they often feel insignificant and like mere cogs in a giant production process. The value of work and the contribution people make can have little meaning if the experience of employment destroys personality and dehumanizes the workplace, if individuals and basic human values are not fully respected. A leader's inner work is necessary to help him or her to become more sensitive and caring in relation to others, and to help him or her become directly concerned about the well-being of those they serve. Leadership is more than a job; it is, in fact, about being able to make a difference in the lives of others, and give a deeper sense of purpose to work. The conviction that one's life and work have significance can provide 'a foundation for both meaningful human activity and utilizing one's individual and unique abilities'.[13] Ideally, a leader can strive to help others experience work not only as part of a service or production process, but the means to the experience of social connection, personal significance, and community. Belonging to a larger, caring community can help people to feel that they are important, that they have worth, that they matter; it can generate a sense of being understood and appreciated beyond their usefulness as workers. Research has provided evidence that developing good-quality relationships with others is central to healthy interpersonal and social functioning and plays a crucial role in increasing resilience, happiness, and a sense of well-being in people at work.[14] This orientation goes a long way towards establishing a healthy workplace culture and is an essential aspect of good leadership.

---

12    L. Fry, 'Toward a Theory of Spiritual Leadership', *The Leadership Quarterly* 14 (2003), 712.

13    Fry and Nisiewicz, *Maximizing the Triple Bottom Line through Spiritual Leadership*, 140.

14    Ibid. 145.

Leaders who think, act and feel like this have the potential to grow in many ways. Those leaders who truly endeavour to care for the well-being of others tend to be consistent in their words and deeds, reflect an ethical way of being, foster good relationships, and so have a positive impact on the group or organizational culture.[15] By working on his or her inner life, a leader has the opportunity not only to increase spiritual, emotional and psychological well-being, but to develop a more honest, trustworthy, caring, humane, and principled way of being in their leadership of others. This kind of leader reflects essential values such as integrity/honesty, trust/loyalty, humility, courage, patience, meekness, endurance, kindness, empathy, compassion, forgiveness, acceptance, gratitude, excellence, and adventure. Such values help to clarify what makes for good leadership and a successful human being.[16]

## Leading from Within

Leading from within essentially involves moving from an ego-centred self to the experience and expression of what it means to be fully human. Leading from within has a positive impact, with the result that a leader, operating at that level of being, is significantly less influenced by negative emotional states, is less inconsiderate, more other-centred, more compassionate and more sensitive to the difficulties facing others.[17] Leaders who have discovered, or rediscovered, their inner life acquire a strong desire to serve first, rather than being concerned by personal status or self importance. Through the experience of positive change in themselves, they are more likely to encourage others to explore their inner spirit, and to grow and succeed in whatever way is possible for them. Being other-centred, they are

15    Ibid. 96.
16    Ibid. 128.
17    Fry and Kriger, 'Towards a Theory of Being-Centered Leadership: Multiple Levels of Being as Context for Effective Leadership', 1680.

always concerned about their followers' growth, ongoing organizational healing, and forming a sense of real community.[18] Additionally, such leaders can be expected to have a high degree of unconditional regard for the other, become more intuitive, foster equality, and make less of a distinction between leader and follower.[19] To put it in simple and popular terms, such leaders will be more unselfish, compassionate, loving, and altruistic in their dealings with others because they are more integrated within themselves.

However, there is a dark side to exploring the inner life. The desire to be fully and authentically human can take years; it requires an openness to a variety of challenging experiences and the willingness to struggle with what is inauthentic and false in the self. The journey to one's innermost being initiates a process of personal transformation, a transformation prompted by one's own need to change, instead of demanding that others, or situations, change first; it involves letting go of the small self, the ego self, one's self pre-occupations and any hint of self-inflation.[20] It soon becomes apparent that much personal healing and growth needs to take place in the self and in one's relationships in this process. Authentic and effective leadership is founded on such ongoing, dynamic engagement with the self. Transformation and personal integration do not happen without a lot of effort. The indispensable impetus, experiences and insights that lead to significant change can only emerge when one has committed to undertaking this demanding journey. This kind of personal work helps to develop skills and knowledge, and provides a catalyst for appreciating inner freedom, practising compassion, and being respectful in all relationships. This inner work is as necessary as outer work; one needs to be an expert practitioner of the inner life, as well as a proactive and efficient practical leader in one's public life. Parker Palmer writes: 'Go far enough on the inner journey, they tell us – go past ego toward true self – and you end up not lost in narcissism but returning to the world, bearing more gracefully

---

18    Ibid. 1681–2.
19    Ibid. 1685.
20    J. Langille, 'There Is Nothing between God and You', in T. Keating and C. Bourgeault (eds), *Spirituality, Contemplation and Transformation* (New York: Lantern Books 2008), 61.

the responsibilities that come with being human'.[21] Exploring the reality of who one is as a person and as a leader means confronting the routine ways of thinking in which we imprison ourselves, the ways in which we hold ourselves captive with unreasonable and inhumane expectations, the external pre-occupations that blind us to our own internalized oppression, and the fears which often lurk just below the level of consciousness that determine our behaviour. To be a good leader, it is imperative to know one's strengths and weaknesses, to be aware of personal needs and ambitions, vulnerabilities and blind spots. It is essential to identify with one's life story and to be able to process self-relevant information. This involves recognizing the ability of ego to distort or exaggerate the truth; it means being conscious of one's warts and flaws. It is important for leaders to appreciate the importance of this inner work because

> ... by failing to look at our shadows, we feed a dangerous delusion that leaders too often indulge: that our efforts are always well-intentioned, our power always benign, and the problem is always in those difficult people whom we are trying to lead.[22]

Leaders are obviously concerned with the public aspects of leadership, and this is a necessary dimension of their work. However, the real tragedy is that they often ignore what is going on inside themselves: the thoughts, ambitions, motivations, dreads, the hurts and memories that emanate from within. Every leader needs to understand and confront the dark or shadow side of his or her personality. If they do not, there is the undeniable danger that they will project this unknown and often unacknowledged self onto their co-workers and the organizations they serve. Leaders are always projecting themselves, for better or worse; and what they do not transform in themselves, they will project onto others. This is why leaders must know the darkness inside; otherwise they will, consciously or unconsciously, inflict the consequences of this darkness on others. We can imagine the

---

21    P. Palmer, *Let Your Life Speak: Listening to the Voice of Vocation* (San Francisco, CA: Jossey-Bass, 2000), 73.
22    Ibid. 79.

violence leaders inflict on themselves and others in neglecting to admit and transform the failings in self. Palmer confirms that:

> A leader is someone with the power to project either shadow or light onto some part of the world and onto the lives of the people who dwell there. A leader shapes the ethos in which others must live, an ethos as light-filled as heaven or as shadowy as hell. A *good* leader is intensely aware of the interplay of inner shadow and light, lest the act of leadership do more harm than good.[23]

There are many varieties of leaders, ranging from the inept to the efficient to those who are really good and conscientious. We all know leaders who create more obscurity than enlightenment, who are blinded by their own ambition, who manipulate power for their own success and disengage in the face of hardship, struggle, doubt and fear. To be a fully authentic human being and a truly effective leader, one must undertake this indispensable journey to move beyond unexamined fears and a reactive self. Those who undertake this journey are the people who have the opportunity to become great leaders.[24] Inner work is the only way of experiencing the regeneration necessary to mature as a person; there is no other way to become an excellent leader; there is no shortcut to being a positive and enlightened influence on others and the world.

## Inner Work Is Personal but Never Private

Although inner work is always deeply personal, for those in leadership it is never private. For leaders, in particular, genuine inner growth always has a social dimension because it involves a lot more than a purely personal, interior progress. There is a profound and dynamic unity between inner growth and one's relationship with others. In this gradual process of transformation,

---

23   Ibid. 78.
24   West-Burnham, *Rethinking Educational Leadership: From Improvement to Transformation*, 110.

the self is rehabilitated from the inside out and this initiates a shift in values; it influences priorities, affects the way one connects with people, and creates a new perception of a better self.[25] There are, of course, degrees and intensities of transformation – no one person can achieve complete transformation once and for all. It is very much a developmental process. For this process to be beneficial, one must be willing to engage in the honest, ongoing exploration of one's inner and outer world. One must strive to uncover what is counterfeit in the self; and be equally willing to continually evaluate the more sinister aspects of personality, thinking, memory, fears and anxieties, which operate in the daily exercise of leadership. It is only then that a leader will do more good than harm, and cast more light than shadow.[26] Without this journey into the 'dark side' leaders may continue to be complicit in their own self-delusions, in the false belief that power and authority automatically confer infallible knowledge and insight, and that long experience and hard work are the only means to success as a person and leader. Research shows that the most essential ingredient for good leadership is a level of self-awareness that makes it easier to self-regulate, to experience congruence between one's inner and outer world, and come to terms with the reality of self at the deepest level. When leaders know themselves and have a clear sense of who they are, and what they stand for, they have a powerful anchor for their decisions, confidence in their actions, and a genuine openness to critique. Most importantly, they learn to trust their own feelings and judgements.[27]

We have great respect for leaders who are guided by internal moral standards and are not susceptible to group, organizational or social pressures. We need leaders who are originals, who act beyond self-interest, who strive to achieve consistency between their actions and beliefs, and who do not compromise their ethical standards to achieve success, profits, or short-term gains.[28] Such leaders exercise self-control over their emotions

25    Palmer, *Let Your Life Speak: Listening to the Voice of Vocation*, 92.
26    Ibid. 92.
27    Northouse, *Leadership: Theory and Practice*, 264.
28    J. Reynolds, 'Transformational Leadership', in J. Reynolds and K. Takamine (eds), *Authentic Leadership after God's Own Heart* (Charleston, USA: CreateSpace, 2013), 23.

and personal desires, and strike a balance between humility and wisdom
in order to achieve the openness and truthfulness that is at the heart of
virtuous leadership It takes great character, optimism and resilience to lead
and empower others. It takes imagination to create a vision of how things
might be. It takes courage to dream dreams in a cynical world and speak
from the heart among sceptics. No one has ever been attracted to leaders
who are false or pretentious in any way and so we look for men and women
who do not engage in leadership activities merely for status, prestige or
personal rewards. We ask of our leaders:

> Do not promise what you can't deliver, do not misrepresent, do not hide spin-doctored
> evasions, do not suppress obligations, do not evade accountability, do not accept that
> the 'survival of the fittest' pressures of business release any of us from the responsibil-
> ity to respect another's dignity and humanity.[29]

These are the challenges of those who will lead as talented, effective and
transformative leaders. The move beyond the unexamined self is the gateway
that leads to accomplished leadership. All good leaders have to travel this
path. They need these moments of insight and transformation to guide them
beyond habitual and unreflective ways of being, towards knowledge and
personal insight, which cannot be found except by journeying into the self.

## Conclusion

Becoming an effective and authentic leader is not easy. There is no doubt
that 'Leadership is a journey, not a destination. It is a marathon, not a
sprint. It is a process, not an outcome'.[30] Considering the demands life
makes and the reality of human limitations, there are many temptations to
distract a person from exploring his or her values and beliefs. As the journey

---

29    Northouse, *Leadership: Theory and Practice*, 436.
30    B. George and P. Sims, *True North: Discovering Your Authentic Leadership* (San
      Francisco, CA: John Wiley and Sons Inc., 2007), 3.

progresses, the desire to grow personally and improve as a leader can wane; disappointment and opposition often set in. Only the deepest conviction can sustain people who wish to cultivate a more personally integrated self in the service of others and dedicate themselves to the welfare of an organization in pursuit of the common good. The quest for authentic leadership is a lifelong developmental process; it is something to aspire to, something one continually discovers and grows into. In the busy and complex world of the self, with all the daily challenges and tensions, authentic and effective leadership can never be completely experienced; it can only become known incrementally in the discovery of better ways of being, in finding healthier emotional and relational ways of working together, and in being committed to implementing the reforms, decisions and policies that change our world for the better. When such personal progress is made, insight and courage increase, real leadership skills develop, an open mind and an open heart paves the way for transformation, and men and women, like Mandela and Suu Kyi with their strengths and weaknesses, emerge to be great leaders and a compelling force for genuine and sustainable change in our world.

# Bibliography

Fry, L., 'Toward a Theory of Spiritual Leadership', *The Leadership Quarterly* 14 (2003), 693–727.

Fry, L., and Kriger, M., 'Towards a Theory of Being-Centered Leadership: Multiple Levels of Being as Context for Effective Leadership', *Human Relations* 62 (II) (2009), 1667–96.

Fry, L., and Nisiewicz, M., *Maximizing the Triple Bottom Line through Spiritual Leadership* (California: Stanford University Press, 2013).

Fry, L., and Whittington, J., 'In Search of Authenticity: Spiritual Leadership Theory as a Source for Future Theory, Research, and Practice on Authentic Leadership', in W. Gardner, B. Avolio and Fred Walumbwa (eds), *Authentic Leadership Theory and Practice: Origins, Effects, and Development. Monographs in Leadership and Management* (Greenwich, CT, USA: JAI Press, 2005), 183–200.

George, B., *Mindful Leadership: Compassion, Contemplation and Meditation Develop Effective Leader* (2014), <http://www.billgeorge.org>, accessed 6 June 2015.

George, B. and Sims, P., *True North: Discovering Your Authentic Leadership* (San Francisco, CA: John Wiley and Sons Inc., 2007).

Granberg-Michaelson, W., *Leadership from Inside Out: Spirituality and Organizational Change* (New York: Crossroad Publishing Company, 2004).

Kriger, M., and Seng, Y., 'Leadership with Inner Meaning: A Contingency Theory of Leadership Based on the Worldviews of Five Religions', *The Leadership Quarterly* 16 (2005), 771–806.

Langille, J., 'There Is Nothing between God and You: Awakening to the Wisdom of Contemplative Silence', in Thomas Keating and Cynthia Bourgeault (eds), *Spirituality, Contemplation and Transformation: Writings on Centering Prayer* (New York: Lantern Books, 2008), 57–80.

Northouse, P., *Leadership: Theory and Practice* (New Delhi: Sage Publication, 2013, 6th edn).

Palmer, P., *Let Your Life Speak: Listening to the Voice of Vocation* (San Francisco, CA: Jossey-Bass, 2000).

Reynolds, J., 'Transformational Leadership', in J. Reynolds and K. Takamine (eds), *Authentic Leadership after God's Own Heart* (Charleston, USA: CreateSpace, 2013), 16–30.

Thompson, S., 'Spiritual Leadership – The Invisible Revolution', in P. Houston, A. Blankstein and R. Cole (eds), *Spirituality in Educational Leadership* (California: Corwin Press, 2008), 151–170.

West-Burnham, J., *Rethinking Educational Leadership: From Improvement to Transformation* (New York: Continuum, 2009).

Zhu, W., Newman, A., Miao, Q., and Hooke, A., 'Revisiting the Mediating Role of Trust in Transformational Leadership Effects: Do Different Types of Trust Make a Difference?', *The Leadership Quarterly* 24 (2013), 94–105.

DEE MCKIERNAN

## 3 The Purpose of Higher Education in Counselling Psychology and Supervision: What Are We Teaching? What Are We Learning?

## Introduction

> In teaching, the teacher asks you to join him/her in their world.
> In learning, the teacher joins you in your world.[1]

Counselling psychology initially arose as a branch of psychology which offered another approach to the helping profession, specifically in relation to the 'use of self' in the therapeutic context. It stems from the work of Abraham Maslow, Carl Rogers and Rollo May, who encouraged a more holistic, humanistic approach to understanding the human person. This approach to the helping profession was one that deliberately moved away from the 'medical model', which, at the time, was more concerned with 'psychopathology', 'mental illness' and 'disorders' than the human person. Carl Rogers, an influential American psychologist and one of the founding fathers of the humanistic approach to psychotherapy, questioned this focus on problems, rather than on the 'person', in psychotherapy and the helping professions. Rogers proposed that clients need to be at the centre of the therapeutic process and not the assumed psychopathology and certainly not a set of techniques or skills and methods.

---

1    M. Carroll and M. Gilbert, *On Being a Supervisee: Creating Learning Partnerships* (London: Vukani Publishing, 2011, 2nd edn).

Woolfe identifies a number of factors that set counselling psychology apart from other professions at the time.[2] Firstly, it seemed clear that significant emphasis and value was placed on the therapeutic relationship within the profession of counselling psychology. Secondly, there was a distinct shift away from the medical model towards a more holistic and humanistic approach to the individual. Thirdly, it seemed important to not only facilitate but encourage a strong sense of health and well-being, as opposed to merely responding to illness and pathology within the individual.

As the profession has developed over the years, it has illustrated through numerous research- and evidence-based findings that the quality of the therapeutic relationship is one of the core principles of the profession and indeed the principle that has the most potential to bring about change.[3] It has also been indicated that the therapeutic relationship is a strong predictor of outcome in individual psychotherapy across diverse treatment orientations and modalities[4]

Counselling psychology has developed and grown significantly in the last thirty years, both in the UK and in Ireland, having evolved from sections and special interest groups to divisions within the British Psychological Society (BPS) and the Psychological Society of Ireland (PSI). This evolution and development of the profession of counselling psychology has been influenced by the humanistic, existential, psycho-dynamic, systemic

2    See R. Wolfe, 'Counselling Psychology in Britain: An Idea Whose Time Has Come', *The Psychologist* 3 (12) (1990), 531–5.

3    See A. Roth and P. Fonagy, 'What Works for Whom?' in *A Critical Review of Psychotherapy Research* (London: Guildford, 1996); M. A. Hubble, B. L. Duncan, and S. D. Miller, (eds), *The Heart and Soul of Change: What Works in Therapy?* (Washington, DC: American Psychological Association, 1999), 133–78; M. Cooper, *Essential Research Findings in Counselling and Psychotherapy: The Facts Are Friendly* (London: Sage, 2008).

4    A. O. Horvath and R. P. Bedi, 'The Alliance', in J. C. Norcross (ed.), *Psychotherapy Relationships That Work: Therapist Contributions and Responsiveness to Patients* (New York: Oxford University Press, 2002), 37–70.; D. J. Martin, J. P. Garske, and M. D. Davis, 'Relation of the Therapeutic Alliance with Outcome and other Variables: A Meta-analytic Review', *Journal of Consulting and Clinical Psychology* (68) (2000), 438–50.

and cognitive behavioural traditions, to name but a few. As a result, counselling psychologists work in various arenas, such as schools, colleges and academic environments, healthcare services, industrial agencies, and many national counselling services both in Ireland and abroad. Counselling psychologists work with individuals, couples, families, and various vulnerable groups of society. They work as part of multidisciplinary teams and are also involved in the teaching, training and supervision of other psychologists and psychotherapists. In addition, they are involved in research and various psycho-educational programmes, as well as being consulted regarding, and being involved in the writing of, policy documents for the government.

## Holistic Personal Development

The science of counselling psychology is described in Ireland as a science that integrates theory, practice and research to 'facilitate personal and interpersonal functioning across the life span [for individuals] with a focus on emotional, social, vocational, educational, health-related, and developmental concerns'.[5] Counselling psychology is rooted in the discipline of psychology, but places great emphasis on the importance of the therapeutic relationship between psychologist and client. As a result, the profession not only requires a holistic view of the human person, and indeed human nature; it has a responsibility to be holistic in its provision of education, research, theory and practice to the greater public.

The education and training of counselling psychologists in Ireland falls under the umbrella of higher education, education that occurs 'beyond school, especially to degree level at a university or similar educational establishment'.[6] In the Irish context, higher education is provided by seven

---

5    Psychological Society of Ireland, 'Counselling Psychology' (2014). Available at: <http://www.psihq.ie/page/art/66/0>, accessed 10 March 2015.
6    J. Pearsall and B. Trumbell, *The Oxford English Reference Dictionary* (Oxford: Oxford University Press, 2002).

universities, fourteen institutions and seven colleges of education,[7] with
a number of other third-level institutions that provide additional training and education in various other areas, including medicine, law and art.
Currently, there are three universities in Ireland that offer education and
training in counselling psychology to honours graduates of accredited psychology programmes: University College Cork, Trinity College Dublin,
and the University of Ulster. The aim of the 2011 National Strategy for
Higher Education in Ireland is to transform Ireland's higher-education
sector over the next two decades. The National Strategy aims to ensure
that higher education will connect more appropriately with the wider
social, economic and enterprise needs of modern Irish society.[8] This only
increases the need for interdisciplinary and comprehensive research on
the role of higher education, to highlight its potential impact on policy,
procedure and professional practice in the Irish, and indeed European,
cultural and social context.

The education and training of counselling psychologists makes particular reference to ethical complexity in social and organizational contexts and
fosters an acute awareness of cultural diversity and issues relating to inclusive
practice. As a result, counselling psychology 'has positioned itself between
the science of psychology and the therapeutic practices of counselling and
psychotherapy' and has 'constructed an identity that espouses the complementary aspects of "scientist practitioner" and "reflective practitioner".'[9]
These holistic perspectives of the human person, combined with the reflective qualities of engaging in scientific, reflective, therapeutic work, results
in the constant growth, development and evolution of the education, training and role of the counselling psychologist. The profession is, by its very
nature, broad, encompassing, and inclusive and the education of counselling
psychologists is what Mezirow would deem inherently 'transformative'.[10]

7    Higher Education Authority (2014), 'Higher Education Authority', <http://www.
     hea.ie/en/about-hea>, accessed 10 March 2015.
8    Higher Education Authority, 2014.
9    R. Wolfe, S. Strawbridge, B. Douglas, and W. Dryden, *Handbook of Counselling
     Psychology* (London: Sage, 2010).
10   J. Mezirow, *Education for Perspective Transformation: Women's Re-entry Programs
     in Community Colleges* (New York: Teacher's College, Columbia University, 1978a)

The education and skills training of counselling psychologists place an emphasis on personal therapy for trainees within this profession. Debate continues regarding whether this should be a compulsory component of the training.[11] Some regard it as necessary, whereas others question the impact of mandatory therapy on personal and professional development.[12] Despite this, holistic personal development is currently a strong component of the training, and indeed the practice, of counselling psychologists in Ireland.

The role of the counselling psychologist involves the 'use of self' as an instrument of change in the therapeutic process.[13] This 'use of self' is left over from its humanistic roots and traditions, along with an acute understanding that, as individuals, we all have emotional, social, vocational, educational and developmental histories, which have the potential to impact on client relationships in a therapeutic context. This 'use of self' is one of the elements that makes this profession unique and has various educative aspects.[14] Orlinsky et al. found that engaging in personal therapy in training had two main educational purposes: firstly, to enhance the professional development and relational capacities of the trainee psychologist and, secondly, to increase the personal development capacities and well-being of the therapist.

---

and J. Mezirow, 'Perspective Transformation', in *Adult Education*, 28 (San Francisco, CA: Jossey-Bass, 1978b) 100–10.

11    H. Wiseman and G. Shefler, 'Experienced Psychoanalytically Oriented Therapists' Narrative Accounts of Their Personal Therapy: Impacts on Professional and Personal Development', *Psychotherapy* 38 (2) (2001), 212–41; P. Atkinson, 'Personal Therapy in the Training of Therapists', *European Journal of Psychotherapy and Counselling* 8 (4) (2006), 4407–10; J. C. Norcross, 'The Psychotherapist's Own Psychotherapy: Educating and Developing Psychologists', *The American Psychologist* 60 (2005), 840–50.

12    A. Grimmer and R. Tribe, 'Counselling Psychologists' Perceptions of the Impact of Mandatory Personal Therapy on Professional Development, an Exploratory Study', *Counselling Psychology Quarterly* (14) (2010), 4.

13    V. Wosket, *The Therapeutic Use of Self: Counselling Practice, Research and Supervision* (London: Routledge, 1999).

14    D. Orlinsky et al., 'Utilization of Personal Therapy by Psychotherapists: A Practice-Friendly Review and a New Study', *Journal of Clinical Psychology* 67 (8) (2011), 828–42.

According to the British Psychological Society, the practice of counselling psychology requires 'a high level of self-awareness and competence in relating the skills and knowledge of personal and interpersonal dynamics to the therapeutic context'.[15] The psychologist's self-awareness and holistic personal development are vital as they facilitate the acquisition of experiential and transformative knowledge, which thereby enables the psychologist to detect transference, counter-transference and other important dynamics of the therapeutic relationship. Atkinson argues that personal therapy is an integral part of training for future therapists.[16] By engaging in individual personal therapy, the trainee practitioner gains direct experience of the therapeutic process and can learn from and observe a qualified therapist, while also being part of the process. Consequently, this makes it a dynamic, transformative learning experience for the trainee and the qualified therapist.

In many cases, and particularly in Ireland, this need for self-awareness and a commitment to holistic personal development and continuing professional development is not only a training requirement, but a job requirement. Irvin Yalom, a prolific American existential psychiatrist at Stanford University, proposes that 'personal psychotherapy is the most important part of psychotherapy training'.[17] Engagement in personal therapy has both educational and therapeutic benefits for the client, or trainee practitioner, as it is, by its very nature, transformative, because therapy is concerned with the process of change. The trainee can increase their knowledge and skill base by being the receptor of the same therapy process. This process allows the practitioner to increase their self-awareness and engage in holistic personal development at the same time, both of which have transformative qualities. After all, it is only by learning about ourselves that we can create a space in which we can learn about others.

This multi-dimensional approach of counselling psychology highlights the importance of holistic personal development for the student, the practitioner and the educator alike and illustrates both the importance of lifelong

---

15    British Psychological Society, 2015.
16    Atkinson, 2006.
17    I. Yalom, *The Gift of Therapy* (New York: Harper Collins, 2002).

learning and the valuable place it has within the counselling psychology profession. The profession accepts the natural, evolving nature of individuals and society. It recognizes the impact this has on both practitioners and the profession, as well as recognizing the potential impact the profession can have on individuals and society. Holistic personal development and continuing professional development are considered so important that they are required in order for counselling psychologists to achieve accreditation and registration with the Psychological Society of Ireland (PSI) and in the British Psychological Society (BPS).

Counselling psychology involves lifelong learning.[18] As practitioners, we develop and grow, through a series of phases, from pre-training through to qualification, accreditation, and registration and beyond. The profession is dynamic by nature, implicitly involved with the process of change. With this in mind, it seems not only rational and logical, but imperative that if we encourage, and in some cases expect, our clients and supervisees to embrace change, then we, too, need to be not only open, but also willing to embrace change ourselves.

## Education as Transformative

Supervision is a practice in which all counselling psychologists engage, particularly those involved in regular therapeutic work with clients or groups. It is a formal, regular agreement between the practitioner and their supervisor, whereby they meet to discuss the intricacies of client work, professional and ethical concerns, and case management issues. Hawkins and Shohet describe it as a 'joint endeavour in which a practitioner with the help of a supervisor, attends to their clients, themselves as part of their client–practitioner relationships and the wider systemic context'.[19] The aim

18    E. Faure et al., *Learning to Be* (Paris: Unesco, 1972).
19    P. Hawkins and R. Shohet, *Supervision in the Helping Professions* (Buckingham: Open University Press, 2014, 4th edn)

of supervision for practitioners is to 'improve the quality of their work, transform their client relationships, continuously develop themselves, their practice and the wider profession'.[20] Supervision is a shared learning process between supervisor and supervisee, very often collaborative in nature, and so the relationship between the supervisor and the supervisee is an important one. Davys and Beddoe state that the 'quality of the relationship between supervisor and practitioner has been identified as the most powerful determinant of the success or quality of the subsequent supervision relationship'.[21]

Kierkegaard wrote that 'Life can only be understood backwards; but it must be lived forwards'. Supervision, as it pertains to counselling psychology, requires a similar outlook. The practitioner engages in the process of looking back over their work with clients in detail, reflecting on that work with their supervisor and consequently learning from that experience and reflection. This process is transformative in nature in that it has the potential to bring about a change in the supervisee, and subsequently the client, through the therapeutic relationship. The process of supervision allows the supervisee to learn from this reflection and in-depth analysis and embody their learning by bringing it back into the therapeutic relationship with the client. This often acts as a catalyst for change, thus enabling the supervisee to move forward with the client. Davys and Beddoe contend that this reflection on practice and experience is 'the most valuable context for reflection in [...] learning'.[22]

Supervision requires the supervisee and supervisor, in the present, to take an in-depth look into the past in order to bring about change in the future. Supervision is a safe place – a sacred space, if you will – which has the potential to encourage profound learning and growth for the supervisee. However, in the supervisory relationship, it is not only the supervisee who learns; the supervisor also learns from the relationship. Many theories or models of supervision are 'driven from the experience of the supervisee

---

20   Ibid.
21   A. Davys and L. Beddoe, *Best Practice in Professional Supervision: A Guide for the Helping Professions* (London: Jessica Kingsley, 2010) 50.
22   Ibid. 13.

rather than from the wisdom and knowledge of the supervisor.'[23] This shared process places an emphasis on the supervisory relationship by moving the supervisor into a position of 'facilitator', as opposed to that of an 'expert' working with a 'novice', thereby transforming the nature of the exchange. The exchange becomes a shared learning experience, whereby both supervisee and supervisor can benefit. As a result, supervision has the potential to be both dynamic and transformative. Ryan describes supervision as 'an inquiry into practice … supervision interrupts practice. It wakes us up to what we are doing. When we are alive to what we are doing we wake up to what is, instead of falling asleep in the comfort stories of our clinical routines.'[24]

Jack Mezirow's theory on 'transformational learning' has become widely influential, particularly in cross-professional and supervisory contexts.[25] The process of supervision is 'transformative' and collaborative in nature, with multi-dimensional aspects; it involves transformative learning and teaching for the supervisor and the supervisee with, a knock-on effect for clients and groups in the therapeutic context. Jack Mezirow originally formulated his theory on learning by observing a group of women who were returning to education, after an extended break from the academic system. Mezirow was curious about this process and was particularly interested in what influenced their successful return to college and, more specifically, the elements that helped and hindered this process. Mezirow's initial research findings indicated that the subjects seemed to experience a kind of 'personal transformation' or change when they returned to college and began their new academic career.[26]

Mezirow recognized that education brings about change, and that this change is not just confined to theories and concepts, but is a more fundamental change. He called this 'transformative learning'. This change

23    Davys and Beddoe, *Best Practice in Professional Supervision: A Guide for the Helping Professions*.
24    S. Ryan, *Vital Practice* (Portland, UK: Sea Change Publication, 2004).
25    Mezirow, *Education for Perspective Transformation* and Mezirow, 'Perspective Transformation'.
26    Ibid.

or 'transformation' Mezirow was referring to became the theoretical basis for his research findings and his subsequent theory, the transformational learning theory. The transformational learning theory proposes that when students reflect critically on their own underlying assumptions and subjective experience, transformation occurs. Mezirow goes on to state that 'A defining condition of being human is that we have to understand the meaning of our experience'.[27] Mezirow suggested that transformational learning occurs in response to, or as a result of, what he termed a 'disorienting dilemma'. This occurs when the individual comes into contact with a dilemma, in the face of which their view of the world is no longer helpful or valid and requires a shift in perspective or change. Transformation occurs when a number of unexamined assumptions are thrown into crisis, and the individual is forced to re-evaluate preconceived notions. This could occur in response to a life crisis, trauma or major life transition. Cranton describes the disorienting dilemma as the very 'catalyst for transformation'.[28] Put simply, education has the potential to be 'transformative'. As Ryan suggests 'Supervision interrupts practice [...] It wakes us up'.[29]

Clark proposed that transformational learning is learning that induces more far-reaching change in the learner than other kinds of learning.[30] This highlights the influence and impact of transformational learning in the supervisory context. The learning in question is experiential learning. Clark proposes that these learning experiences shape the learner and produce a significant impact or paradigm shift.[31] This shift subsequently affects the learner's future experiences. Most learning occurs at the boundary of knowing and not knowing; this is where the learner sits on the edge of knowing and courageously steps outside their comfort zone into a transitional zone where new learning can occur.

27    Mezirow, 'Transformative Learning: Theory to Practice'.
28    P. Cranton, 'Teaching for Transformation', *New Directions for Adult and Continuing Education* 93 (2002), 63–72.
29    S. Ryan, *Vital Practice* (Portland, UK: Sea Change Publications, 2004).
30    M. C. Clark, 'Transformational Learning', in Merriam (ed.), *An Update on Adult Learning Theory, New Directions for Adult and Continuing Education* (San Francisco, CA: Jossey Bass, 1993), 47–56.
31    Ibid.

Berger explains that it is in this 'liminal space that we can come to terms with the limitations of our knowing and thus begin to stretch those limits' to acquire new knowledge.[32] In the context of supervision, the supervisee can, at this point, explore options for new roles, relationships and actions, and acquire new knowledge and skills. According to Mezirow, 'transformative learners move toward a frame of reference that is more inclusive, discriminating, self-reflective, and integrative of experience'.[33] As a result, subsequent actions and interventions are more considered and reflect good professional practice.

If we consider these findings in both therapeutic and supervisory terms, it becomes clear that the learning that occurs during supervision has a knock-on effect, and in many cases directly impacts on the therapeutic relationship and the therapeutic process. Supervision offers a space for reflection, where assumptions can be questioned, and blind spots revealed, and ultimately enlightenment can occur, inspiring new insights and transformational learning.[34]

In the profession of counselling psychology and supervision, the relationship, be it therapeutic or supervisory, is a collaborative, reflective learning process which occurs in relation to an 'other'. In fact, the relationship is often the main mechanism or medium through which change and transformational learning can occur.[35] The work of the counselling psychologist is almost always in relation to an 'other', and this relationship is a key element in both therapeutic and supervisory work. Rogers famously stated, 'If I can provide a certain type of relationship, the other person will discover within himself the capacity to use that relationship for growth, and change and personal development will occur'.[36]

---

32    J. G. Berger, 'Dancing on the Threshold of Meaning: Recognising and Understanding the Growing Edge', *Journal of Transformative Education* 4 (2004), 335–61.

33    Mezirow, 1997, 5.

34    Mezirow, 2009

35    Ibid.

36    C. R. Rogers, *On Becoming a Person: A Therapist's View of Psychotherapy* (Boston, MA: Houghton Mifflin, 1961), 32–3.

Collaborative learning which occurs in supervision is not merely transferred from one to another, from 'teacher' to 'learner'; instead, it is co-created. This kind of education assumes that the learner has the necessary knowledge and wisdom and recognizes that it is merely the task of the educator to draw this information from the supervisee. Conroy states that 'the approach and process of supervision is contemplative and evocative'.[37] To evoke, as the word suggests, is to draw out, or invite. This position assumes that the supervisee has experience, wisdom and valuable knowledge that is useful to the supervisory process and that, by connecting with this knowledge, it can bring about new insights.

The profession of counselling psychology and supervision has an important role to play in the therapeutic arena and has multi-dimensional aspects. As psychologists and supervisors, we have direct impact both *on* and *within* the therapeutic relationship *and* the supervisory relationship. The work is, by nature, active, dynamic and constantly in flux. In addition, the collaborative work within the supervisory relationship is multi-dimensional in terms of its aim, influence and ultimately its impact. It aims to facilitate growth and learning in the supervisee, which in turn impacts on their clients, the organization and the wider clinical rhombus within which the supervisee and the supervisor both work. It seems clear that by working in collaboration, we learn in collaboration, so it is fundamental, perhaps now more now than ever, to ask: what are we teaching? And what are we learning in the process?

Patricia Cranton proposes that when educators are led to examine their own practice critically and thereby acquire alternative ways of understanding what they do, transformative learning about teaching can take place.[38] As Carroll suggests, we move 'from reflection-in-action, to reflection-on-action to reflection-for-action'.[39] We learn that education, and indeed

37    M. Conroy, *Looking into the Well: Supervision of Spiritual Directors* (Chicago: Loyola University Press, 1995), 39.

38    Cranton, 'Teaching for Transformation', 2002.

39    M. Carroll, 'Levels of Reflection: On Learning Reflection', *Psychotherapy in Australia* 16 (2) (2010), 29.

learning, can be active, engaging and transformational and not just passive, instructive and lifeless.

## Vocational Education

Vocation is described in the Oxford English dictionary as 'A strong feeling of suitability for a particular career or occupation', 'a person's employment or main occupation, especially regarded as worthy and requiring dedication' and as 'a trade or profession'.[40] Vocational education traditionally referred to the education of religious groups. However, more contemporary perspectives consider vocation to be an alignment or congruence between an individual's belief or value system and their education and work life choices. The education and training of counselling psychologists certainly falls into this category of vocational education. Counselling psychology educates and trains individuals to work with others, and often involves a sense of vocation or a feeling on the part of the trainee psychologist that their value system suits or matches their choice of career.

The counselling psychology profession focuses on the individual and, as mentioned earlier, places significant value on the relationship between the therapist and the client – that is, the therapeutic relationship. Yalom proposes that 'the relationship with the client should take top priority' and that 'therapy should not be theory driven, but relationship driven'.[41] Indeed, this relationship is one of the core components of the work carried out by counselling psychologists. We also know that the relationship or therapeutic alliance is a strong predictor of outcome in individual psychotherapy across diverse treatment orientations and modalities.[42] The therapeutic

---

40   J. Pearsall and B. Trumbell, *The Oxford English Reference Dictionary* (Oxford: Oxford University Press, 2002).

41   Yalom, *The Gift of Therapy*, 2002, xviii.

42   A. O. Horvath and R. P. Bedi, 'The Alliance', in J. C. Norcross (ed.), *Psychotherapy Relationships that Work: Therapist Contributions and Responsiveness to Patients* (New York:

relationship is often a moderating factor in the process of change and is usually a key component in the helping professions.

Much of the work of a counselling psychologist involves, or is in relation to, another individual. The work is collaborative in nature and necessitates an acute awareness both of the 'self', the 'other' and the potential impact of the 'self' on the other. In counselling psychology, the aim is to alleviate distress and increase the psychological well-being of clients. We do this by educating and training individuals in the skills necessary in order to work therapeutically and collaboratively with individuals – essentially, how to 'be' in relation to an 'other'.

This is not an easy task and is not simply about the transfer of knowledge; it involves encouraging individuals to think critically, to engage in experiential learning, and to reflect on that experience, so as to bring about more learning – to learn from the inside out, as it were. Conroy proposes that 'supervisors also must create the space within themselves to be able to receive [supervisees'] experiences', illustrating the importance of an awareness of the potential impact on another and the importance of creating and cultivating space for another.[43] Mary Bumpus and Bradburn Langer pose the question: is 'supervision something we do or something we are?'[44]

## Conclusion

The science of counselling psychology and supervision requires an understanding and acceptance of one's own personal history, combined with an explicit knowledge and understanding of psychological theories. The

---

Oxford University Press, 2002); D. J. Martin, J. P. Garske and M. D. Davis, 'Relation of the Therapeutic Alliance with Outcome and other Variables: A Meta-analytic Review', *Journal of Consulting and Clinical Psychology* (68) (2000), 438–50.

43   Conroy, *Looking into the Well*, 51.

44   M. R. Bumpus and B. Langer, *Supervision of Spiritual Directors: Engaging in Holy Mystery* (London: Morehouse, 2005).

education and training is vocational in that it allows students to work in a particular way with various client populations. Many educational institutions now also check applicants to determine their suitability for the role, to see if they are appropriately attuned and sufficiently resilient to be capable of attending to the needs of others in what can be an extremely challenging role. Can the individual truly embody the attitude, ethos and philosophy of counselling psychology and, if not, is this something that can be taught? In essence, the profession of counselling psychology is often vocational by nature as it requires a willingness to engage in, and a capacity for, holistic development and lifelong learning in both students and educators alike.

As previously mentioned, the 'use of self' is necessary in the therapeutic and supervisory context and the profession recognizes that an in-depth knowledge of self is crucial when relating therapeutically to others. The 'use of self' as an instrument of change is implicit in the profession of counselling psychology. This understanding of self and increased self-awareness also links in with the notion of vocation, specifically as in, providing a service to others. As Conroy suggests, it is 'the privilege of companioning others'[45] in leadership, justice and service.

## Bibliography

Atkinson, P., 'Personal Therapy in the Training of Therapists', *European Journal of Psychotherapy and Counselling* 8 (4) (2006), 4407–10.
Berger, J. G., 'Dancing on the Threshold of Meaning: Recognising and Understanding the Growing Edge', *Journal of Transformative Education* 4 (2004), 335–61.
Bumpus, M. R., and Langer, B., *Supervision of Spiritual Directors: Engaging in Holy Mystery* (London: Morehouse, 2005).
British Psychological Society, *Division of Counselling Psychology, Professional Practice Guidelines* (2014), available at: <http://www.bps.org.uk/sites/default/files/documents/professional_practice_guidelines_-_division_of_counselling_psychology.pdf>, accessed 11 March 2015.

45   Conroy, *Looking into the Well*, 1995, 93.

Carroll, M., 'Levels of Reflection: on Learning Reflection', *Psychotherapy in Australia* 16: 2 (2010).

Carroll, M., and Gilbert, M., *On Being a Supervisee: Creating Learning Partnerships* (London: Vukani Publishing, 2011, 2nd edn).

Clark, M. C., 'Transformational Learning', in S. Merriam (ed.), *An Update on Adult Learning Theory, New Directions for Adult and Continuing Education* (San Francisco, CA: Jossey Bass, 1993), 47–56.

Conroy, M., *Looking into the Well: Supervision of Spiritual Directors* (Chicago: Loyola University Press, 1995a).

Conroy, M., 'The Ministry of Supervision: Call, Competency, Commitment', in *Presence: An International Journal of Spiritual Direction* (1) (1995b), 12–24.

Cooper, M., *Essential Research Findings in Counselling and Psychotherapy: The Facts Are Friendly* (London: Sage, 2008).

Cranton, P., 'Teaching for Transformation', *New Directions for Adult and Continuing Education* 93 (2002), 63–72.

Davys, A., and Beddoe, L., *Best Practice in Professional Supervision: A Guide for the Helping Professions* (London: Jessica Kingsley, 2010).

Faure, E. et al., *Learning to Be* (Paris: Unesco, 1972).

Grimmer, A., and Tribe, R., 'Counselling Psychologists' Perceptions of the Impact of Mandatory Personal Therapy on Professional Development, an Exploratory Study', *Counselling Psychology Quarterly* (14) (2010) 4.

Hawkins, P., and Shohet, R., *Supervision in the Helping Professions* (Buckingham: Open University Press, 2014, 4th edn).

Higher Education Authority (2014). 'Higher Education Authority', <http://www.hea.ie/en/about-hea>, accessed 10 March 2015.

Horvath, A. O., and Bedi, R. P., 'The Alliance', in J. C. Norcross (ed.), *Psychotherapy relationships that Work: Therapist Contributions and Responsiveness to Patients* (New York: Oxford University Press, 2002), 37–70.

Hubble, M. A., Duncan, B. L., Miller, S. D. (eds), *The Heart and Soul of Change: What Works in Therapy*? (Washington, DC: American Psychological Association, 1999), 133–78.

Martin, D. J., Garske, J. P., and Davis, M. D., 'Relation of the Therapeutic Alliance with Outcome and other Variables: A Meta-analytic Review', *Journal of Consulting and Clinical Psychology* (68) (2000), 438–50.

Mezirow, J., *Education for Perspective Transformation: Women's Re-entry Programs in Community Colleges* (New York: Teacher's College, Columbia University, 1978a).

Mezirow, J., 'Perspective Transformation', in *Adult Education*, 28 (San Francisco, CA: Jossey-Bass, 1978b), 100–10.

Mezirow, J., 'Transformative Learning: Theory to Practice', in P. Cranton (ed.), *Transformative Learning in Action: Insights from Practice. New Directions for Adult and Continuing Education*, no. 74 (San Francisco, CA: Jossey-Bass, 1997), 5–12.

Norcross, J. C., 'The Psychotherapist's Own Psychotherapy: Educating and Developing Psychologists', *The American Psychologist* 60 (2005), 840–50.

Orlinsky, D., Schofield, M., Schroder, T., and Kazantzis, N., 'Utilization of Personal Therapy by Psychotherapists: A Practice-Friendly Review and a New Study', *Journal of Clinical Psychology* 67 (8) (2011), 828–42.

Pearsall, J., and Trumbell, B., *The Oxford English Reference Dictionary* (Oxford: Oxford University Press, 2002).

Psychological Society of Ireland, 'Counselling Psychology' (2014). Available at: <http://www.psihq.ie/page/art/66/0>, accessed 10 March 2015.

Rogers, C., 'A Theory of Therapy, Personality and Interpersonal Relationships as Developed in the Client-centered Framework', in S. Koch (ed.), *Psychology: A Study of a Science. Vol. 3: Formulations of the Person and the Social Context* (New York: McGraw Hill, 1959), 184–256.

Rogers, C. R., *On Becoming a Person: A Therapist's View of Psychotherapy* (Boston, MA: Houghton Mifflin, 1961).

Roth, A., and Fonagy, P., '*What Works for Whom?*', *A Critical Review of Psychotherapy Research* (London: Guildford, 1996).

Ryan, S., *Vital Practice* (Portland, UK: Sea Change Publications, 2004).

Wiseman, H., and Shefler, G., 'Experienced Psychoanalytically Oriented Therapists' Narrative Accounts of Their Personal Therapy: Impacts on Professional and Personal Development', *Psychotherapy* 38 (2) (2001), 2129–41.

Wolfe, R. (1990) 'Counselling Psychology in Britain: An Idea Whose Time Has Come' *The Psychologist* 3 (12), 531–5.

Wolfe, R., Strawbridge, S., Douglas, B., Dryden, W., *Handbook of Counselling Psychology* (London: Sage, 2010).

Wosket, V., *The Therapeutic Use of Self: Counselling Practice, Research and Supervision* (London: Routledge, 1999).

Yalom, I., *The Gift of Therapy* (New York: Harper Collins, 2002).

ANDREW O'REGAN

# 4    Transformative Leadership in Irish Voluntary Organizations: Lessons from the Field

## Introduction

Over the past twenty-five years or so, there has been considerable growth in the number and range of programmes at third-level institutions devoted to the education of managers and leaders of organizations in the third, or non-profit, sector. While these programmes have taken a variety of forms, an increasing amount of graduate programmes at master's level are being offered. Much of the initial work in this educational field took place in the United States; however, such programmes can now be found worldwide. This may be seen as an expression of the growth in the number of third-sector organizations over the last fifty years and, linked to this growth, an increasing academic interest in this area in a range of social and human science disciplines. Of course, the very provision of such programmes implies, among others things, that (i) a distinct curriculum is required and can be identified and delivered, and (ii) that the postgraduate space is the correct place for such programmes. In this chapter, it is not my intention to critique curricula or the structures of formal educational progression Rather, I wish first to explore why an individual might be involved in action in third-sector organizations before considering what challenges the individual's reasons for being involved might pose in developing educational provision for managers and leaders of these organizations. The approach is as follows: findings from research with individuals with experience of leading third-sector organizations are presented, then these findings are considered in the light of particular ideas from the fields of philosophy, sociology, and leadership studies, and, finally, the implications for the provision of third-sector or non-profit management and leadership education are considered.


## Experience of Leading Third-Sector Organizations


Some years ago, I sought to understand the meaning and sense-making of individuals who had committed much of their lives to involvement in third-sector organizations in Ireland. The research involved asking seven individuals to explain why they had so committed themselves and how they had come to be doing what they were doing by telling of their lives. The seven comprised four women and three men. They were aged between their early forties to their late fifties. All had been educated to postgraduate level in the humanities, the social sciences and education. All had been deeply involved in third-sector organizations as volunteers or staff or both and had either established organizations or led significant or transformational organizational change. Each was asked to tell their life story relative to their engagement with the organizations they had chosen to found, work in, or volunteer for. Through these life stories, I sought to understand the subjective experience of an individual over the course of their life.[1] The life stories were collected during in-depth, unstructured and iterative interviews. The relevance of such life stories lies not in their accurate portrayal of lives lived, but in the manner in which they are constructed and used in the present to make sense of the past, the present and a possible future.[2]

1     R. Atkinson, 'The Life Story Interview', in J. F. Gubrium and J. A. Holstein (eds), *Handbook of Interview Research; Context and Method* (Thousand Oaks, CA: Sage, 2002), 121–140.

2     J. F. Gubrium and J. A. Holstein, 'Narrative Practice and the Coherence of Personal Stories', in *Sociological Quarterly*, 39: 163–87 (Oxford: Blackwell Publishing, 1998); J. A. Holstein and J. F. Gubrium, *The Self We Live By: Narrative Identity in a Postmodern World* (New York: Oxford University Press, 2000).

The value of such personal narratives lies precisely in their interpretation, rather than their re-construction, of the past.[3]

The aim of interpretation was to illuminate the meanings given to lived experience by the storytellers or narrators. The analytical process sought to identify (a) meanings attached to experience, and (b) themes within and across the life stories.

*Interpretation: The Lived Experience*

Within the lived experience as recounted by the narrators, common or recurring elements may be presented as: (i) the presence of early significant others in their lives, (ii) early reflexive experiences and a sense of difference, (iii) the experience of epiphany, (iv) the search for a work context that supports the expression of self, (v) the rigorous and ongoing testing of values with experience, (vi) a willingness to undertake personal responsibility for making change happen, (vii) an ability to give organizational expression to an enactment of values, and (viii) in life, regularly reaching and recognizing a time to move on. These elements are presented and considered below.

THE PRESENCE OF EARLY SIGNIFICANT OTHERS IN THEIR LIVES

The narrators variously identified the importance of the impact of other individuals on their lives, particularly in relation to the formation of their values during their childhood or the development of a critiquing eye during their later education. However, the identification of specific individuals as substantial influencers was more muted than I had anticipated. Indeed, the narrators, rather than identifying such individuals, were more likely to highlight significant early experiences, a developing awareness of significant thought, or cognitive and interpretative systems later in life. While the expectation that such significant others would be identified by the

---

3   C. Kohler Riessman, 'Analysis of Personal Narratives', in J. F. Gubrium and J. A. Holstein (eds), *Handbook of Interview Research; Context and Method* (Thousand Oaks, CA: Sage, 2004), 695–710.

storytellers lay in my own biases, it may be that their relative absence is due to the narrators' preference for using incident as a way of encapsulating meaning. However, within the scheme of their lives, it seems more likely that the tendency not to identify single influencers reflects the degree to which the narrators have struggled with socially presented value systems and worked to develop their own value systems.

## EARLY REFLEXIVE EXPERIENCES AND A SENSE OF DIFFERENCE

The narrators variously recalled a sense of being different or of seeing things differently from others during their childhood. This sense of difference was not expressed as a conclusion in hindsight, but as a recollection of a reflexive awareness at the time. Such reflexivity was coupled with strong childhood sensitivity to aspects of the human condition and, in teenage years, to aspects of the social environment. In particular, their narratives were illustrative of an early sense of self, of self in relation to others in society, and of a distinction or difference between that self and others, in terms of perception of the world or of personal interests.

## THE EXPERIENCE OF EPIPHANY

Denzin[4] uses the concept of epiphany to describe singular events that have an impact on the lives of individuals by changing their perspective on some aspect of their experience of the world. In the telling of their stories, the narrators in this research often referred to particular events with such an emphasis. However, the notion of sudden and momentary revelation suggested by 'epiphany' may be too restrictive. Taking a longer temporal view might suggest that epiphany is a crystallizing moment in a more complex and longer process of perspective and value change. Indeed, several of the narratives described defining personal struggles that stretched over many years. Whether the experience of 'epiphany' is singular and distinct or long and laboured, the central characteristic remains similar, however: that is, the

---

4    N. K. Denzin, *Interpretative Biography* (London: Sage, 1989).

narrators experienced a sense of arriving at a point at which they saw the social world differently to how they had previously viewed it. Furthermore, this new perspective led them to reassess their own relationship to the social world and thereby influenced their actions in it.

## THE SEARCH FOR A WORK CONTEXT THAT SUPPORTS THE EXPRESSION OF SELF

While it may not have been formally expressed as such, all the narrators displayed a concern about pursuing activities which were consistent with their personally held values and which supported, in some manner, their own development. Given the realities of economic life and their own financial resources (or lack thereof), for most of them, this concern inevitably meant a close attention to their work context. Hence the pursuit of value-driven activities has had to be managed in the context of making a living as well. Nevertheless, it is clear that the wage requirement is the subservient need and that for the narrators their own identification with their work life is a central requirement of their commitment to their employment. This search for a work life that is consistent with an expression of self reflects one dimension of a concern that the fullest enactment of one's life should be consistent with the expression of self. To the degree that individual participation in society is organized around formal work settings, then the involvement with ensuring a consistency between work life and self-enactment simply reflects a context-specific example of a more embracing concern.

## THE RIGOROUS AND ONGOING TESTING OF VALUES WITH EXPERIENCE

As the narrators detailed their lives in the course of the interviews, a recurring pattern of rigorous and ongoing testing of personally held values with personal experience was recounted. Hence the development of personal values is shown as an ongoing, experiential, reflective, and reflexive process. This ongoing testing of values with experience is seen in a continual interrogation of the self so as to ascertain whether one's actions and place in the world are consistent with one's values.

## A WILLINGNESS TO UNDERTAKE PERSONAL RESPONSIBILITY FOR MAKING CHANGE HAPPEN

All the narrators displayed a desire to contribute to organizational and social change, as well a strong belief in their own capacity to do so. Their personal orientation towards social reality is characterized by socially directed action and a determination to effect change. This belief in their own capacity is reflected also in a personal ease when it comes to assuming responsibility for organizing action. Their self-belief is not expressed in an egotistical manner but as a strong commitment to their values and the importance of these values in their lives. Their capacity for effecting action seems to derive from the central position of their values in their lives. In this manner, their commitment and drive to act in society seems to stem from both other-directed and self-directed motivations. Thus, while their action for social change is directed specifically at a social reality, it is also directed at an expression of self that is consistent with personally held values.

## AN ABILITY TO GIVE ORGANIZATIONAL EXPRESSION TO THE ENACTMENT OF VALUES

All the narrators displayed an orientation towards acting in a manner consistent with their espoused values. Additionally, all had played and were continuing to play central roles in the establishment and leadership of non-profit organizations. In some cases, this took the form of providing leadership, at times transformational leadership, for extant organizations. Of particular interest is the link between a set of personally held and espoused values and the value basis and mission of the organizations the narrators chose to be associated with.

The narrators may be seen to give expression to their values not only through socially oriented action, but also specifically through the formally organized expression of values. In this manner, these organizations may be viewed as an organizational expression of meaning. For these narrators, one of the results of establishing or becoming involved in such organized expressions is that their personal value systems are provided with a social space in which these value systems can be communicated to, and enacted for, others. Indeed, the ability to articulate and communicate to others the attribution of meaning in action seems to be a crucial force in the narrators' capacity to initiate and develop organized action. The narrators variously gave evidence of this capacity to generate meaning in an organizational context for others. While this is most clearly exemplified in those cases in which the narrators were individually central to the establishment of organizations and hence articulated the founding values of those organizations, the ability to communicate the integration of values and action with others is likely to have been important wherever and whenever narrators led organizational change.

## IN LIFE, REGULARLY REACHING AND RECOGNIZING A TIME TO MOVE ON

In tracing the pattern of their lives, all the narrators recounted the experience of reaching a time when they felt or knew that they needed to move on from what they were doing and, in so doing, walk away from achievement, position and organizations in which they had a considerable personal investment. This recognition of a time to move on was always explained in personal development terms rather than in terms of the requirements of a given organization. As such, it seems to indicate an orientation towards the needs of the self rather than the needs of the organizations. Given the narrators' central involvement and personal identification with the relevant organizations, this capacity to separate the self from the organization is noteworthy. Indeed, such a lack of conflation of self and organization is not always achieved in organizational life, either in the non-profit or other sectors. In their presentation of their stories, the narrators show little, or perhaps, no evidence of a need for an organizational role to provide self-affirmation.

This point about not requiring an organization for self-affirmation is a rather nuanced one. Insofar as the organization is central to the 'value expression in action' of the individual, then the organization is seen to be central to the individual's expression of self in society. As such, the organization is important to the individual narrator, but not as an organization; rather, as a vehicle for the expression of values. Hence, as the individual's need to express or to emphasize particular values changes, the degree of personal fit with the organization can change also. Personal values remain the central driving force of individual action; therefore, the personal relevance of the organization can become diminished, in which case the individual looks to direct their action elsewhere.

*Interpretation: Emerging Themes*

In and beyond the details of the individual lives, a number of themes consistently emerged. In the interviews, these were seen to run through the life story, to reflect an approach to social engagement, or to characterize perspectives on the human condition. They can be distinguished from the recurring narrative elements in the lived experience outlined above in that they are not specific to an event or time. As presented here, they are abstractions from the stories and are identified in analysis by me as the researcher rather than having been specified in interview by one or other of the narrators. They are presented and discussed below under the headings of (i) a capacity for empathy, (ii) the nature of the relationship with the self, (iii) the nature of the relationship with the other, (iv) the expression of self in action and in communion with others, (v) the relationship with values and belief, (vi) the interpretation of the relationship between living and dying, (vii) a spiritual nature, (viii) a search for meaning and for place, and, (ix) the experience of life as a self-creative process.

The first four themes – (i) a capacity for empathy, (ii) the nature of the relationship with the self, (iii) the nature of the relationship with the other, and (iv) the expression of self in action and in communion with others – may be seen to combine to form the narrators' orientation towards the social world. The remaining five themes – (v) the relationship with values and belief, (vi) the interpretation of the relationship between living and dying, (vii) a spiritual nature, (viii) a search for meaning and for place, and, (ix) the experience of life as a self-creative process – are illustrative of the narrators' experience of the human condition as essentially spiritual rather than material. They may be seen to shape the narrators' orientation to the metaphysical world.

## A CAPACITY FOR EMPATHY

In speaking with all the narrators, I was left with a sense of their deep capacity for relating with empathy to others. This capacity was expressed also as a profound sense of a common humanity, a common human condition, or, in some instances, a sense of a common thread in all life. Such orientations also supported a sense of justice, particularly social justice, and a motivation to act on related issues.

The capacity for empathy for others expressed and displayed by the narrators is an important dimension of how they relate to the social world in which they find themselves. What is particularly notable is the manner in which the empathetic orientation appears to arise from the integration of the generic and specific – that is, their understanding of the human condition and their sensitivity to the place in which a specific other finds him- or herself. Hence, what is expressed is not just a concern for the plight of an 'other', but also a concern for the plight of this other as a human being.

## THE NATURE OF THE RELATIONSHIP WITH THE 'SELF'

Encountered as individuals, the narrators each projected a sense of self that seemed grounded in a deep self-knowledge. I describe this as 'self-possessed' – not to signify self-absorption, but rather their strong focus on their ways of being in the world. In proposing the term 'self-possessed', I have two meanings in mind. Firstly, I intend it to encompass the idea of 'possession of one's self', as in, owning one's self; that is, the individual is not determined by another's or society's value system. Secondly, I intend it also to encompass the idea of 'being possessed by one's self', as in, being owned by the self; that is, a kind of possession by the self so that one's actions are always predicated on the self. The term 'self–possessed' has deliberately been chosen for this dual meaning, for such a duality is exhibited to varying degrees among the narrators. On the one hand, they are self-possessed in the sense that they are not driven by externally generated impulses, such as the wants and needs of a consumer society. On the other hand, they are self-possessed, in the sense that they are never free of an insistent demand to be consistent with their own self, to maintain integrity between their values and their actions. From this imperative, it appears that there is no escape, nor, indeed, any desire to escape, so that there is an underlying and constant tension between the repose of self-containment and the restlessness of constant search. The particular nature of the relationship with self, displayed by the narrators, is central to their orientation to the world. One way of looking at it is that the world becomes the theatre in which they write, direct and perform the plays of their own lives.

## THE NATURE OF THE RELATIONSHIP WITH THE 'OTHER'

The perception of a shared humanity is another of the threads running through the narrators' interpretations of their experience of the world. This perception seemed to be strongly based on empathy or sympathy. As a personal disposition, it appears to be evident early in life and can be found reflected in references to a childhood sense of difference. This sense of a shared experience of the human condition serves to create bonds with all and to do so in a way that breaches the barrier between the individual and the other. Living, therefore, becomes a relational act and the measure of a life is relationally based. While it may be argued that living is relational for everyone, what stands out for the narrators in this research is their awareness of this relational aspect and its importance to them. The manner in which the narrators relate to others in their social world is conditioned or shaped by an orientation to all that is grounded in 'honouring' their individual humanity. This orientation reflects their sensitivity to the impact of their relationships with others on those others, which in turn is based on a empathy or sympathetic capacity.

## THE EXPRESSION OF SELF IN ACTION AND IN COMMUNION WITH OTHERS

Linked to the themes of 'relationship with the self' and that of the 'relationship with the other' is a pattern of self-expression through inter-action and social engagement. Thus, while some of the narrators actively sought time for introspection and reflection, self-expression for these narrators was achieved through action in, and communion with, the community outside of the familial circle. Meaning is not an introverted experience, but is found by these storytellers in engagement with others; hence we can see the importance of the external object or other event in their experience of meaning. In apparent contradiction to this social orientation, however, the storytellers are self-reliant and self-contained and do not need to be in a communal space.

## THE RELATIONSHIP WITH VALUES AND BELIEF

Questions about the narrators' religious belief and practice elicited a variety of responses in the interviews, ranging from deep engagement, to lifelong struggle, to disillusionment and abandonment. In all cases, however, the line of questioning was accepted as entirely valid and my enquiry into the relative importance of the religious dimension of their lives was treated with regard by all the narrators. While their individual level of engagement with this dimension varied substantially, they had all been born and reared in a society in which religious belief constituted the dominant espoused value basis for individual and social action. Given this, it was perhaps inevitable that each would have a story of personal engagement with this religious belief as a potential value system. The various paths this engagement took reflected the basic possibilities open to them: embracement and explora- tion; disenchantment and relative disengagement; and challenge and rejec- tion. Nonetheless, these stories, whether of engagement, disenchantment, or rejection, are illustrative of, on the one hand, the relative influence of religious belief in Irish society, and on the other, of the narrators' vigorous personal engagement with the question of values and the search for values by which to guide their lives.

## THE INTERPRETATION OF THE RELATIONSHIP BETWEEN LIVING AND DYING

As in any discussion on religious belief, the question of the nature of the relationship between the life lived and the mortal condition constituted a fulcrum and all the narrators exhibited a deep awareness of the relationship between living and dying. In broaching this topic in interview, it was notice- able that it was not responded to with the rhetorical air that a twenty-year-old might adopt. All the narrators were older and had enough life experience to deal with the question in a forthright and personal manner. They were aware of their own mortality and reflected on the relevance of that mortality for the task of meaning-making in their own lives. Their search for an interpretation of the relationship between living and dying suggests that death, and how to make life sensible in the face of death, or how to make death itself sensible, remained an existential mystery of deep concern for these storytellers.

## A SPIRITUAL NATURE

All the narrators expressed a view that they had a spiritual element within themselves, to varying degrees. For some, this spiritual element provided a – or perhaps *the* – medium of interpretation. As such, it structured the logic of their personal meaning and their personal engagement with the world. Thus these narrators believe in the value in the human individual, beyond the physical or the economic dimensions. Indeed, the chief value in the human individual is seen by them to lie in this possession of a spiritual dimension. Through their spiritual nature, these lives present themselves as an ongoing search for spiritual expression. Spirituality is not understood as an addition to human existence, but rather as the very core of it. Indeed, spirituality was described by one narrator as the essence of being human and the search for spiritual expression as central to human existence. For other narrators, the articulation of spirituality was neither so clear, nor so centrally positioned within their lives.

While recognizing that, for these narrators, the importance of their spiritual engagement with the world is varied, the common spiritual thread is all the more remarkable, given the range of religious, agnostic and atheistic positions they held. It seems that a degree of spiritual attunement to the world is a common aspect of their orientation to their social and physical environment.

## A SEARCH FOR MEANING AND PLACE

One of the most insistent themes to emerge from these life stories is the experience of what might be characterized as a restless search for meaning, or of life being experienced as such. It is easily identifiable in all the life stories and it is linked to a search for a place where this meaning is recognized and celebrated. Whatever the cause of this restlessness, obviously felt to varying degrees and at varying times in the passage of the individual lives, it finds a foil in dissatisfaction with the normative, institutionalized explanations presented by society. This dissatisfaction seems grounded in an experiential and interpretative dissonance; a dissonance between personal experience and interpretation, on the one hand, and normative, institutionalized explanations offered on the other. The nature of this search for meaning is not a flippant tripping from moment to moment or from value to value. A practice of rigorously interrogating proposed values is evident. Further, values are not subject to a single examination but are continuously tried and reflected on in lived experience over and over again.

## LIFE AS A SELF-CREATIVE PROCESS AND A JOURNEY OF SELF-REALIZATION

All these life stories share a theme that remains largely unarticulated by the storytellers – that is, the notion of the individual life as a process or journey of self-creation or self-realization. Viewed as such, life constitutes a process in which the individual must rise to the challenge of being human. Part of this is the challenge of living; part of this is the challenge of finding meaning; and part of this is the challenge of making one's own life meaningful. Life becomes a challenge to be embraced, not a challenge to seek protection from. This demands a degree of creativity, as the challenge lies in creating the human in the living moment. In doing so, meaning is created for the self and others. From this arises the importance of choice and action, for it is in choice and action that meaning and value are identified and given presence.

The foregoing interpretation and analysis may be posited as a concern with the expression and enactment of self through action in society consistent with self-articulated and self-espoused values. This orientation on the part of these narrators can be characterized as being existentialist in character.[5] As such, their voluntary activity is seen to result from their attention to their perception of the existential dichotomy of being in which

---

5   H. J. Blackham, *Six Existentialist Thinkers* (London: Routledge and Kegan Paul, 1961, 2nd edn).

our humanness, and the relationship between social reality and subjective meaning, are embedded in the tension between two counterpoising tendencies. On the one hand, human beings desire and attempt to express their humanness through their actions on the world. On the other, the world presents itself as an already constituted reality that must be understood and mastered if the potentialities of consciousness are to emerge and develop.[6]

What is particular about this group of individuals is that they have been closely and continually involved in organized voluntary activity over the course of their lives, either as founders or leaders of organizations. It seems, therefore, that in the case of these narrators, the personal requirement for values enactment in society acts as an impulse towards involvement in value-oriented organizations. For it is in such social, value-oriented organizations that they find or can create the social space for self-enactment consistent with their articulated and espoused values. What emerges from these life stories is a reflection of the individual as a participant in voluntary action which is complex, multi-faceted and closely attuned to the subjective perception and expression of self.

Questions remain, however, regarding the degree of transferability of the interpretation outlined above. Specifically, it may be asked to what degree these stories reflect the particularities of (a) exceptional individuals who are not reflective of the wider population involved in voluntary action, (b) the social and human services sub-sectors of the third sector, and (c) the cultural and generational attributes of a specifically Irish cohort.[7] Nevertheless, there remains the underlying theme of individuals struggling with issues of self-identity, choice and values, personal integrity, the interpretation of social experience, and the expression or construction of self. Of course, such issues are recurring dilemmas for our reflexive selves and hence inevitably find multiple expressions in the disciplinary discourses in the human and social sciences. We now turn to consider some of these.

6    G. R. Jones, 'Life History Methodology', in G. Morgan, *Beyond Method* (London: Sage, 1983), 147.
7    A. O'Regan, *Imaging the Voluntary Actor: Interpreting Narratives of Intent and Meaning* (Baden-Baden: Nomos, 2009).

# Perspectives from Philosophy, Sociology and Leadership Studies

## Philosophy

In philosophy, the discourse in existential thought is centrally concerned with human freedom, personal choice and the world as the environment of humans. The social world is held to be dominated by ideological super-structures which inhibit self-understanding and which must be transcended in order to realize one's full potential.[8] Specifically, human freedom is the freedom to choose 'not only what to do on a specific occasion, but what to value and how to live'.[9] Human freedom is treated as a profoundly practical problem, a question of daily praxis. Despite powerful philosophical arguments countering the possibility of free will, 'in many human beings, the experience of choice gives rise to the conviction of absolute responsibility that is untouched by philosophical arguments'.[10]

Existentialism proposes a model of the human being in which existence is seen as preceding essence. Hence, humans are not predetermined by biological evolution or psychological predisposition. Nor are they post-determined by social context. Each is free to choose. However, the price of such freedom is high, for each must create, by his or her choice, his or her own essence. And so,

> For man, to be is to choose oneself: nothing comes to him either from within or without that he can receive and accept. He is entirely and helplessly abandoned to the insupportable necessity of making himself be, even down to the last detail.[11]

8    G. Burrell and G. Morgan, *Sociological Paradigms and Organisational Analysis* (England: Heinemann, 1979).

9    M. Warnock, *Existentialism* (Oxford: Oxford University Press, 1970), 2.

10   G. Strawson, 'Free Will', in *Concise Routledge Encyclopaedia of Philosophy* (London: Routledge, 2000), 264.

11   J.-P. Sartre, *L'être et le néant*, as cited in F. Copleston, *Contemporary Philosophy* (London: Search Press, 1972), 116.

This act of self-creation is purposeful, both for the self and in relation to others. Or as Marcel put it:

> I affirm myself as a person in the measure that I assume the responsibility of what I do and what I say. But before whom am I or before whom do I recognize myself as responsible? ... both before myself and before others; this conjunction is character-istic of personal commitment.[12]

Existentialist thought distinguishes between the character of being which applies to humans and the character of being which applies to things and to humans only in so far as they are things. Humans, unlike things, are not predetermined and must choose their life. Hence, human freedom and the nature of that freedom have an ontological grounding. 'Furthermore, men are conscious of the contrast between themselves and things, of their relations with other man, of their eventual deaths, and of their power to choose and become what they are not.'[13] The challenge of the indi-vidual life is to live in acts of authentic choice, to realize one's individual freedom and not to deny it by behaving as a mere thing, as something determined.

The absolute nature of human freedom is such that choice is neither conditional on an individual's past or on some set of external values. The individual transcends him- or herself insofar as he or she cannot be identi-fied with the past but, through choice, is in an act of continual self-creation:

> For Sartre the philosopher cannot determine a universally valid set of objective values, nor can he tell the individual what his moral choices should be. But he can make clear the inevitability of choice of some kind, the nature of choice, and the difference between authentic and unauthentic choice, so that a man may realize what he is about and commit himself with open eyes.[14]

---

12    Homo Viator, 26, as cited in Copleston, 117.

13    A. R. Lacey, *A Dictionary of Philosophy* (London: Routledge and Kegan Paul, 1976), 64.

14    Copleston, *Contemporary Philosophy*, 135

Or as Blackham has it:

> For nothing can be achieved once and for all or objectively established for mankind; human existence is realized in personal being, and personal being is a difficult and precarious individual attainment constantly striven for and never permanently possessed, but upheld, drawn on, and rewarded by the rich responsiveness of an objective world.[15]

The being which pertains to humans, which provides their freedom and separates them from the world has an epistemological consequence. As Blackham points out:

> ... the scission which makes the existing individual aware of himself and of the world in which he is makes him a question to himself and life a question to him ... The reason why there can be no objective, universal, and certain answer to them is not merely the present inadequacy of our knowledge but because man is and remains in his being a question, a personal choice, and the objective world is and remains in its being a question, open possibility: both are at any time other than and more than anything that can be said of them.[16]

This separation of humankind and the world which is so central to existentialist thought distinguishes it from other philosophies such as materialism, idealism and theology, which 'in their typical forms abolish ideally the separation of man and the world, and thereby destroy his being which lies in living the tension of the ideal and the actual'.[17] Hence Copleston characterizes existentialism thus:

> ... we can say that existentialism in general is the form taken in a particular historical epoch by the recurrent protest of the free individual against all that threatens or seems to threaten his unique position as an existent subject, that is to say, as a free subject who, though a being in the world and so part of nature, at the same time stands out from the background of nature ... existentialism represents the reassertion of the free man against the collectivity or any tendency to depersonalization.[18]

15   Blackham, *Six Existentialist Thinkers*, 161–2.
16   Ibid. 152.
17   Ibid. 154.
18   Copleston, *Contemporary Philosophy*, 137.

Casting the net wider, Blackham puts it more vigorously:

> Man not only manifests himself in history by the deeds of all individual men known and unknown, but also fights in the individual for his authenticity against the great objectivities, the universals, abstract and concrete, which he has made, against the premature *rigor mortis* which creeps in from all quarters. The danger is not only from the devouring maw of the industrial machine, bureaucratic administration, and the totalitarian State, and from the banditry of militant ideologies with their incessant fire of propaganda, but also not less in the holy places of security, in science and morals and law, in Christianity and in humanism. Faith in science, or reason, or duty, or *homo faber*, or Christ, if it stands between the individual and his total responsibility hides him from himself.[19]

## *Sociology*

In the field of sociology, where the nature of the relationship between the individual and society is a central question, there are two main perspectives. The dominant one is that 'sociology should only be concerned with social structures which determine the characteristics and actions of individuals, whose agency or special characteristics therefore become unimportant'.[20] The alternate view is that structures are not to be seen as determining, but rather that individuals create the world around them. While there are a number of views which seek a position between these two extremes, that proposed by Berger and Luckmann is most appealing. They conceive of a 'dialectical process in which the meanings given by individuals to their world become institutionalised or turned into social structures, and the structures them become part of the meaning-systems employed by individuals to limit their actions'.[21]

Adopting an interpretative position, Berger and Luckmann note that unlike other animals, humans have no species-specific environment, no

---

19    Blackham, *Six Existentialist Thinkers*, 163.
20    N. Abercrombie, S. Hill and B. S. Turner, *Dictionary of Sociology* (England: Penguin, 1994, 3rd edn), 10.
21    Ibid. 10

environment firmly structured by our own instinctual organization and that our relationship to our environment is characterized by a world-openness. The development of the individual takes place both biologically and psychologically in a relationship with their environment. This environment is both a natural and a human one. The developing human being not only inter-relates with a particular natural environment, but with a specific cultural and social order, which is mediated to them by the significant others who have charge of them. Ways of becoming and being human are as numerous as man's cultures. Humanness is socio-culturally variable. Thus, while it is possible to say that humans have a nature, it is of more consequence to say that humans construct their own nature, or, more simply, that humans produce themselves. Central to this ongoing process is the individual's experience of the self and of the self in society. Firstly, the individual both *is* a body and *has* a body: 'man's experience of himself always hovers in a balance between being and having a body, a balance that must be redressed again and again'.[22] A human experiences the self as both objective and subjective reality. Secondly,

> ... man's self-production is always, and of necessity, a social enterprise. Men together produce a human environment, with the totality of socio-cultural and psychological formations ... Man's specific humanity and his sociality are inextricably intertwined. *Homo Sapiens* is always, and in the same measure, *Homo Socius*.[23]

Humans experience society as both an objective and a subjective reality.

As we move into the twenty-first century, sociologists seek to elucidate the social changes effected by the social, economic, political, cultural and technical dynamics which shape the overall processes of globalization. Increasingly, terms such as 'post-industrial economy' and 'postmodern society' are used to refer to a changing economy and society. While many of the aspects of industrial society and modern society are maintained, such

22    P. Berger and T. Luckmann, *The Social Construction of Reality: A Treatise on the Sociology of Knowledge* (London: Allen Lane, 1967, quote taken from Penguin reprint 1991, 68).
23    Ibid. 69

as choice, diversity and criticalness, modernity is characterized by a valuing of order and uniformity, whereas postmodern societies embrace ambiguity, diversity and uncertainty. In modernity, the state sought to impose control, but under the conditions of globalization, the state is substantially weakened and the market acts to socialize and normalize. With its focus on the individual and choice as the basis of a market society and its celebration of diversity and multiplicity, social space becomes fractured and contested.[24]

In this social space of diversity, norm and value uncertainty, and a market offering an unending array of commercial identities, the individual is faced with relentless choice. The distinction between social and personal identity becomes blurred as processes of individualization increase. Social identity changes from a given, a factor of birth, to a personal task of self-construction. Whereas humans have always been born into social contexts which provided and shaped their social identity, now, in a postmodern context, increasingly we are bereft of this and are left to our own devices. Individualization concerns the conversion of identity from a social given into a task to be achieved.[25] Life is increasingly lived as an individual project. While some hold that in this situation we become slaves to the market,[26] others see in it an opportunity for an individual engagement with moral choice and social responsibility. Bryan S. Turner states that:

> The requirement that we recall our unconditional responsibility towards the other without trying to reinvent the existential security of rules and expert systems takes us to the heart of post-modernity. In this respect, processes of globalization and individualization offer new opportunities for responsible political engagement beyond the now permeable walls of the nation state.[27]

24    S. Seidman, *Contested Knowledge: Social Theory Today* (Oxford: Blackwell Publishing 2004, 3rd edn).

25    U. Beck and E. Beck-Gernsheim, *Individualization* (London: Sage, 2002).

26    Zygmunt Bauman, *Work, Consumerism and the New Poor*, Issues in Society series (Buckingham: Open University Press, 1998).

27    B. S. Turner, *The Cambridge Dictionary of Sociology* (Cambridge: Cambridge University Press, 2006), 461.

## *The Study of Leadership*

The topic of leadership has long been a matter of great interest in human societies.[28] In the twentieth century, the systematic study of leadership developed in tandem with the study of organizations and management. Initial attention to the traits and skills of the 'leader' moved on to consider the situation or context of the organization. The adaptability of the leaders to the environment, rather than a constant and enduring set of characteristics, became significant. As the focus of investigation turned to the followers and the relationship between the leader and the followers, research sought to understand the drivers, patterns and functioning of this relationship. Much of this work describes the leader–follower relationship as a set of transactions through which both parties achieved desired outcomes. In such transactions, shared goals or values are neither presumed nor required. Towards the end of the century, particularly as we moved into a knowledge economy, greater attention has been paid to the capacity of organizational leaders to motivate employees towards the goals of their organizations and, at the same time, towards developing their own individual capacities. The ability of leaders to engage or change the power dynamic on intrinsic rather than extrinsic motivation has been judged as essential to improving competitive ability in the contemporary organizational world. The discourse on leadership in this space is conceived as being concerned with the transformation of followers, hence the distinction between transactional and transformational leadership.

In contemporary work, a new concept, that of 'authentic leadership', is emerging. Intrapersonal, interpersonal and developmental perspectives on authentic leadership emphasize respectively the leader's self-knowledge, self-regulation and self-concept; a relationship between the leader and followers which affects both; and leadership as a capacity which develops in over a lifetime. The core components of authentic leadership are identified as self-awareness, an internalized moral perspective, openness to the

---

28    K. Grint (ed.), *Leadership; Classical, Contemporary, and Critical Approaches* (Oxford: Oxford University Press, 1997).

perspectives of others (referred to as balanced processing) and a presentation of a true self to others (relational transparency).[29]

> Its roots are also in various expressions of the humanistic movement in psychology
> including Maslow's theory of self-actualization and Carl Rogers' concept of the fully
> functioning person. Central to both of these is the idea that individuals can develop
> to modes of understanding and interacting with their social environments so as to
> become more truly independent of others' expectations of them (individual, group,
> and cultural) and guided more by the dictates of universal truths and imperatives.
> Such individuals manifest congruence between how they feel on the inside and how
> they act, between what they say and what they do. They have realistic self-perceptions,
> free from the blind spots and misperceptions of self that are common to most people.
> At the same time they are accepting of themselves, their nature, and of others too.
> … They have strong convictions which guide their behaviour not so much to avoid
> doing 'wrong' things as to always try to do the 'right' things including treating others
> with respect and dignity. They know where they stand on their fundamental values
> and on key issues. Authentic leaders behave the way they do because of personal
> conviction rather than to attain status, rewards, or other advantages.[30]

In his conceptualization of meta-motivations and meta-needs, Maslow
argues that self-actualizing individuals with meta-motivations devote themselves to a task outside of themselves in which an inner and outer required-
ness coincide. Work and play become indistinguishable. Their vocation
becomes a defining characteristic of the self:

> The tasks to which they are dedicated seem to be interpretable as embodiments or
> incarnations of intrinsic values … The tasks are loved (and introjected) BECAUSE
> they embody these values. That is, ultimately it is the values that are loved rather
> than the job as such.[31]

Writing in a different and indeed earlier context, Frankena focuses on the
internalized moral perspective and balanced processing individual agency
when he noted that

29   P. G. Northouse, *Leadership; Theory and Practice* (Thousand Oaks, CA: Sage, 2013,
     6th edn).
30   R. L. Hughes, R. C. Ginnett and G. J. Curphy, *Leadership: Enhancing the Lessons of
     Experience* (McGraw-Hill International, 2009, 6th edn), 186.
31   A. H. Maslow, *The Farther Reaches of Human Nature* (England: Penguin/Arkana,
     1971; 1993 edn), 296–7.

Moral philosophy arises when ... we pass beyond the stage in which we are directed by traditional rules and even beyond the stage in which these rules are so internalised that we can be said to be inner-directed, to the stage in which we think for ourselves in critical and general terms and achieve a kind of autonomy as moral agents.[32]

In her study of altruism, Monroe proposes five concepts as being of critical importance for altruism: cognition, worldview, canonical expectations, empathy/sympathy, and views of self. Monroe proposes 'the altruistic perspective', a way of seeing the world and especially of seeing oneself as an individual linked to others through a shared humanity. Behaviour flows from this sense of self. Attempts to act in a manner inconsistent with this sense of self in relation to others incurs great psychological costs. As she outlines her theory (in relation to the case of ethical political acts), key factors are (a) the prime force behind such acts are related to our individual identity rather than conscious choice, (b) in general, our everyday lives do not involve decisions which challenge our sense of self, (c) core identity supersedes and shapes our consciously held moral values, (d) actions which touch our basic sense of self involve self-recognition not choice, (e) in action, the individual discovers rather than creates their identity, and (f) behaviour is influenced by the perspective on oneself in relation to others, not the objective existence of a particular characteristic.[33]

## Education for Non-Profit Leadership

The argument for specific management education for practitioners in the third sector is made on a number of grounds. Typically, these highlight characteristics of non-profit organizations that distinguish them from

32   W. K. Frankena, *Ethics*, Foundations of Philosophy series (New Jersey: Prentice Hall, 1973), 4.

33   K. Renwick Monroe, *The Heart of Altruism: Perceptions of a Common Humanity* (New Jersey: Princeton University Press, 1996), 238.

for-profit or public-sector organizations.[34] Indeed, a case for such education provision is evidenced empirically by the growth in the availability
of, and presumable demand for, such education.[35] Internationally, different
approaches to developing non-profit management education have been
pioneered.[36] Such variation, in part, reflects the different background,
context, and role of the sector in different countries.[37]

Despite international growth in targeted non-profit education provision, in Ireland many managers in non-profit organizations seek to up-skill
through the pursuit of courses primarily designed for the for-profit market
and delivered in a for-profit paradigm. This trend seems at variance with,
on the one hand, the dominance in the US of non-profit programmes
that are linked to schools of public administration, and, on the other, the
central funding role played by government agencies in resourcing the Irish
non-profit sector.[38] The fact that non-profit managers in Ireland choose
such programmes may stem from a variety of factors, including programme
availability, the pursuit of certification that might offer greater opportunities for inter-sectoral career development, and a perception by potential
students and employers that non-profit programmes are not as 'hard-edged'
as for-profit programmes. Taking such a course of action, non-profit managers are then required to engage in a kind of translation exercise where
for-profit-based concepts and perspectives must be adapted to suit the
non-profit context. In order to make the assertion that the management
of non-profit organizations requires specific and contextualized education

34   M. O'Neill and D. Young, *Educating Managers of Non-profit Organizations* (New
     York: Praegar, 1988).
35   N. B. Wish and M. Roseanne, 'Curricular Variations in Non-profit Management
     Graduate Programs', *Non-profit Management and Leadership* 9 (1) (Fall 1998), 99–109.
36   M. O'Neill, 'Non-profit Management Education: History, Current Issues, and the
     Future', in M. O'Neill and K. Fletcher (eds), *Non-profit Management Education, US
     and World Perspectives* (Praeger, 1998).
37   L. M. Salamon and H. K. Anheier, 'Social Origins of Civil Society: Explaining the
     Non-profit Sector Cross-Nationally', *Voluntas* 9 (1998), 213–48.
38   F. Donoghue, G. Prizeman, A. O'Regan and V., Noel, *The Hidden Landscape: First
     Forays into Mapping Non-profit Organisations in Ireland* (Dublin: Centre for Non-
     profit Management, Trinity College Dublin, 2006).

compelling, such a translation exercise needs to be viewed as more than simply regarding the output of non-profit organizations as product, for a given market, against a measured price, in a competitive product and funding environment. In practice, one impact of this choice of for-profit education by non-profit managers is that they experience communication difficulties with their non-profit audiences as their learned management language references the for-profit world. While the value of better management is acknowledged in the Irish non-profit sector, the applicability of for-profit management training and education to practitioners in the non-profit field remains problematic.

Across western democracies, there has increased attention to public service management as demand increases, costs rise, budgets are constrained, and a global market economic model demands efficiencies in all sectors. The same dynamic impacts the non-profit sector, particular via the perspectives of many of the providers of funding, whether they be in the public sector or in the private philanthropic sector. The market and the management approaches developed and pursued by the for-profit sector in a competitive environment have become the dominating paradigm of 'good' or legitimate management. The increased use and legitimization of management methods and management thinking seems to be one of the most visible manifestations of organizational change in both public and non-profit organizations.

The constant themes in the analysis of managerialism are the dominance of ideas and practices emanating from the business world. Currently, central ideas are instrumental rationality, agency, and progress. Employing instrumental rationality, an organization is a vehicle for a special purpose (the mission); this purpose is distinguishable from methods for achieving it, and members are expected to use the most efficient and effective means to reach this end. Agency means that the organization and various stakeholders, such as managers, employees, customers, donors – virtually everybody – are seen as independent agents who are striving for their interest, who are capable of initiative, creativity, and intelligence, and who are responsible for their own actions. The centrality of progress, finally, means that managerialism puts the main emphasis on the future. Organizations, people, nation states, and any other kinds of agentic actors always have to

improve and innovate; otherwise, it is expected that they will fall behind
the competition. Past and present are thus subtly devalued. The emphasis on progress typically goes hand in hand with acceleration and work
intensification.[39]

The distinction between management and leadership has long been
debated without resolution and it tends to be shaped by the contemporary
themes in the discourse on leadership.[40] However, in broad terms, it tends
to be summarized in terms of management concerns with system maintenance and efficiency, and leadership concerns with system change and
effectiveness.[41] In the context of an organization, however, the two roles are
less easy to distinguish and any given individual is likely to be performing
both roles at the same time.[42] Nonetheless, the distinction between system
maintenance and system change is useful in that it highlights a necessary
driving force in many areas of non-profit organizational leadership – that
is, a dissatisfaction with the current state of things and a determination
to effect change. For example, the seven individuals whose life narratives
were the subject of the analysis above had all developed coherence systems
based on radical perspectives on society. These personalized coherence systems or social perspectives or interpretations of the social world informed
and gave meaning to their actions in the world. They were informed, variously, by (i) radical feminism, post-structural perspectives in individual
and community empowerment, (ii) Catholic liberation theology, radical
Christianity, (iii) civic republicanism, Christianity, (iv) feminist analysis of
power relationships and their impact on equality, (v) social justice, practical

39    M. Steinbereithner, G. Donnelly-Cox, F. Maier, M. Meyer and A. O'Regan, 'Faces
      and Antecedents of Managerialism in Austria and Ireland', paper presented to the
      International Society for Third-Sector Research, 9th International Conference, Kadir
      Has University, Istanbul, Turkey, 10 July 2010.
40    R. Gill, *Theory and Practice of Leadership* (Sage, 2006).
41    L. J. Mullins, *Essentials of organisational Behaviour: Utilizing Human Resources* (New
      Jersey: Prentice Hall, 2011, 5th edn).
42    H. Mintzberg, *The Manager's Job: Folklore and Fact*, Harvard Business Review Classic
      (Harvard Business School Publishing Corporation, 1990).

engagement, (vi) human rights and the idea of truth, and (vii) practical engagement from a social justice perspective.[43]

Yet in third-level management education, irrespective of the sector the particular programme is aimed at, we find increasingly the institutionalization of a managerialist approach as the legitimate – indeed, the only – paradigm for such education.[44] This is influenced by the global dominance of a market paradigm and an increasingly careerist understanding of the purpose of the attainment of educational qualifications. It is particularly the case in the area of postgraduate and post-experience education. Indeed, as universities are increasingly required to develop lines of self-funding and to understand their role in society as serving an employment-skills market, there is increasing pressure to adopt such an approach.[45]

Yet, if we consider the experience of these leaders working in the Irish third sector, the capacity for and the urge towards leadership is developed experientially, part of which (but only part), is educationally based. Furthermore, the role and impact of education in this context is not in relation to the inculcation of a set of technical skills, but rather the development of the human individual and the individual's capacity for social agency. In this context, the role of formal education begins on the very first day of school and is far from being confined to the tertiary level.

## Conclusion

The immediate problem facing those who would develop and offer professionalizing education to leaders or potential leaders of third sector, non-profit or voluntary organizations is how to shape an offering which

---

43  O'Regan, *Imaging the Voluntary Actor*.

44  Non-profit Academic Centers' Council – see their curriculum guidelines as an example.

45  D. Maskell and I. Robertson, *The New Idea of a University* (Haven Books, 2001); S. Collini, *What Are Universities For?* (London: Penguin Books, 2012).

addresses two distinct issues. Firstly, much leadership in the sector seems to arise from individuals pursuing a holistic engagement of the self with the social world as experienced in their lives. Hence, a limited, time-specific intervention needs to engage specifically with the individuality of the participant. Secondly, there is a tension between a managerialist framing of the leadership role as one of system maintenance on the one hand and the system critique and articulation of alternate meanings by individuals active in these social and organizational spaces on the other. In other words, how is it possible to separate the knowledge of the practice of management from the social paradigm it has developed and upholds? Engaging with these dilemmas is a major challenge. Resolving them within the constraints of a postgraduate offering may not be feasible.

# Bibliography

Abercrombie, N., Hill, S., and Turner, B. S., *Dictionary of Sociology* (England: Penguin, 1994, 3rd edn).

Atkinson, R., 'The Life Story Interview', in J. F. Gubrium, and J. A. Holstein (eds), *Handbook of Interview Research; Context and Method* (Thousand Oaks, CA: Sage, 2002), 121–140.

Bauman, Z., *Work, Consumerism and the New Poor.* Issues in Society series (Buckingham: Open University Press, 1998).

Beck, U., and Beck-Gernsheim, E., *Individualization: Institutionalized Individualism and Its Social and Political Consequences* (London: Sage, 2002).

Berger, P., and Luckmann, T., *The Social Construction of Reality: A Treatise on the Sociology of Knowledge* (London: Allen Lane, 1966).

Blackham, H. J., *Six Existentialist Thinkers* (London: Routledge and Kegan Paul, London, 1952, 1961 edn).

Burrell, G., and Morgan, G., *Sociological Paradigms and Organisational Analysis* (England: Heinemann, 1979).

Collini, S., *What Are Universities For?* (London: Penguin Books, 2012).

Copleston, F., *Contemporary Philosophy* (London: Search Press, 1972).

Denzin, N. K., *Interpretative Biography* (London: Sage, 1989).

Donoghue, F., Prizeman, G., O'Regan, A., and Noel, V., *The Hidden Landscape: First Forays into Mapping Non-profit Organisations in Ireland* (Dublin: Centre for Non-Profit Management, Trinity College Dublin, 2006).

Frankena, W. K., *Ethics*, Foundations of Philosophy series (New Jersey: Prentice Hall, 1973).

Gill, R., *Theory and Practice of Leadership* (London: Sage, 2006).

Grint, K. (ed.), *Leadership; Classical, Contemporary, and Critical Approaches* (Oxford: Oxford University Press, 1997).

Gubrium, J. F., and Hostein, J. A., 'Narrative Practice and the Coherence of Personal Stories', *Sociological Quarterly* 39 (Oxford: Blackwell Publishing, 1998), 163–87.

Gubrium, J. F., and Holstein, J. A., *The Self We Live By: Narrative Identity in a Post-modern World* (New York: Oxford University Press, 2000).

Hughes, R. L., Ginnett, R. C., and Curphy, G. J., *Leadership: Enhancing the Lessons of Experience* (New York, NY: McGraw-Hill International, 2009, 6th edn).

Jones, G. R., 'Life History Methodology', in G. Morgan, *Beyond Method* (London: Sage, 1983).

Lacey, A. R., *A Dictionary of Philosophy* (London: Routledge and Kegan Paul, 1976).

Maskell, D., and Robertson, I., *The New Idea of a University* (CA: Haven Books, 2001).

Maslow, A. H., *The Farther Reaches of Human Nature* (England: Penguin/Arkana, 1971).

Mintzberg, H., *The Manager's Job: Folklore and Fact*, Harvard Business Review Classic (Boston, MA: Harvard Business School Publishing Corporation, 1990).

Monroe, K. R., *The Heart of Altruism: Perceptions of a Common Humanity* (New Jersey: Princeton University Press, 1996).

Mullins, L. J., *Essentials of Organisational Behaviour: Utilizing Human Resources* (New Jersey: Prentice Hall, 2011, 5th edn).

Northhouse, P. G., *Leadership: Theory and Practice* (London: Sage, 2013, 6th edn).

O'Neill, M., 'Non-profit Management Education: History, Current Issues, and the Future', in M. O'Neill and K. Fletcher (eds), *Non-profit Management Education, U.S. and World Perspectives* (London and Westport, CT: Praeger, 1998).

O'Neill, M., and Young, D., *Educating Managers of Non-profit Organizations* (New York: Praegar, 1988).

O'Regan, A., *Imaging the Voluntary Actor: Interpreting Narratives of Intent and Meaning* (Baden-Baden: Nomos, 2009).

Riessman, C. K., 'Analysis of Personal Narratives', in J. F. Gubrium and J. A. Holstein (eds), *Handbook of Interview Research; Context and Method* (Thousand Oaks, CA: Sage, 2002), 695–710.

Salamon, L. M. and Anheier, H. K., 'Social Origins of Civil Society: Explaining the Non-profit Sector Cross-Nationally', *Voluntas* 9 (1998), 213–48.

Seidman, S., *Contested Knowledge: Social Theory Today* (Oxford: Blackwell Publishing, 2004, 3rd edn).

Steinbereithner, M., Donnelly-Cox, G., Maier, F., Meyer, M., and O'Regan, A., 'Faces and Antecedents of Managerialism in Austria and Ireland', paper presented to

the International Society for Third-Sector Research, 9th International Conference, Kadir Has University, Istanbul, Turkey, 10 July 2010.

Strawson, G., 'Free Will', in Professor E. Craig and E. Craig (eds), *Concise Routledge Encyclopaedia of Philosophy* (London and New York: Routledge, 2000), 293.

Turner, B. S., *The Cambridge Dictionary of Sociology* (Cambridge: Cambridge University Press, 2006).

Warnock, M., *Existentialism* (Oxford: Oxford University Press, 1970).

Wish, N. B., and Mirabella, R. M., 'Curricular Variations in Non-profit Management Graduate Programs', *Non-profit Management and Leadership* 9 (1), Fall 1998, 99–109.

CATHERINE BREATHNACH

# 5 Irish Third-Level Education: The Challenge of Transformational Learning, a Case Study

## Introduction

Statistics demonstrate the significant and historical under-participation of Irish adults in third-level education; the older the cohort, the starker the outcomes. The Higher Education Authority identified north Dublin as a 'black spot in terms of third-level numbers.'[1] In 2006, participation of adults in higher education was low.[2] In response, in 2009, an innovative adult learning BA degree at All Hallows College in north Dublin was established. It continued to develop until 2014, when the closure of the college was announced. The last students graduated from the programme in 2017.

In a rapidly changing world, this type of situation pertaining to participation in higher education has serious implications for individuals personally and professionally, for their communities, as well as for the economy and society more generally. Referencing this experience of 'liquid modernity' in his discussion of transformational learning, Illeris identified three key questions for adult learners in a world that has become increasingly

---

1    Central Statistics Office, <http://www.cso.ie/en/statistics/education/principalstatistics/>, accessed 12 March 2015; S. McGuinness et al., *Predicting the Probability of Long-Term Unemployment in Ireland Using Administrative Data* (Dublin: ESRI, 2013), <http://www.esri.ie/publications/latest_publications/view/index.xml?id=3999>, accessed 29 January 2018; Aontas, <http://www.aontas.com/blog/2012/08/how-many-people-are-participating-in-adult-educati/>, accessed 29 January 2018; S. McCoy et al., *Leaving School in Ireland: A Longitudinal Study of Post-School Transitions*, research series no. 36 (Dublin: ESRI, 2014).

2    P. J. O'Connell, D. Clancy, and S. McCoy, *Who Went to College in 2004? A National Survey of New Entrants to Higher Education* (Dublin: Higher Education Authority, 2006).

complex and unpredictable: how to relate to oneself? How to relate to one's existence? How to relate to the outside world as it is today?[3] It may be suggested that this approach runs counter to the current dominant paradigm evident in Irish higher education and related government funding, which may be said to be concerned primarily with a narrow understanding of the demands of the economy.[4]

This chapter explores the experience of the adult learning BA (ALBA) programme at All Hallows College as a case study of transformational learning in the Irish higher education context, and the challenges it experienced.

## Transformational Learning and Adult Learners

Jack Mezirow named the concept of transformational learning (TL), defining it as learning that results in change in a person's structures of meaning and understanding.[5] This definition perhaps reflected the perspectives of Paulo Freire and others who regarded adult education as a process of emancipation through the naming of one's world with a view to changing it.[6] Mezirow observed that TL entails critical reflection with the potential for profoundly changing the way we make sense of our experience of the world, other people and ourselves.[7] Illeris, reflecting on this perspective, developed the definition further. Building on research in individual psychology since

---

3    K. Illeris, *Transformative Learning and Identity* (London and New York: Routledge, 2013).

4    For example, 'Funding Basic Research in Science', *The Irish Times*, 19 March 2015; O. Feely, 'The Intrinsic Value of Our Universities Must Be Preserved', *The Irish Times*, 23 April 2015.

5    J. Mezirow, 'Perspective Transformation', *Adult Education* (1978), 100–10.

6    P. Freire, *Pedagogy of the Oppressed* (New York: Continuum, 1970).

7    J. Mezirow, *Fostering Critical Reflection in Adulthood* (San Francisco, CA: Jossey-Bass 1990), xiii.

the 1970s, Illeris proposed a redefinition of TL as 'comprising all learning that implies change in the identity of the learner'.[8]

Both Mezirow and Illeris published reviews of the literature on TL indicating a number of core and interdependent TL characteristics. These are themes discussed by others also, including Chaves in his discussion of the involvement and retention of adult students.[9] These characteristics included the following:

- Purposeful and heuristic: Based on trusting and respectful relationships, TL is a process that focuses on patterns of understanding and behaviour. It is a process that manages the transition from present circumstances to change, and which offers experiential growth for learners and facilitates their realization that important changes are possible and worthwhile.
- The provision of emotional support and confidence-building: Learners require emotional support during the process of TL. This begins by building confidence in the learner, and being sensitive to his or her structures of meaning. As collaborative learners, educators communicate that they respect what students know and what they seek.
- Modelling: An important aspect of the role of the 'teacher' is to model the behaviour and values underpinning the TL process.
- Critical reflection: Critical reflection involves the analysis of one's own interpretation from different perspectives through reasoning the presuppositions on which beliefs are based. The availability and generation of contrast and comparisons enables creative exploration of the meaning of situations. The competences required for this include developing new criteria for assessing situations (evaluation), developing new perspectives on a situation (divergence) and the ability to find alternatives in a given situation (new ways of seeing, new questions to ask, new ways to use things).

8   Illeris, *Transformative Learning and Identity*, 40.
9   C. Chaves, 'Involvement, Development and Retention: Theoretical Foundations and Potential Extensions for Adult Community College Students', *Community College Review* 34 (2) (2006), 139–52.

- Imaginative, creative and experiential: The TL process is not simply a 'rational' process. Imagination, experience, creativity and emotional involvement are also significant dimensions.
- Social, collaborative and dialogical: The identification of one's dilemma as a shared and negotiable experience, in the sense that a dilemma is an interpretation of an experience or situation, supports critical reflection as a process of testing taken-for-granted premises. The role of dialogue is therefore particularly important. Interaction with others enables the identification of alternative perspectives, and the provision of models for functioning within a new perspective. Through dialogue, attempts to understand what is valid in our own and other's assertions can occur. Such dialogue can therefore be understood as a means to help the learner challenge presuppositions, explore alternative perspectives, transform old ways of understanding, and act on new perspectives. Consequently, TL may be understood as being centrally involved in creating and facilitating dialogical communities that enable new learners to engage in rational discourse and action.
- Confronts power and engages with difference: The process uncovers and addresses interests of power, conflict and cultural difference. A 'dialogical' community embraces diversity.
- Innovative and flexible: TL often occurs where learners reach their previous limits, go beyond these and feel the tension, anxiety and emotions associated with the new or unknown experience. Such exposure often encourages emotional intensity and innovation. It can develop the capacity to respond adequately to new choices in a sustainable manner: '... we must be able to meet and control continuous innovations and unpredictable changes'.[10]
- Change action: Change begins with individual perspective transformations, before social transformations can succeed. Acting on insights derived from transformed perspectives is a logical result. Therefore, the individual perspective transformation process includes taking action, which often means some form of social action. This in turn can include

10    Illeris, *Transformative Learning and Identity*, 31.

collective political action. This brings to mind the approach inherent in both action research methodology, and Kolb's Learning Cycle of integrated learning tasks.[11]


## A Case Study: ALBA, the Adult Learning BA Degree at All Hallows College


*Background to the Model of Learning*

Following the Vietnam War (1962–75), the US government initiated a scheme to enable war veterans to continue their education at third level. Colleges experienced difficulty integrating and responding to the needs of these returning soldiers, not surprisingly, given the complexity of their life experiences. At DePaul University, Chicago, the School for New Learning (SNL) was established to provide an approach to higher education required in these circumstances. This approach related to both content and particularly to the mode of delivery and andragogical methodologies applied.[12] The programmes offered by SNL are based on a competency-based approach (learning outcomes), continuous assessment, valuing and recognition of both prior formal and informal learning. Access is based on learner 'readiness' rather than previous educational attainment. SNL operates on the basis of on-campus, online, blended learning and satellite provision centres. It also has developmental partnerships with other organizations in the USA and internationally. A particular aspect of this model of education is its primary focus on methodology, and the possibility to apply this both appropriately and responsively to the cultures and needs of alternative locations and groups of learners.

11   D. A. Kolb, *Experiential Learning: Experience as the Source of Learning and Development* (Englewood Cliffs, NJ: Prentice Hall, 1984).

12   M. S. Knowles, *The Modern Practice of Adult Education: From Pedagogy to Andragogy* (Englewood Cliffs, NJL Prentice Hall, 1980).

## *ALBA*

DePaul University in the United States was established by the Congregation of the Mission (the Vincentian Order). There were strong links between this order and members of the order in Ireland who had responsibility for All Hallows College in north Dublin.[13] One of the Irish Vincentians, Fr Joe McCann, identified an opportunity to start a degree programme based on the SNL model at All Hallows College that would respond to the needs in north Dublin.[14] This was actively supported by SNL. Dublin City University (DCU) accredited the degree in 2008, and the programme opened its doors in 2009. It continued to develop until the college announced its wind-down in 2014. Enrolment for the programme ceased at that point.

This degree, the BA for Personal and Professional Development, was specially designed to meet the needs of adult learners, and was colloquially known as ALBA – the adult learning BA. The programme philosophy and pedagogy was firmly set in andragogical adult learning dialogical methodology, was learning-outcomes focused, and valued the experience of each student as being at the heart of the learning that took place. In particular, Kolb's set of integrated learning tasks, or learning cycle, provided the architecture for the programme's learning process.[15] There was also an emphasis on Gardner's multiple intelligences theory,[16] Bloom's taxonomy of higher-order thinking, as well as other adult learning theories.[17] Classes were run at night, weekends and intensively during holiday periods. Blended learning was the next item on the programme's agenda.

13    <https://www.cmglobal.org/>, accessed 29 January 2018; <http://vincentians.ie>, accessed 29 January 2018.
14    As discussed by O'Connell et al. (2006).
15    Kolb, *Experiential Learning: Experience as the Source of Learning and Development*, 1984.
16    H. Gardner, *Multiple Intelligences* (New York: Basic Books, 2006).
17    L. W. Anderson et al., *A Taxonomy for Learning, Teaching and Assessing* (London: Longman, 2001).

*The Policy Context*

The period in which the ALBA degree was established coincided with a time of significant review and policy-level challenge in higher education in Ireland, and also in both EU and broader international contexts.

As Keeling observed, the European Commission had become increasingly involved in higher education.[18] Since 1999, and the adoption of the Bologna Declaration, various EU policy objectives had been pursued in this domain. These included, for example, an academic credit transfer system (ECTs) achieved through the establishment of national qualification frameworks in participating member states. The EU Council resolution on 'Learning Outcomes' and validation for non-formal and informal learning, and its resolution on a 'Renewed Agenda for Adult Learning', emphasized that adult learning should embrace the shift to a policy based on learning outcomes in which the autonomous learner is central, regardless of where he or she learns.[19] In relation to the Recognition of Prior Learning (RPL), the European Commission identified that this is an essential contribution to the EU ambition to achieve smart, sustainable and inclusive growth.[20] The commission's consultation process showed an overwhelming consensus on the importance of formally recognizing skills gained through life and work. In particular, it stated that national systems should focus on the following aspects of validating prior learning:

- The identification of learning outcomes;
- Their documentation;
- Their assessment against agreed standards;
- Their certification.

---

18    R. Keeling, 'The Bologna Process and the Lisbon Research Agenda: The European Commission's Expanding Role in Higher Education Discourse', *European Journal of Education* 41 (2) (2006), 203–223.
19    EU Council Resolution 20/12/2011 C372/1 on learning outcomes; EU Council Resolution 2011/C372/01 Final on a renewed agenda for adult learning.
20    EU proposal to the EU Council 5/9/2012 COM (2012) 485 Final.

The European University Association[21] has suggested that qualifications frameworks based on learning outcomes have become the central part of the Bologna process, describing them as the basic building blocks of the Bologna package of educational reforms, and endorsed these as the methodological approach at the heart of the paradigm shift from teacher- to student-centred learning. Learning outcomes imply an approach which focuses on what the student will know, understand and be able to demonstrate as a result of the learning process.[22] This also reflects the characteristics of Bloom's taxonomy of higher-order thinking.[23]

Reservations have been expressed from both philosophical and technical perspectives regarding the possible dangers of a narrow interpretation and application of the learning outcomes approach to education.[24] As Kennedy et al. have pointed out, however, this can be avoided if learning outcomes are written with a focus on higher-order thinking and application of skills.[25] They have suggested that the chief advantage of learning outcomes is the clarity and precision they can bring to learning from the perspectives of the learner, teacher and employer. The second major advantage is that the link between the development of knowledge, understanding and skills to *one* set of 'inputs' and approaches to learning is broken. This enhances flexibility in developing effective and alternative learning approaches and occasions, utilizing life experiences, recognition of prior learning and embracing diversity among learners. This focus on learning outcomes is also reflected in the growing interest among institutions of third-level education in North America in adopting a 'competencies-based'

21    EUA Qualifications Frameworks, <http://www.eua.be/eua-work-and-policy-area/ building-the-european-higher-education-area/bologna-basics/>, 14 April 2015.
22    M. Keane, 'Guide to Writing Module Learning Outcomes at DCU' (Dublin: DCU, 2009).
23    Anderson et al., *A Taxonomy for Learning, Teaching and Assessing* (2001).
24    S. Adam 'An Introduction to Learning Outcomes' (Dublin, 2006), <http://www. dvresources.dcu.ie>, accessed 23 November 2013.
25    D. Kennedy et al., 'Writing and Using Learning Outcomes: A Practical Guide' (Articles C 3.41), in E. Froment, J. Kohler, L. Purser and L. Wilson (eds), *EUA Bologna Handbook – Making Bologna Work* (Berlin: Raabe Verlag, 2006), 2–28.

approach to learning. It has been reported that the numbers of such institutions in the USA with an interest in this grew from 20 to 250 in 2014 alone.[26]

Within the Irish context specifically, the *National Strategy for Higher Education to 2030* published in 2011 included a number of observations regarding the challenges faced by higher education in terms of lifelong learning, and the types of approaches required to address policy objectives in this domain. It can be suggested that the challenges identified and conclusions reached in relation to lifelong learning in the report related to three core elements in particular. These were as follows.

In common with other EU states, there is a relatively poor performance within the Irish higher education system in relation to support for lifelong learning. The report suggested that innovative approaches to research-led teaching and learning, programme design, student assessment and quality assurance are needed.

There is a social and economic requirement for the constant upgrading of employee skills and competences, and this requirement will increase. There is a need to equip graduates with essential generic foundation skills as adaptive, creative, rounded thinkers and citizens, in addition to the comprehensive understanding of their relevant disciplines. This necessitates a new emphasis on nurturing creative and innovative minds.

There is a need to increase the variety and diversity of provision, improve the interface between higher education and further education and training in order to develop 'progression' routes in education to create and enhance human capital. This relates particularly to expanding pathways to higher education.[27]

26  P. Fain, 'Lumina-Funded Group seeks to lead conversation on competency-based education', 12 December 2013, <https://www.insidehighered.com/news/2013/12/luina-funded-group-seeks-lead-conversation-competency-based-education>, accessed 29 January 2018; F. Mili, 'The Multi-Faceted Potential of Competency-Based Education: Four Benefits of CBE', in *Competency-Based Education Digest*, 4 February 2015, <http://www.evollution.com/opinions/multi-faceted-potential-competency-based-education-benefits-cbe/>, accessed 29 January 2018.

27  Solas, *Further Education and Training Strategy 2014–2019* (Dublin: Solas/Department of Education, 2014).

Depending on the manner in which these policy objectives are implemented, it can be suggested that they are consistent with and can support transformative learning for adults in higher education. This was the educational policy context within which ALBA developed. The emergence of the programme also coincided with the onset of the recent economic recession.

## ALBA Student Profiles

Initially starting with very small numbers, within its first year, the programme had to expand rapidly to enrol around sixty people whose jobs had been made redundant at a Dublin-based aviation company. The EU Globalisation Fund, and subsequently the Department of Education and Science, funded their participation. Unlike most of the other ALBA students, in the main, these were male and had a technical educational and occupational background. They were able to undertake the programme on a full-time basis, even though it was primarily designed for those who had to study on a part-time basis and in a non-traditional manner. This was significant as the state does not provide fees support to part-time students; only to those studying full-time.

Each of the ALBA students had a unique story because, as adult learners, the decision to study for a degree posed challenges not just for themselves but also for their families and communities. For this reason, it is difficult to describe a 'typical' ALBA student. The following list gives an insight into the diversity of the students, and the ways in which they were non-typical of the traditional third-level student population. In addition to being mature students over twenty-three years of age, characteristics of many of the students included:

- Those who were the first from their family or community to attend university;
- Those who were unemployed, and often had a sense of hopelessness about the future;

- Those who were early school leavers, a number had left school when they were thirteen or fourteen;[28]
- Those who had had a bad earlier experience of formal education, sometimes due to undiagnosed learning difficulties, for example, dyslexia;
- Those in employment but who were precluded from promotion because they had no third-level qualification;
- Those who held a level 5 or 6 qualification or other pre-university qualification and wished to progress;
- Those who had been carers in the home and wanted to return to paid employment;
- Those who had complex lives and responsibilities preventing them from studying in the traditional full-time manner at third level;
- Those who had retired and were seeking an interest, and had a love of a particular subject matter;
- Those who already had a third-level or professional qualification but were attracted by the wide-ranging subjects they could study in ALBA, and the manner in which they were explored on the programme, and who sometimes wished to pursue a change of professional direction.

It can be seen, therefore, that ALBA students held a distinctly different profile to the traditional third-level student.

*Programme Structure*

The primary focus of the ALBA programme was to enable those who had not previously had the opportunity to participate in higher education and to complete their degree to do so. Access was based on a person's readiness to engage, rather than on previous educational attainment. Readiness was determined by the potential student in consultation with programme staff

---

28 Detailed analysis of previous educational attainment of ALBA students is currently being undertaken.

in a supportive environment. This took place at a Learning Assessment Seminar (LAS) held over two weekends. A number of LAS were held annually, and there were multiple dates at which students could start the programme during the academic year.

Building on the supportive relationship established between the programme staff and potential students during the LAS, each student embarked on the programme by undertaking the two 'Foundations in Adult Learning' modules. During these modules, students were introduced to theories and practices of adult learning and given the space to develop an understanding of themselves as adult learners, and a deeper understanding of the programme. On completion of these modules, each student was allocated a 'mentor' to provide holistic academic mentoring support to them throughout their studies. In particular, mentors acted as advisors and thinking partners for students when making decisions regarding the design and completion of their mentees' own course of studies. This always took place in the context of knowledge of the particular life circumstances of each student. In general, the mentor allocated to a student had been one of the tutors involved in the delivery of the Foundations in Adult Learning modules in which the student had participated.[29]

The ALBA programme was structured on the basis of the achievement of thirty-six learning outcomes (180 ECTs) for the ordinary-level degree (level 7) and forty-eight learning outcomes (240 ECTs) for the honours-level degree (level 8). These were achieved through a framework of four learning strands: Adult Learning, Human Development, Arts and Ideas, Professional Focus (a choice between Business, Pastoral Studies, Community Development, Family Studies, Adult Education, Facilitation or a specially designed professional focus area building on previous experience and interest). Those seeking a level 8 degree also undertook a Capstone suite of outcomes and modules.

There were a number of core learning outcomes that all students were required to achieve. These included all the outcomes in the Adult Learning

---

29   The importance of this mentoring system and approach was identified in the work of C. Ó Mathúna, Transformative Adult Education: Transformative Learning Experiences, in the Self-Evaluation of Participants in the BA for Personal and Professional Development (AlBA), All Hallows College, Dublin, on Completion of the First Year of Studies (PhD Thesis, unpublished, 2013).

Strand. These encompassed essential competences required when undertaking academic study at third level.[30] Four core ethics courses were also required, one in each strand area. In addition, each student was required to complete a minimum of one learning outcome in each of the three subsections of the Human Development Strand (Communities and Societies, Institutions and Organizations, Individual Development) and the Arts and Ideas Strand (Interpreting the Arts, Creative Expression, Reflection and Meaning).

Out of the thirty-six learning outcomes of the level 7 degree studies, thirteen specific outcomes were required, with a further six required from specific sections of the programme, though students could decide which these would be. All the remaining seventeen learning outcomes were completely determined by the choices of each student, with the proviso that nine of the outcomes had to be achieved within each strand and one had to be designated for a 'Final Project' to allow for full grade classification of the final result. Therefore, in many ways, each student's level 7 degree programme was largely self-designed by the student within established parameters. This allowed students to develop and enhance their individual study focus or area of specialization. Students could complete outcomes through taught modules, guided reading courses, independent learning projects (ILP), and recognition of prior learning through transfer of credit for formal learning or ILP for informal experiential learning analysed using an appropriate theoretical framework.

Once a student completed thirty-five of these outcomes, they could opt to either graduate with an ordinary-level degree at level 7, or continue to the Capstone content, which provided the honours level 8 degree. The level 8 element consisted of an additional twelve learning outcomes related to taught modules in Globalization, Creativity, Interdisciplinary Studies and Research Methods, and four independent study projects, including an Internship, Externship, Summit Seminar and Advanced Project. The Summit Seminar was a reflection and presentation on each student's

---

30   Foundation Studies: understanding learning, oneself as a learning and the programme; Scholarly Writing; IT; Quantitative Reasoning; Critical Thinking; Collaborative Learning; Ethical Acting. The final outcome in this strand, the Summit Seminar, was the last outcome completed before the student completed their studies and was a review of the student's personal learning journey through the programme, undertaken by the student.

individual learning journey by the students themselves. If the students chose to graduate at level 7, the Summit Seminar was presented at that point as the thirty-sixth learning outcome.

Any full-time, third-level student in any course is expected to complete sixty ECTs annually. This is equal to twelve learning outcomes on the ALBA programme. The defined maximum part-time study requirement on the ALBA programme was forty-five ECTs, or nine learning outcomes annually. Depending on an individual student's circumstances and potential opportunities to transfer ECTs for previous formal learning at level 6 or higher, he or she could achieve more than this number of ECTs or learning outcomes in a given academic year.

The ALBA academic year comprised four semesters (autumn, winter, spring and summer) rather than the traditional two (autumn and winter). This enabled part-time students in particular to accelerate their progress in a manner which would be impossible otherwise. They could also plan their annual academic work in the context of their other life commitments.

## Programme Awards

The programme awards were degrees at level 8 (honours) and level 7 (ordinary), and for those who wished to complete their studies at an earlier stage, a level 8 certificate or diploma in Personal and Professional Development. Just prior to the announcement of the wind-down of All Hallows College, additional non-major awards were also accredited by DCU. These were non-major level 8 certificate and diploma 'Short Awards' in Professional Development in the professional focus areas encompassed by the degree.

## Academic Programme Governance and Quality Assurance

All learning outcomes were specified in terms of the required knowledge, skills and competence to the defined required standards of the award being sought. Academic assessment was generally carried out through a process of continuous assessment. The design, assessment, documentation and recording of all learning outcomes and their achievement by students, and related modules, had a chain of documented evidence to ensure and demonstrate that a student received a quality learning experience resulting in the defined learning outcomes, and a fair and transparent assessment of that learning. The process was ensured and assured by the involvement of appropriate and academically highly qualified external examiners appointed by the accrediting institution, and other academic external and internal advisory and oversight committees, as appropriate to different stages of the programme accreditation and oversight process. A high-level representative of the accrediting institution also directly oversaw the student assessment process. This all took place in the context of a strict quality assurance policy and practice at both the level of the delivery and accrediting institutions.

The manner in which the programme operated ensured continuous innovation in terms of content, methodology and structure in response to emerging need and opportunity. An example of this was the capacity of the programme to expand dramatically at a very early stage. Equally, the wind-down of All Hallows College provided the final demonstration of this capacity as it required the flexibility of the programme delivery mechanism to be stretched to its limits in order to provide the full range of learning outcomes to an ever-decreasing number of remaining students. At the point of wind-down of All Hallows College being announced, the next phase of development of this aspect of the programme was in preparation. This was the formal embedding of data collection and review for the purposes of continuous innovation and research.

## Student Retention and Award Achievement

During the final year of operation, a research project was undertaken to evaluate the experience and impact of the ALBA programme. This included a survey undertaken by online questionnaire in January 2017. There was an 85 per cent response rate, and this was a representative sample.[31] Since 2009,

---

31    C. Breathnach, C. Kelly, C. Kilgallon, and S. Larkin, *The ALBA Programme 2009–17: A Case Study in Learner-Centred, Flexible, Competence-Based Irish Higher Education* (Dublin: Higher Education Competence-Based Learning Project, DCU-All Hallows College, 2017).

209 students registered and engaged fully with the programme. Of these 169 (or 81 per cent) graduated with an award, 72 per cent with a degree. 19 per cent withdrew from the programme before achieving an award. In general this was due to financial or health reasons, and most stated their hope to return to complete degree studies at a later stage. The remaining students achieved a Certificate or Diploma, again indicating their intention to complete a degree in the future. 44 per cent of students had been early school leavers. Of these, 32 per cent achieved a level 8 degree and 48 per cent a level 7 degree. 45 per cent of students had completed their full-time formal education having undertaken the Leaving Certificate. 30 per cent of these achieved a level 7 degree and 60 per cent a level 8 degree. Of those who had graduated by January 2017, 40 per cent had already progressed to postgraduate or vocationally related further study. Two had already embarked on PhD studies.

### The Business Model

As with any new enterprise, investment is required at its inception to enable sustainability. In particular, All Hallows College and a number of religious orders generously supported the endeavour through the provision of a number of scholarships. The recent research mentioned above into the operation of ALBA indicates that the model lends itself to a self-financing social enterprise approach to delivery. There are three main reasons for this.

The first reason was that the core programme acted as a 'hub' mechanism supporting the delivery and potential delivery of a number of courses, accredited and unaccredited, at degree level and lower. This was primarily directed at a local adult learning market, but had the capacity to expand to encompass regional, national and international markets without incurring significant additional programme delivery costs. This was in terms of both blended learning and campus-based provision. This, therefore, created the possibility for the generation of additional income through fees without the need for significant additional resourcing. Additional investment in marketing had the strong potential to pay dividends.

The second reason was that the programme operated with a small core staff. The bulk of staff employed on the programme was employed on an adjunct basis. This included both lecturers and mentors. This not only kept costs of delivery to a minimum; it also ensured flexibility of delivery in terms of time and location, in addition to content innovation.

The third reason was that the delivery of the programme did not require large-scale, sophisticated facilities. The core delivery and quality requirement was the andragogical and disciplinary expertise of the faculty.

### *The Core Characteristics of the ALBA Programme Delivery in Terms of Transformative Learning*

Ciarán Ó Mathuna, in his research into the first-year experiences of ALBA students, found that even at that early stage, students experienced personal, academic and social transformations.[32] These were enabled, according to the students, by the supportive and adult learning environment, the relationships with mentors and fellow students, the course content and structure, and the foundations in adult learning modules, in particular. Students started to graduate from the programme in 2012, with the first larger group graduating in 2013. Observations made prior to graduation by students reflecting on their experience of the programme in the context of their Summit Seminar presentations, while anecdotal, suggest the change in meaning structures and identity referred to by Illeris and Mezirow.[33] Examples include the following:

> Although I was apprehensive about returning to education, the ALBA course has helped me believe in myself and realise my potential ... The course is unique in that it allows students to bring all their experiences to date with them, while at the same time you are challenged by new understandings and concepts. Before I began this journey, I had a lot of self-doubt, however, the positive experiences I have had on

32    Ó Mathúna, *Transformative Adult Education*, 2013.
33    Summit Seminar presentations have been recorded since summer 2014, primarily for examination processes. See Illeris, *Transformative Learning and Identity*, 2013; Mezirow, *Fostering Critical Reflection in Adulthood*, 1990.

ALBA has given me new-found confidence in my ability and belief in the future. (Paul, 2014)

ALBA has shown me a new world that I never thought I would see. A world that has given me confidence to be the person I was meant to be. ALBA has changed 'I can't' into 'I can'. (Miriam, 2013)

Overall my academic experience in All Hallows has been transformative. They deliberately challenged many of the preconceptions we had about our own capacities and abilities … My ability to express myself in a way that articulates precisely how I feel, think and experience has multiplied. (Mark, 2013)

I have challenged and pushed myself to overcome self-inflicted obstacles to my learning. I have also become a critical, objective, lateral thinker. I work in administration. I was studying theory and concepts in college whilst putting it into practice in my work. (Margaret, 2013)

This type of student impact is suggestive of the dimensions of TL described earlier. This has been further confirmed by the research into the programme undertaken in 2017. The core characteristics of the ALBA programme delivery and process demonstrated these TL dimensions in the following ways. Application to and acceptance onto the programme occurred through a rigorous yet accessible and open method, via a Learning Assessment Seminar, and the development of a personal learning plan. These occurred at various and multiple times during the year. The ALBA model actively enabled student independence and self-directed learning through programme flexibility and choice underpinning the learning-design methodologies. There was a concentration on quality, competency-based learning outcomes achieved by students, rather than 'inputs'. As such, it was a student-centred process. The range and integration of learning outcomes completed during the course of studies ensured students engaged with multi-faceted approaches to thinking about and engaging with issues and problems posed through the study of programme content. This included, for example, traditional academic analysis, creative and imaginative approaches and personal reflection techniques. Building on this, ALBA actively valued prior informal experiential and formal learning, and recognized this for credit purposes. The programme engaged in continuous assessment of student learning and achievement in terms of the demonstration of competency. This approach ensured the integration of the assessment process within the process of learning. This flexibility ensured a procedure which was responsive to the complexity of student lives. These approaches were supported through the one-to-one holistic academic mentoring provided, and the collaborative working methods utilized. The collaboration recognized that the previous experience of participants was a valuable learning resource to all involved, and provided a supportive peer, dialogical, learning community. This ensured there was a real-world focus to the learning occurring, integrating theory and practice. This actively facilitated the development and application of critical reflection. There was also a recognition that staff and students were co-educators, demonstrating mutual and equal respect for each other in this context.

ALBA had a focus on non-traditional learners, on lifelong learning and diversity among the mature student population in terms of gender, age, occupational and educational background, and nationality. The programme resulted in students who not only developed key discipline-specific knowledge and skills, but also developed an expertise in lifelong learning, adaptability, a change-action orientation, and related self-awareness, self-confidence and a set of values. The programme also achieved the continued participation of the vast majority of students to the point of graduation.

In these ways, it can be suggested that the ALBA model demonstrated a process of TL, in particular because it was

- Purposeful and heuristic;
- Emotionally supportive and built self-confidence;
- Modelled the values of TL through the approaches and behaviours utilized;
- Enabled critical reflection;
- Supported imaginative, creative and experiential learning;
- Social, collaborative and dialogical learning;
- Confronted issues of power and engaged with difference, valuing diversity;
- Innovative and flexible;
- Change-action oriented.

*Some Challenges Experienced*

During its existence, the programme encountered a number of systemic challenges, in particular. Such challenges provide significant learning for the development of innovative programmes in the context of the established institutional setting of much of Irish third-level education. It might be said that this setting is often dominated by the needs and assumptions of earlier eras, and a narrow understanding of economic and employment-market needs, rather than those of future-focused, twenty-first-century higher education provision.

The programme had a short-term planning horizon due to the original low level of financial investment in programme development. This inhibited multi-semester planning and the building of a programme-embedded staff (full time, part time and adjunct), as contracting took place on a short-term basis only. All staff involved in the programme needed a sound grasp of the andragogic philosophy of the programme. Due to the circumstances outlined, professional development happened informally and depended on the voluntary commitment of staff.

There was a need for an IT system structure based on the achievement of learning outcomes, continuous assessment using multiple assessment methodologies, and multiple points of entry to the programme. Attempting to graft the ALBA model requirements onto the traditional model of IT administration resulted in the process being unnecessarily cumbersome, labour intensive and costly. It also made it difficult to monitor the progress of individual students in the programme.

The traditional Central Applications Office (CAO) marketing calendar, based on a single annual intake of students, does not meet the needs of a degree such as ALBA, which responds to the particular needs and availability of adult learners rather than school leavers. As with any enterprise, success depends on the ability to reach the market and build sustainable relationships with it in the long term. ALBA needed to develop a well-resourced, programme-specific marketing model, which would reflect the niche mature student markets to which the programme appealed, and the related networked and 'localised' approach and communications strategy required.

There was a perception that the programme was very costly because of the nature of the methodology applied. However, this perception is not borne out by the facts and may have resulted from an assumed cost base linked to traditional models of higher education delivery which did not apply to the ALBA model of education. It must also be noted that no course can be self-financing until it reaches a certain scale. The programme experience demonstrated that the required scale was achievable. Part-time students, most of whom are likely to be 'mature' students, are currently ineligible for state grant aid towards tuition fees, unlike full-time students. Aside from issues of equity, this creates significant financial challenges for such students who wish to participate in and access higher education, with knock-on effects for education providers. It also inhibits the achievement of current EU and Irish policy in relation to enabling educational progression.

The adjunct nature of most of the ALBA faculty ensured the necessary flexibility in delivering the programme in terms of the hours and location of delivery, as well as the responsive development of programme content. A number of permanent All Hallows College staff with standard contracts engaged with the ALBA programme and actively participated in 'out of normal teaching hours' delivery. This was also the case for ALBA administrative support staff. This was a result of their personal commitment to the programme. Such staff availability is likely to pose a challenge, however, in many traditional third-level educational settings. Staff employed on an adjunct basis must also be meaningfully and actively valued as members of the academic community.

## Conclusion

This discussion suggests that the ALBA programme demonstrated the core aspects of transformative learning identified, including the retention of non-traditional students to graduation. In the process, the programme also provided a particular and successful approach to the implementation of both EU and Irish policy on lifelong learning in higher education, encompassing a learning-outcomes, student-centred approach, educational progression and recognition of prior informal and formal learning. Unfortunately, while the research completed in 2017 has shown promising impacts, it will be up to others to trace the long-term impact of the programme on its graduates given the closure of All Hallows College.

The ALBA experience does, however, raise questions regarding the capacity of many institutions of higher education to support the development of twenty-first-century and lifelong-learning-focused innovative programmes. In the first instance, these relate to system-support concerns such as the marketing and IT functions, and the necessity for appropriate levels of start-up investment to enable long-term sustainability and effectiveness. It also challenges the accepted timing of traditional onsite educational delivery at third level, and its effective staff resourcing.

There is, however, a deeper issue to be considered. This relates to the experience of traditional higher education as a transformational learning process, whether for mature learners or the school-leaver cohort. Transformational learning aims to equip students to cope with the demands of a continuously and rapidly changing environment, in which they have to adapt constantly and confidently, and be lifelong learners. The literature on TL has suggested that this requires such students to be able to respond to three key questions: how do I relate to myself? How do I relate to my existence? How do I relate to the world as it is today? This requires critical thinking and an education that reaches beyond the current paradigm, which is focused narrowly on discipline-specific skills and narrowly perceived requirements of the economy only. It requires empowered and creative minds. As we have seen in this discussion, the challenge in responding to this agenda relates not only to educational content and methodology, but also to the need for the organizational development of our institutions of higher education to serve the needs of society. Meeting these challenges within an organizational culture embedded in a bygone era could be daunting, no matter how good the intentions of those involved may be. The prize of serving the needs of society, however, will be worth the effort.

# Bibliography

Adam, S., 'An Introduction to Learning Outcomes' (Dublin, 2006), <http://dvre-sources.dcu.ie>, accessed 23 November 2013
Anderson, L. W., Krathwok, D. R., and Bloom, B. S., *A Taxonomy for Learning, Teaching and Assessing* (London: Longman, 2001).

Breathnach, C., Kelly, C., Kilgallon, C., and Larkin, S., *The ALBA Programme 2009–17: A Case Study in Learner-Centred, Flexible, Competence-Based Irish Higher Education*, (Dublin: Higher Education Competence-Based Learning Project, DCU-All Hallows College, 2017).

Chaves, C., 'Involvement, Development and Retention. Theoretical Foundations and Potential Extensions for Adult Community College Students', *Community College Review* 34 (2) (2006), 139–52.

Fain, P., 'Lumina-Funded group seeks to lead conversation on competency-based education', 12 December 2013, <https://www.insidehighered.com/news/2013/12/lumina-funded-group-seeks-lead-conversation-competency-based-education>, accessed 29 January 2018.

Freire, P., *Pedagogy of the Oppressed* (New York: Continuum, 1970).

Gardner, H., *Multiple Intelligences* (New York: Basic Books, 2006).

Illeris, K., *Transformative Learning and Identity* (London and New York: Routledge, 2013).

Keane, M., 'Guide to Writing Module Learning Outcomes at DCU' (Dublin: DCU, 2009).

Keeling, R., 'The Bologna Process and the Lisbon Research Agenda: The European Commission's Expanding Role in Higher Education Discourse', *European Journal of Education* 41 (2) (2006), 203–223.

Kennedy, D., Hyland, A., and Ryan, N., 'Writing and Using Learning Outcomes: A Practical Guide' (Articles C 3.4–1), in E. Froment, J. Kohler, L. Purser, and L. Wilson (eds), *EUA Bologna Handbook – Making Bologna Work* (Berlin: Raabe Verlag, 2006), 2–28.

Knowles, M. S., *The Modern Practice of Adult Education: From Pedagogy to Andragogy* (Englewood Cliffs, NJ: Prentice Hall, 1980).

Kolb, D. A., *Experiential Learning: Experience as the Source of Learning and Development* (Englewood Cliffs, NJ: Prentice Hall, 1984).

McCoy, S., Smyth, E., Watson, D., and Darmody, M., *Leaving School in Ireland: A Longitudinal Study of Post School Transition* (Dublin: ESRI, 2014).

McGuinness, S., Kelly, E., and Walsh, J. R., *Predicting the Probability of Long-term Unemployment in Ireland Using Administrative Data* (Dublin: ESRI, 2013).

Mezirow, J., *Fostering Critical Reflection in Adulthood* (San Francisco, CA: Jossey-Bass, 1990).

Mezirow, J., 'Perspective Transformation', *Adult Education* (1978), 100–10.

Mili, F., 'The Multi-Faceted Potential of Competency-Based Education: Four Benefits of CBE', *Competency-Based Education Digest*, 4 February 2015, <http://www.evollution.com/opinions/multi-faceted-potential-competency-based-education-benefits-cbe/>, accessed 29 January 2018.

O'Connell, P. J., Clancy, D., and McCoy, S., *Who Went to College in 2004? A National Survey of New Entrants to Higher Education* (Dublin: Higher Education Authority, 2006).

Ó Mathúna, C., Transformative Adult Education: Transformative Learning Experiences, in the Self-Evaluation of Participants in the BA for Personal and Professional Development (ALBA), All Hallows College, Dublin, on Completion of the First Year of Studies (PhD Thesis, unpublished, 2013).

Solas, *Further Education and Training Strategy 2014–2019* (Dublin: Solas/Department of Education, 2014).

# PART II

# Transformation and Justice

SHEENA HYLAND

# 6 Small Group Learning: Reflections on a Pedagogic 'Gold Standard'

## Introduction

Built on structures, values and practices that are often derived from the past, universities are today under intense pressure to speed up, modernize and respond to the needs of the market economy. Higher education is increasingly globalized, corporatized and entrepreneurial, and focused on employability and economics. After decades of widening participation, Morley warns that the economics of austerity and privatization could see higher education 'move from expansion to contraction, with a reinforcement of social hierarchies and privilege'.[1] In this climate, higher education is arguably at risk of being re-positioned as a 'private positional good and luxury product' rather than as a public good or right.[2] Discourse on the value of higher education as a public good has largely been eclipsed by questions concerning the cost of education and the rate of return on one's 'investment'. It is the 'perceived needs of the economy', rather than academic or social imaginaries, which is crucial in driving change in higher education.[3]

After decades of raised aspirations and momentum behind widening participation, the sector now faces the very real possibility of contraction,

---

1    L. Morley, 'Imagining the University of the Future', in R. Barnett (ed.), *The Future University: Ideas and Possibilities* (London: Taylor and Francis, 2012), 26.
2    Ibid. 27.
3    Ibid. 26.

particularly in relation to access for the poorest students.[4] As elitist participation patterns continue to prevail in higher education, we are reminded
that participation is intimately linked to power as universities serve not
only as sites of knowledge production and legitimization, but as sources
of 'capital and dissemination and symbolic control', all of which play a
fundamental role in perpetuating social inequality.[5] As the sector becomes
increasingly associated with the hyperactivity and hypermodernity of the
knowledge economy, the equation of learning with earning risks becoming ever more deeply entrenched. While universities undoubtedly serve
an important function in driving economic growth, it is critical that we
develop new ideas and ways of thinking about higher education beyond its
exchange value in the labour market. Although discourses concerning the
role and value of universities in supporting social mobility tend to stress
its potential for enhancing personal income and wealth among those from
lower socio-economic groups, equity of access to intellectual opportunity
and capital, as well as the potentially transformative experiences that can
come with learning, tend to be overlooked.[6]

In this chapter, I reflect on the experience of teaching in a learning environment that is rapidly vanishing from today's higher education landscape.
As lecturer in the Department of Philosophy at All Hallows College for
ten years, I witnessed first-hand the immense value of teaching philosophy
to small yet diverse groups of students and seeing how engagement with
the discipline had a profoundly transformative effect on the students' self-
esteem, personal identity and intellectual development. Combining the
'gold standard' of Oxbridge-style instruction[7] with the pedagogic ideal of
Socratic exchange and debate, small group learning positions the academic

---

4    Only 4 per cent of the UK's poorest people enter higher education (David et al.,
     2009; Hills Report, 2009), while only 5 per cent of this group currently enter the
     top universities in UK league tables (HESA, 2010).
5    Morley, 'Imagining the University of the Future', 29.
6    J. Mezriow, 'Learning to Think Like an Adult: Core Concepts of Transformation
     Theory', in J. Mezirow (ed.), *Learning as Transformation: Critical Perspectives on a
     Theory in Process* (San Francisco, CA: Jossey Bass, 2000), 1–33.
7    D. Mills and P. Alexander, *Small Group Teaching: A Toolkit for Learning* (York:
     Higher Education Academy, 2013).

teacher as an intellectual 'midwife' who assists others in the labour of giving birth to knowledge .[8]

## 'Discussion Learning' Approach

A 'discussion learning' approach can encourage students to develop intellectual independence by 'scaffolding' learning while they make sense of the subject-matter for themselves and take ownership of their learning.[9] In this environment, students become partners in a 'learning community' where there is no clear master–apprentice transfer of knowledge. Moreover, smaller learning groups can also open up more lateral power dynamics between the teacher and the students, which may be empowering for some, particularly first-generation higher education students. Christensen writes of the discussion learning approach:

> In discussion teaching, partnership – a collegial sharing of power, accountability and tasks – supplants hierarchy and asymmetry in the teacher–student relationship. The discussion process itself requires students to become profoundly and actively involved in their own learning, to discover for themselves rather than accept verbal or written pronouncements. They must explore the intellectual terrain without maps, step by step, blazing trails, struggling past obstacles, dealing with disappointments. How different from simply following others' itineraries![10]

Unlike traditional formal lectures, the intimacy and interpersonal dynamics of small group sessions provides academic teachers with a valuable insight into the prior experience and knowledge of their students, as well as their burgeoning academic interests and agendas. Teaching in these small group

---

8   Plato, *Theaetetus*, 369 BCE–367 BCE.
9   C. R. Christensen, 'Premises and Practices of Discussion Teaching', in C. R. Christensen et al. (eds), *Education for Judgment: The Artistry of Discussion Leadership* (Boston, MA: The Harvard Business School Press, 1991).
10  Christensen, 'Premises and Practices of Discussion Teaching', 24.

sessions gave me access to the backgrounds and learning experiences of my students as they were developing and an opportunity to tailor classroom discussions and develop resources for more individualized learning. This allowed me to adapt my teaching practice accordingly and explore module content in a manner that resonated with my students' backgrounds, lives and developing academic interests.

Moreover, collaborative learning experiences in the small group sessions can provide students with immediate formative feedback on their independent class preparation.[11] Learning in small groups can involve an interactive unpacking of topics and ideas, encouraging students to see disciplinary knowledge not as a fixed and ready-made product to (passively) consume, but as a continually evolving site of knowledge requiring ongoing intellectual engagement and exchange. This social interaction and discussion, key features of small group sessions, encourages students to actively 'do philosophy' together as intellectual partners. Not only is discussion-based learning the oldest form of intellectual instruction; it is a form of pedagogy that is particularly suited to the study of philosophy. Stretching as far back as the Ancient Greeks, philosophical inquiry has been dialogical and dialectical in nature, encouraging participants to discuss and question ideas as a means of deepening knowledge.

This approach conceives of learning as a community effort that takes place through dialogue and critical engagement with philosophical ideas. Even Plato's dialogues underscore the notion that knowledge formation is a process requiring participants to play an active role in their own learning. This is not the unidirectional flow of expertise from teacher to student. In much of the academic literature related to small-group teaching the role of the teacher is 'to facilitate rather than dictate what is being learned'.[12] I attempted to apply this approach in my teaching by providing appropriate 'scaffolding' around which my students could 'construct' their own learning.[13] Although module content and associated suggested reading

---

11    W. G. Moore, *The Tutorial System and Its Future* (Oxford: Pergamon, 1968).

12    Mills and Alexander, *Small Group Teaching*, 12.

13    See, for example, R. B. Barr and J. Tagg, 'A New Paradigm for Undergraduate Education', *Change*, 27 (6) (1995), 13–25; E. DeCorte 'New Perspectives on Learning

were set by me as the teacher, student understandings of these set texts and/or ideas were collaboratively scrutinized and critically challenged through student discussions. As the facilitator, I considered it my role to subtly direct discussion, ensuring that students maintained a focus on the topic at hand, insofar as possible. At times, I found it a challenge to know when it was appropriate to rein in the conversation as discursive detours sometimes led to unexpected insights. It could also be difficult to move on from a topic or idea that triggered unusual levels of enthusiasm and engagement amongst students.

Christensen stresses that a respectful 'learning community' is critical to the success of discussion learning and that teachers play a key role in setting the tone of the sessions.[14] In an effort to promote 'collaboration and comradeship', the teacher-facilitator must create an environment underpinned by the values of civility, a willingness to take risks, an appreciation of diversity, and the freedom for the group to 'venture into intellectual *terra incognita*, where explorers need one another's help and support'.[15] I understood that creating such a learning environment meant that I too had to take risks and be vulnerable with the group so that they understood that the process of learning is rarely a straight line from zero to success. I aimed to be open about my own academic journey, my defeats and successes, and the hard work involved. I wanted my students to feel that they belonged to a supportive community. As Christensen writes:

> [I]f we want our students to take the risks that make creativity possible, we must show we are willing and able to assist them when they stumble. To make independence practical, and enfranchise all the members of the group, we must support students

---

and Teaching in Higher Education', in Burgen (ed.) *Goals and Purposes of Higher Education in the 21st Century* (London: Jessica Kingsley Publishers, 1996); L. S. Vygotsky, *Thought and Language* (Cambridge, MA: The MIT Press, 1962); L. S. Vygotsky, *Mind in Society: The Development of Higher Psychological Processes* (Cambridge, MA: Harvard University Press, 1978).

14  Christensen, 'Premises and Practices of Discussion Teaching'.

15  Ibid. 26.

when their comments depart from the consensus of the moment or their proposals collide with firmly held convictions of the class.[16]

Although I aimed to create a 'safe' environment for learning[17] based on an 'atmosphere'[18] of mutual respect and the sense of belonging to a group of learners on a shared intellectual journey, participant anxiety[19] and the specific group dynamic (including psychodynamic behaviours, such as projection, introjection and transference) presented an obstacle to full engagement for some students.

My attempts to build a 'safe' pedagogic space based on trust amongst participants, where students could feel free to express their ideas and where 'failure' was accepted as an important part of the learning process, was, at times, challenged by students' own prior educational experiences and their views on the educative process. The collaborative unpacking of learning in the small group sessions was the exception rather than the rule in their experience, and some expressed anxiety and/or reluctance about contributing what they saw as 'half-formed opinions' or incomplete knowledge in front of their peers and, I suspect, in front of their teacher. I came to see how students' prior learning environments, particularly in contexts where learning processes were largely hidden from peers and teachers and where 'good academic performance' was equated with a good grade and finished product, played an important role in shaping how comfortable students were sharing their ideas in the sessions

Cognizant of the potential influence of these prior learning experiences on their new educational context, I wanted to ensure that that perceived criticisms would not damage students' self-esteem or be demoralizing or an obstacle to the enjoyment and engagement of students. Although I attempted to 'engineer' a particular learning environment, I also had to learn to relinquish the idea of having absolute control over all aspects and

16    Ibid.
17    G. Brown and M. Atkins, *Effective Teaching in Higher Education* (London: Routledge, 1988).
18    T. Douglas, *Groupwork Practice* (London: Tavistock, 1978).
19    J. Heron, *The Complete Facilitator's Handbook* (London: Kogan Page, 1999).

effects of the group, both positive and negative. The intimacy and nature of the small group learning environment transformed the student–teacher hierarchy, but it did not eliminate it. Sessions were student-centred, but my disciplinary expertise and professional status had an impact on the group dynamics. As the 'authority' in the room, I was given additional power and influence within the group and this was, at times, a motivating factor for more active student engagement in classroom discussion. Moreover, this close interaction also gave students a sense of my work as an academic. I talked to students about the nature of undertaking and disseminating research in a professional context. When questions were put to me that I could not answer, I was comfortable disclosing my lack of knowledge regarding the matter in question and, where it seemed useful or relevant to the module, suggested that we follow it up at the next weekly session. I wanted to encourage students to see disciplinary expertise as a lifelong process (rather than as an endpoint to learning) and 'incomplete knowledge' as a normal part of developing expertise.

The close relationship built with students in the small sessions offers students an insight into what it means to be a professional academic. In my practice, I slowly started noticing over the years that many of my students were developing a sense of themselves as emergent academics. In classroom discussions, I noticed that students would frequently refer to themselves as 'philosophers' and had come to see themselves as novice practitioners linked to a wider 'community of practice'.[20] This process of 'identity transformation'[21] positively influenced student engagement with the curriculum and appeared to play a role in student participation in extra-curricular activities associated with the discipline, organizing events that appealed directly to their own academic interests.[22] In the class discussions, it was evident that many students were reading beyond the strict requirements of

20 E. Wenger, *Communities of Practice: Learning, Meaning and Identity* (Cambridge: Cambridge University Press, 1998).

21 G. Hughes, 'Talking to Oneself: Using Autobiographical Internal Dialogue to Critique Everyday and Professional Practice', *Reflective Practice* 10 (4) (2009), 451–63.

22 Such as taking up leadership roles in the Philosophical Society, organizing and attending events related to philosophy within and external to All Hallows College.

the module, and through their own developing intellectual areas of interest, students brought new and interesting perspectives to the material in the module.

## Assessment

Many of the opportunities and benefits of learning in small groups are under-supported in the traditional curriculum and modes of assessment. The personalized discussion learning approach cultivated in the classroom may not be 'built into' the structure of the curriculum or modes of assessment and in my own experience I found that there was little time to explore those areas of inquiry that triggered particular enthusiasm and engagement amongst students. This presented a problem for my teaching practice. How could I develop and implement assessment options that would better support the established strengths of small-group learning and the achievement of the intended learning outcomes (ILOs)? Was there any room within my institution's assessment regime to optimize the learning opportunities taking place in the more student-centred pedagogy of the small group sessions?

I was restricted to assessment that consisted of three-hour terminal examinations (worth 50 per cent of the module marks), short non-invigilated 500-word essays (worth 20 per cent of the module marks), and longer non-invigilated 1,500-word essays (worth 30 per cent of the module marks). In the three-hour written terminal examination, students were required to answer three out of a selection of six essay questions and were not informed of the questions in advance of the examination. This mostly summative, high-stakes assessment exercise encouraged a more superficial and strategic approach to learning than had been developed in the small group sessions. Examination answers tended to be 'safe' and I noticed that most students answered the same questions in examinations. While these essays were mostly well written and relevant and used appropriate terminology, they did not demonstrate the extent and level to which students were engaging with philosophical ideas in the classroom. Under time and performance pressure, the conditions of the examination were considerably less conducive to the exploration, development and reflection of ideas that were possible in other non-timed and non-invigilated conditions.[23]

This left me with few new assessment options. In classroom discussions, it was increasingly evident that students were developing their own specific areas of interests in the module and I was struck by the idea that I could allow students to come up with their own essay titles. This would give them an opportunity to explore their own academic interests and, I hoped, encourage greater enthusiasm and deeper engagement with the curriculum. I announced to my students that they would be responsible for developing the focus and title of their own essays (long and short) for the module. Students were asked to arrange to meet me to discuss their ideas for their assignments to ensure that they had a developing sense of the direction of their essay and ideas for the essay title. I assumed that these meetings would be brief and that students would be full of ideas. To my surprise, a number of students found the task very difficult, especially those already struggling with the discipline. Many students were unable to clearly articulate the area or topic(s) they would focus on in the essay. I had to suppress the urge to suggest areas of focus and let students come to their own decisions about their essay. Once the direction of the assignment was established, developing an essay title also proved challenging. Suggested titles were often too broad or too ambiguous and, careful not to impose my own preferences, I tried to explain how greater clarity and focus would help students write a better essay.

I quickly discovered that this exercise was only practicable with a small group of students. It would be too time-consuming to provide such attention to each student in a larger group. On average, the meetings lasted one hour and often included follow-up email exchanges as students continued to reflect on their essay-topic decision. In some cases, it felt as though the

23   J. Biggs and C. Tang, *Teaching for Quality Learning at University: What the Student Does* (Maidenhead: Society for Research into Higher Education/Open University, 2007).

students were sending me suggested titles to be *approved*. I had intended to encourage an environment where we would work together to *agree* essay topics and titles, but the traditional student–teacher hierarchy re-emerged and students' fears about selecting the 'wrong' topic made the creation of such an environment difficult. I noticed that while students had become far more open and experimental in class preparation and discussion, they held deep anxieties about their academic performance and 'getting it right' in graded assessments. The willingness to take intellectual risks seen in the classroom sometimes failed to translate in the graded assessment.

## Conclusion

Even where there are limitations imposed by assessment regimes, small-group teaching can have a powerful effect on the intellectual and personal development of students. Given the more lateral power dynamics between teacher and student, the atmosphere of intellectual partnership between students, and an environment where students are encouraged to actively seek out and develop their own interests in the discipline, small-group learning can provide students with particularly enriching and transformative educational experiences. In the age of massification in higher education, teaching in small groups is increasingly limited to elite universities with highly competitive entry requirements, such as Oxbridge.

For the vast majority of university students, module 'delivery' typically means large-group formal lectures that involve one 'sage on the stage' and an audience of up to 500 other students. Such teaching contexts arguably re-enforce steep intellectual hierarchies dividing students and teachers, reproducing dynamics in the educational environment that replicate some of the more pernicious inequalities in society more generally. For first-generation students in particular, the absence of meaningful contact with teachers and other students in the classroom may exacerbate feelings of social alienation or of being 'out of place' in higher education. Small-group learning offers an opportunity to close perceived differences between students and even between students and teachers, as the process of learning becomes inextricably social in nature. Learning does not have to be a solitary or competitive exercise, but can be re-imagined as a collaborative, novice 'community of practice'.

# Bibliography

Barr, R. B., and Tagg, J., 'A New Paradigm for Undergraduate Education', *Change* 27 (6) (1995), 13–25.

Biggs, J., *Student Approaches to Learning and Studying* (Melbourne: Australian Council for Educational Research, 1987).

Biggs, J., and Tang, C., *Teaching for Quality Learning at University: What the Student Does* (Maidenhead: Society for Research into Higher Education/Open University, 2007).

Brown, G., and Atkins, M., *Effective Teaching in Higher Education* (London: Routledge, 1988).

Christensen, C. R., 'Premises and Practices of Discussion Teaching', in C. R. Christensen et al. (eds), *Education for Judgment: The Artistry of Discussion Leadership* (Boston, MA: The Harvard Business School Press, 1991).

Dansereau, D. F., 'Cooperative Learning Strategies', in E. Weinstein (ed.), *Learning and Study Strategies: Issues in Assessment, Instruction and Evaluation* (New York: Academic Press, 1988).

DeCorte, E., 'New Perspectives on Learning and Teaching in Higher Education', in Burgen, A. (ed.), *Goals and Purposes of Higher Education in the 21st Century* (London: Jessica Kingsley Publishers, 1996).

Diederich, P. B., *Measuring Growth in English* (Urbana, IL: National Council of Teachers of English, 1974).

Douglas, T., *Groupwork Practice* (London: Tavistock, 1978).

Entwistle, N., *Understanding Classroom Learning* (London: Hodder and Stoughton, 1987).

Exley, K., and Dennick, R., *Small Group Teaching: Tutorials, Seminars and Beyond* (Abingdon: Routledge, 2004).

Heron, J., *The Complete Facilitator's Handbook* (London: Kogan Page, 1999).

Hughes, G., 'Talking to Oneself: Using Autobiographical Internal Dialogue to Critique Everyday and Professional Practice', *Reflective Practice* 10 (4) (September 2009), 451–63.

Jaques, D., and Salmon, G., *Learning Groups: A Handbook for Face-to-face and Online Environments* (Oxon: Routledge, 2007, 4th edn).

Kottler, J. A., and Englar-Carlson, M., *Learning Group Leadership: An Experiential Approach* (London: Sage, 2015, 3rd edn).

Marton, F., Hounsell, D., and Entwistle, N. (eds), *The Experience of Learning* (Edinburgh: Scottish Academic Press, 1997).

Marton, F., and Saljo, R., 'On Qualitative Differences in Learning: Outcome and Process', *British Journal of Educational Psychology* 34 (1976), 4–11.

Mezirow, J., 'Learning to Think Like an Adult: Core Concepts of Transformation Theory', in J. Mezirow (ed.), *Learning as Transformation: Critical Perspectives on a Theory in Process* (San Francisco, CA: Jossey Bass, 2000), 1–33.

Mills, D., and Alexander, P., *Small Group Teaching: A Toolkit for Learning* (York: Higher Education Academy, 2013).

Moore, W. G., *The Tutorial System and Its Future* (Oxford: Pergamon, 1968).

Morley, L., 'Imagining the University of the Future', in R. Barnett (ed.), *The Future University: Ideas and Possibilities* (London: Taylor and Francis, 2012), 26–35.

Nicol, D., and Macfarlane-Dick, D., 'Formative Assessment and Self-regulated Learning: A Model and Seven Principles of Good Feedback Practice', *Studies in Higher Education* 31 (2) (2006), 199–218.

Prosser, M., and Trigwell, K., *Teaching for Learning in Higher Education* (Buckingham: Open University Press, 1998).

Starch, D., 'Reliability of Grading Work in History', *School Review* 21 (1913a), 676–81.

Starch, D., 'Reliability of Grading Work in Mathematics', *School Review* 21 (1913b), 254–9.

Starch, D., and Elliott, E. C., 'Reliability of the Grading of High School Work in English', *School Review* 20 (1912), 442–57.

Tubbs, S. L., *A Systems Approach to Small Group Interaction* (New York: Random House, 2011, 11th edn).

Wenger, E., *Communities of Practice: Learning, Meaning and Identity* (Cambridge: Cambridge University Press, 1998).

Vygotsky, L. S., *Mind in Society: The Development of Higher Psychological Processes* (Cambridge, MA: Harvard University Press, 1978).

Vygotsky, L. S., *Thought and Language* (Cambridge, MA: The MIT Press, 1962).

CIARÁN Ó MATHÚNA

# 7  Adult Learners Returning to Higher Education: Implications for Education Providers

## Introduction

Completed PhD research of adult learners in higher education at All Hallows College shows that students value an andragogical approach to their learning.[1] Recognition of prior learning is important to the adult learner, as is the value of their lived experiences and autonomy in choosing areas of study. The findings of this research present a number of positive challenges for education providers in how to attract, maintain and support adult learners in higher education.

The number of adult and mature students entering into full-time and part-time education is growing year on year. Between 2010 and 2011, 15 per cent of full-time undergraduates were mature students; this was an increase of 2.7 per cent from the previous year, on top of a 6.1 per cent increase on the preceding year.[2] In part-time provision, the number of adult and mature students is as high as 92 per cent. It is estimated that by 2015 the percentage of mature students engaged in full-time education will be

---

1   See Ciarán Ó Mathúna, Transformative Adult Education: Transformative Learning Experiences, in the Self-evaluation of Participants in the BA for Personal and Professional Development (ALBA), All Hallows College, Dublin, on Completion of their First Year of Studies (Unpublished PhD thesis. Dublin: All Hallows College, Dublin City University, 2013).

2   Higher Education Authority, *Education Key Facts and Figures 10/11* (Dublin: HEA, 2012).

18 per cent and that by 2030 it will be 25 per cent.[3] These statistics indicate that the provision of study programmes designed for adult learners will be a growth area in Ireland within the next decade. I will argue that such provision should therefore be founded on the principles of an adult methodological approach: andragogy, rather than pedagogy.

Adult education is not merely the provision of a course which adults attend; it is a philosophy, an approach to learning that arguably has implications for providers of education for adult learners. Programmes of study targeted at adult learners should be designed to support and encourage achievement, not just academically but also personally. This chapter is drawn from the findings of my recent PhD research of adult learners studying for the (level 7) BA in Personal and Professional Development (ALBA) at All Hallows College, Dublin.

## Research Methodology

Thirty-two adult learners in a higher education BA programme were interviewed using narrative interviews. This methodology was chosen as it allowed the participants to self-reflect on their individual experiences. The learners referred to narrative research as a 'voyage of discovery – a discovery of meaning'.[4] Elliot (2008) speaks of the interview enabling the interviewee to tell their 'own account of their lives' and states that it is important not to 'impose a rigid structure on the interview'.[5] The adult

---

3    Department of Education and Science, *National Strategy for Higher Education to 2030* (Dublin: DES Publications Sales Office, 2011).

4    R. Josselson and A. Lieblich, 'A Framework for Narrative Research Proposals in Psychology', in R. Josselson, A. Lieblich and D. P. McAdams, *Up Close and Personal: The Teaching and Learning of Narrative Research* (Washington, DC: American Psychological Association, 2002), 260.

5    Jane Elliot, *Using Narrative in Social Research: Qualitative and Quantitative Approaches* (London: Sage Publications, 2005, 1st edn), 31.

learners were asked to tell the story of their educational experiences. The data was then analysed using a narrative analysis approach, from which findings were drawn.

## Profile

Of the thirty-two students interviewed, sixteen were male and sixteen were female. Of these, seventeen had completed upper second-level education; thirteen had completed lower second-level education. Two had left formal education after primary school. The majority of the male interviewees were unemployed. Of the men who were working, two were working full-time. The profile of the female interviewees was somewhat different, with the majority of the women working, either full-time or part-time, with only two identifying as unemployed and two identifying as retired on health grounds. No member of the students' immediate family had attended or attained third-level education. Almost all of those interviewed expressed the opinion that they had long desired to study for a degree and had always had an interest in learning.

## Adult Learner Experience

Interviewees spoke of the impact of returning to education, on themselves and their families: of time constraints, of not being available, of missing out on family and social occasions. They highlighted barriers encountered and supports enjoyed along the way. There was agreement that returning to study had and was having a profound effect on their family lives. Trying to juggle work and family life, as well as attending lectures and studying, was mentioned as a source of stress, particularly given commitments to their immediate family, but also commitments to extended family, especially elderly parents, and other social commitments. However, it became apparent that the longer the person had been experiencing the routine of attending classes and studying, the less stressful the situation was. All interviewees felt they had underestimated the commitment involved in being a third-level student. Many had not initially accounted for the time commitment involved outside of attending classes.

## Barriers Encountered

The single largest barrier to participation in education, identified by all interviewees, was internal. This ranged from procrastination, to a lack of organization, to a lack of self-belief. Financial barriers, such as the costs associated with being a student, course materials, travel and subsistence, was the next largest barrier. Students' lack of IT skills and the impact this has on their participation was noted by a considerable number of both men and women. Academic language caused difficulties as interviewees struggled to understand new terminology. For example, one female interviewee tells of how she wanted to study for a degree, but did not understand what was meant by the term 'BA', routinely used by lecturers and other staff.

In their return to education, a notable number of female interviewees reported experiencing a lack of support. This ranged from a lack of support from their spouse/partner, their employer and/or their extended families. No male interviewee spoke of experiencing such a lack of support. A number of women relayed stories of actual discrimination and an attitude of indifference towards their return to study. Because the course they were studying is primarily a part-time course, with mostly evening classes, the interviewees felt that the college facilities, such as the library, canteen and student-support services, were focused particularly on the day/full-time students.

## Personal Growth Experiences

All of the adult students interviewed agreed that the single biggest personal impact of returning to education was the personal change they experienced. They had become more self-aware, which ranged from a sense of befriending the self to accepting personal flaws. Adult learners acknowledged a shift from positions previously held to new thinking processes, tolerance and openness. People spoke of being more aware of both their personal strengths and weaknesses. For some, dormant interests were rekindled, while others discovered latent knowledge. Interviewees increased their awareness of how they learnt and of their desire to learn, their enthusiasm for learning and their interest in new areas of knowledge. They noticed how they had become much more relaxed in themselves, more reasoned in their thought processes and emotional responses. Commonly, interviewees referred to themselves as more 'mature'.

Overwhelmingly, interviewees spoke of their confidence levels being increased as a direct result of their participation. People felt they were now more confident to offer an opinion, not just in college, but in wider social situations. Many spoke of entering the course with low levels of personal confidence, which they now felt had been augmented. When speaking of increased confidence, interviewees spoke about their own understanding of themselves, using phrases like 'increased self-esteem', being 'more sure of myself' and being 'more grounded'. People spoke of having a sense of developing as a person as a direct result of the increase in confidence. They spoke with pride when saying they felt they now had more confidence and belief in themselves, in what they do and what they know. The women spoke of validating their own sense of themselves. They spoke of being able to affirm for themselves that they are capable people and that they have a value and a contribution to make. Many spoke of finding their own 'voice' and 'finding the real me'. This acknowledgement of their sense of worth was accompanied by a phrase that was often used when students discussed their academic ability: 'I am better than I thought'. The students spoke of how, prior to the course, they did not feel confident in either social or formal situations if they were speaking to a person who they knew had a third-level qualification. This had reduced due to their participation in higher education.

An equal amount of men and women spoke of being more confident in a variety of social situations. They spoke of being more outgoing and found themselves to be more talkative, more engaging in conversations, both in social settings and at work. A number of people said that in the past they were not willing to offer an opinion during a conversation and now felt comfortable making such contributions. In the past, they would not have had the confidence to engage at this level for fear of being judged as not being intelligent. As this interviewee describes:

> I must say at that stage I wouldn't have that much confidence in meeting people but I always felt sometimes inadequate that I mightn't know as much as they know. (Interviewee 15)

Of those who were working, their new and improved confidence levels were having a positive effect in their employment. For some, it was the ability to speak up, ask questions or seek clarifications. Others spoke about starting new initiatives at work, proposing new ideas and taking the initiative to improve work practices. In describing how they knew their personal confidence levels had increased, interviewees spoke of how they were now better able to communicate. They spoke of how they felt they had the language and ability to articulate their thoughts, views and opinions. They recounted experiences of how they reacted differently in situations, in a calmer, reflective and more assured manner. They thought they were better listeners and more analytical in their approach. The fear they had previously felt in social situations, when speaking with people they did not know, when meeting people in positions of authority or people they perceived to be educated was no longer present. Overall, the major change that people experienced was that they felt they could engage with people in a better, deeper and more meaningful way, which they attributed to course participation.

## Academic Transformations

As regards new academic learning identified by interviewees, most people referenced their ability to research, critique and analyse and present information in an academic style. To be able to write in an academic manner was a new experience and seen as a major achievement. Students described how their thinking had become much clearer, how they were now better able to structure their thoughts to think in a critical way and analyse information. They asked more questions and looked for alternative possibilities, other interpretations and other solutions in everyday life, as well as in their academic ventures. This newly developed approach transformed their life experiences, from reading the newspaper to social interactions. Interviewees spoke of how they had become more reflective and more critically aware of their own personal lives and their relationships. Throughout all the interviews, the phrase 'new horizons' was referred to repeatedly, specifically within the context of the benefits of adult education. Interviewees spoke of their personal horizons being broadened and attributed this to their engagement in higher education. They noted that they had become more socially aware of humanitarian issues and more ethically aware of social and political structures and governance.

This awareness included a new understanding and knowledge of social issues that, as one interviewee described, 'pushed their boundaries' of comfort. There was a genuine sense of discovering that there is more than just one way of seeing and interpreting the world and that society is complex. Each individual spoke of being able to see things from new and different perspectives as a liberating experience.

## What Helped?

The overriding consensus from the adult learners was that they had experienced an open, supportive, encouraging, non-judgemental environment. People spoke of their engagement with the course being a positive experience. They had experienced peer support and peer learning. There was a sense that the individual mattered, that this course was not just about attaining a degree or a new career, but about personal development. Others commented on the holistic approach to learning and said that this approach is encouraging and that they felt the college strived to support students and their academic and personal development.

Interviewees spoke about experiencing this sense of support from the time of the initial contact with the college staff when enquiring about the course. Of particular note is the fact that many of the interviewees spoke warmly of the personalized attention they received when attending an information evening or a one-to-one appointment. This sense of personal interest and of being supported and encouraged continued once the student enrolled on the programme of study. The second largest aspect of support was the physical environment, the location and the ambiance of the college. Interviewees spoke about the sense of peace and tranquillity within the college grounds. One example given was that the college had provided rooms for study groups.

The classroom methodologies and facilitation skills of the tutors were given high praise by those interviewed, who felt they were encouraged to actively participate in their learning. Students' prior experience was valued and classroom discussion was encouraged, with group work and presentations as part of the educational experience. Students had the support of a mentoring system, which they found to be of great value and very supportive. They spoke of their mentors giving them honest and realistic feedback in a supportive manner. The availability of tutors was also repeatedly commented on by the interviewees, who felt they had unprecedented access to their tutors. Tutors were approachable and available outside of the classroom, particularly in the coffee area, where they willingly engaged in discussions with the students, described well by this student:

> In here we're very blessed with how good, how accessible our lecturers are ... they're so accessible all the time, in the coffee dock. Like they never sit apart, they always sit with whoever [sic] at the table and they leave themselves open for, bless them, and can be exhausting they never get a break. So they never hide out in the, you know, in another cafeteria they're always there and they're always accessible. (Interviewee 2)

Allied to these supports was the course structure and content. Students initially had to undertake a 'foundations' course which helped them transition into third-level education. Other compulsory modules included scholarly writing, collaborative learning and information technology. For all other modules, the student is able to choose modules they would like to study in order to achieve the learning outcome required. It was this range of subjects and the autonomy of choice that attracted many of the interviewees to choose the course.

Finally, the fact that this course is designed for adults, accepts adult students only, and uses adult teaching methodologies helped contribute to a positive, supportive and nurturing environment for adult learners.

They felt it was important to be treated like an adult and to be responsible for their own progression through the course, as captured by one student who said she 'liked being treated like an adult with no patronising stuff' (Interviewee 22).

## Implications for Providers

The findings of this research show that it is important for adult learners to have a facilitated transition into third-level education where there is flexibility and choice within the programme of study. Adult methodologies and recognition of prior experience are particularly important to the adult learner. Structured, specific supports, such as mentoring, tutor availability, supportive feedback, IT and scholarly writing classes, are critical in assisting student retention and progression. Such findings have an impact on education providers. A number of these impacts are now explored.

### Assisting Transition

Many adult learners returning to education are unfamiliar with the world of academia. Assisting them in the transition of entering an education programme must be an essential element of any higher education programme. Adult learners need this transition to be managed in a supportive manner, with college policy, procedure and guidelines clearly articulated, without assuming that the student has prior knowledge of terminology used in higher education.

One very practical support to make the transition easier is to provide an orientation programme, which includes orientation to the physical world of the college or institution. This can include tours of the college facilities, including the library and other student support services. Helping students familiarize themselves with ICT access, photocopying and canteen facilities should all be part of this orientation programme.

The provision of a foundations course as part of the initial transition into third-level education is essential for programmes aimed at adult learners. The findings of this study show that students benefited greatly from their initiation through the foundations programme provided. Such a programme must be set up with the aim of helping students to understand the expectations of the institution and the language of academia, along with managing their own expectations. It must include assistance in study planning, how to research and how to write for the academic environment. Another core element of any foundations programme is inclusion of the philosophy of learning, adult development, learning styles and an exploration of the different types of intelligence. Students at this initial stage of returning to study will also benefit greatly from being assisted in discovering their own learning style and intelligence type, along with developing organization skills and self-management for the work ahead.

All providers of adult education programmes need to provide a foundations course of some kind. This course would include: acknowledgement of prior learning; understanding of life experiences, learning styles and learning preferences; adult learning methodologies; an introduction to academic writing; and college orientation.

*Supports*

Adult learners who return to education after a long absence and often with low self-esteem regarding the academic environment need to be supported not just in their transition but throughout their course of study. There are different levels of support needed at various times throughout a course of study as the individuals' life experiences change. At times support is needed in the role of encouragement while at other times it may need to take a more therapeutic form. The types of supports I consider to be appropriate for adult learners are:

- A mentoring system through which students are supported by an experienced member of staff, often through encouragement and honest feedback. Adult learners need someone they can trust and confide in, especially when they are unsure about their ability to produce academic work or sustain the momentum necessary for a prolonged study programme. Such mentors could meet with the students at designated times throughout the academic year.

- The availability of a career guidance counsellor for all students enrolled on an adult education course is essential. Having a service such as this available would undoubtedly ease some of the pressure experienced by adult learners and help them remain focused on their goal of gaining a qualification. It would also assist them in planning for their future, post-qualification.

- Easy access to a counselling service needs to be provided by colleges and institutions enrolling adult students. Providing a counselling service can help to retain students and provide them with the personal tools and strength to cope with personal or family issues that are impinging on their well-being.

## Course Structure

The provision of a flexible range of modules that are outcome-based, containing various assessment methods, may be helpful in developing adult-friendly education programmes. Providers might take the following recommendations into account:

- Provision which will include modular-based, full-time and part-time options, available at multiple times throughout the course, is optimum. Whether it be daytime hours, evening hours, weekday, and weekends, along with intensive programmes over shorter time periods, adults can choose what is best for their particular learning needs. For example, a week-long, full-time course is an option for providers to consider for adults who are busy with various other occupations. There also needs to be clarity regarding the scheduling of provision in order that a person enrolling for a programme can know that they will be able to attend on set days.

- To sustain interest, momentum and active participation, subject choice is an important aspect of provision. Education providers might be more creative in how they can facilitate the achievement of learning outcomes for their students. Within this research study, subject variety, flexibility and choice were key elements for the adult learners.

- Modular-based provision enables adult learners to define the level of their commitment, for example taking one or more modules per college term. Another advantage of modular-based provision is that it allows students greater autonomy in the choices they make. It is therefore imperative that an adequate choice and range of modules are provided. Whilst some modules will undoubtedly need to be core or compulsory modules, there needs to be a wide selection of other modules to choose from.

- A system of learning outcomes is best suited to facilitate the flexible, module-based approach. Under this system, students enrol in a module of study with the expressed intention of achieving a specific learning outcome. The learning outcomes that could possibly be gained through successful completion of the course of study are stated in advance by the course provider. Ideally, decisions regarding learning outcomes will result from collaboration between the provider, the teacher and the student. Through an outcome-based approach, it is possible that students studying the same module may achieve similar or different learning outcomes, through different methodologies, depending on their study emphasis.

- Modules comprising classroom assessment and/or assignments are the popular choice. It is important therefore that whilst maintaining the highest standards of education, the provider acknowledges the preferred choice of assessment. Assessment through assignments allows the students to study in their own time and gain a deeper knowledge and appreciation of the area of study. Group assessments could also be considered, as could assessment of classroom presentations. A combination of more than one of the above methods could provide opportunities for students to perform to their own personal abilities aware of the nature of different learning styles.

## An Andragogical Approach

In order for adult learners to experience best practice, it is vital that provision is andragogically proofed and that all teaching staff have an understanding of appropriate methodologies. An andragogical approach to the facilitating of learning amongst adults is paramount as it ensures that the teaching methods employed are appropriate for the learning cohort. The understanding of andragogy and the application of this approach must be consistent amongst all those entrusted with the provision and teaching of adult-specific courses. Adults learn best when they are engaged as adults, when their life experience is acknowledged and valued, when they are entrusted with an ownership of the learning process, and when learning is facilitated.

To enhance student learning and opportunities, it is important that those responsible for the provision of adult learning incorporate some, if not all, of the following methodologies: facilitated classroom discussion and debate; individual and group research projects; classroom presentations by students; reflective practice; assessed assignments; along with the more traditional provision of information from the tutor. Through these various methodologies, it is envisaged that students will be able to expand and explore their own learning style preference and gain a broader understanding of the educational process.

Finally, adult education providers need to make a conscious effort to develop and increase their students' personal development and confidence levels. It is not sufficient to rely on this happening as a by-product of study. One of the major findings of this research was the growth in personal confidence as a direct result of engagement in the ALBA programme. In order to ensure that such personal development is achieved in adult education programmes, it is important to make deliberate choices to incorporate elements of personal development practice and theory into the course provision, through either standalone or cross-curricular modules. One example of providing direct opportunities for personal development and confidence-building is to take the ALBA experience of providing a compulsory module in communications, along with building classroom presentations into many of the modules on offer.

## Conclusion

Adult learners are a growing population within our education system. The specific attributes of this group, many of whom are part-time learners, needs to be acknowledged and responded to by our institutions of education and course providers. The experience of adult learners captured in the research informs us of the issues that helped and hindered their progression and learning. It is essential that we encourage greater debate concerning adult learners in higher education.

## Bibliography

Department of Education and Science, *National Strategy for Higher Education to 2030* (Dublin: DES Publications Sales Office, 2011).

Elliot, Jane, *Using Narrative in Social Research: Qualitative and Quantitative Approaches* (London: Sage Publications, 2005, 1st edn).

Higher Education Authority, *Education Key Facts and Figures 10/11* (Dublin: Higher Education Authority, 2012).

Josselson, R., and Lieblich, A., 'A Framework for Narrative Research Proposals in Psychology', in R. Josselson, A. Lieblich, and D. P. McAdams, *Up Close and Personal: The Teaching and Learning of Narrative Research* (Washington, DC: American Psychological Association, 2002), 259–274.

Ó Mathúna, Ciarán, Transformative Adult Education: Transformative Learning Experiences, in the Self-evaluation of Participants in the BA for Personal and Professional Development (ALBA), All Hallows College, Dublin, on Completion of Their First Year of Studies (Dublin: All Hallows College: unpublished PhD thesis, 2013).

GARY KEOGH

# 8    Leading Ethical Education: Teaching How to Think, Not What to Think

## Introduction

This essay is contextualized by uncertainty and debate with regard to the education system in Ireland, in Britain, and indeed with regard to the nature of education itself. There are, for example, ongoing debates on both the grassroots and the political level pertaining to Church patronage of Irish primary schools. The organizational management of schools is almost uniformly reflective of a particular social–cultural–religious paradigm which has since evolved drastically. The post-secular dimensions of Irish life are evident in dwindling participation in religious events and a legal system less fully aligned with a particularly Catholic moral framework. I mention the issue of school patronage not because it is the theme of this essay, but rather because it points to the wider issue of multiculturalism and the presently non-existent scaffolding policies which need to be put in place to ensure the peaceful co-existence of diverse and even opposing ethical systems, while also balancing the fundamental rights of children to have access to an education with the pragmatic and financial implications for governments funding religious or denominational education. Through an ongoing process of secularization and multiculturalism, Ireland will be left with a pluralistic character, but with an education system that would, on the face of it, be unable to cope with such plurality. How are ethics to be approached in this uneasy context?

Furthermore, in Britain in the summer of 2014, an undercover 'operation', which became known as 'Trojan horse', highlighted a number of Jewish and Islamic schools which were ignoring legislative best practice policies regarding the education and welfare of children, and indeed ignoring national syllabi.[1] Instead, these schools were promoting their religious ethos with fervour. Subsequent commentaries were bifurcated, as they tend to be in the British media, with those on the right blaming all our problems on immigration, while the liberals were too afraid of being labelled Islamophobic to admit that multiculturalism brings with it significant challenges, manifest in this case in educational policy.

The rapid growth of non-denominational education also provides some context, as newly formed ethics curriculums are implemented, and the current debate regarding the potential introduction of philosophy into the Irish school curriculum is further context – the new Junior Certificate framework has provisions for philosophy-based short courses, though it is unlikely Ireland will go ahead providing philosophy (such as the A-Levels in Britain and other European educational systems do), given the Irish educational system's struggle to recuperate following the financial crash of 2008/2009 and subsequent budgetary refinements in the educational sector. So, in the midst of all of this upheaval, this essay will probe the question of how ethics ought to be approached in the classroom. My main conclusion will be that the best strategy is one of cautious leadership: encourage the deep integration of ethical education, but do so in a way that is open-ended, rather than dictatorial or parochial.

## Why Ethics?

I suppose the first question people might ask is why bother with ethics in schools at all? As I have outlined in the introductory contextualizing of this essay, it seems that ethical models are causing more consternation

1    See N. Harley (November 2014), <http://www.telegraph.co.uk/education/11244547/
     Seven-schools-in-latest-Trojan-Horse-scandal.html>, accessed 29 January 2018. See
     also P. Wintour (July 2014) 'Trojan Horse Inquiry: A Coordinated Agenda to
     Impose Hardline Sunni Islam', <https://www.theguardian.com/uk-news/2014/
     jul/17/birmingham-schools-inquiry-hardline-sunni-islam-trojan-horse>, accessed
     20 December 2017.

than anything else, so why not simply abandon the prospect of teaching ethics all together? You may notice at this point that I have not yet made a distinction between ethics and religious ethics, but this is owing to the fact that the two were essentially one up until the eighteenth century, as I will discuss later. Moreover, particularly within the Irish educational system, for better or worse, the two spheres are scarcely separated. The question 'why ethics?' leads to the wider question of what we view as the role of education in general. Not in a kind of, 'I want my kids to get good grades to get a secure job for themselves' way, but let us consider for a moment why we bother to teach at all: again, not why I teach or why you teach, but why we teach as a civilization. What's the point of all of this?

There was a recurrent theme in the writings of the influential American philosopher of education John Dewey. He did not view the school as an input–output machine where blank slates were filled with information. Rather, he emphasized the sociality and institutional dimensions of the school setting, in a sense viewing the school as a simplified microcosm of society writ large, or, we might say, a microcosm of our future society – though I do not wish to cause upset by terminologically excluding children from the notion of the contemporary society. It was the undeniable relationship between education and society, the recognition of schools as communities, which Dewey felt was absent from schooling:

> I believe that much of present education fails because it neglects this fundamental principle of the school as a form of community life. It conceives the school as a place where certain information is to be given, where certain lessons are to be learned, or where certain habits are to be formed. The value of these is conceived as lying largely in the remote future; the child must do these things for the sake of something else he is to do; they are mere preparation. As a result they do not become a part of the life experience of the child and so are not truly educative.[2]

Dewey's views on education being *primarily* a social institution call into question, perhaps not for the first time, the role of the school and indeed the role of education in general. Though written over 100 years ago, his reflections still offer food for thought; he notes how it is impossible to

---

2    J. Dewey, 'My Pedagogical Creed', *The School Journal* 54 (3) (1897), 77.

consider what the world will be like twenty years from now, and that this must be kept in mind in our endeavour to educate: 'With the advent of democracy and modern industrial conditions, it is impossible to foretell definitely just what civilization will be twenty years from now. Hence it is impossible to prepare the child for any *precise set of conditions*.'[3] Here we notice that although Dewey is relatively old and arguably outdated, he noted that we cannot gear education towards one particular social setting, because we have absolutely no idea what circumstances will characterize the social landscape in twenty years. Thus education cannot be too 'contextualized'. Were we educated to live in a world where social media reigns, for instance? No, and who knows what is coming around the corner?

One last point I take from Dewey pertains to the subject matter of education. The points he raises resonate in modern curriculum studies and have implications for policymakers within the educational spheres:

> I believe, therefore, that the true centre of correlation on the school subjects is not science, nor literature, nor history, nor geography, but the child's own social activities. I believe that education cannot be unified in the study of science, or so called nature study, because apart from human activity, nature itself is not a unity; nature in itself is a number of diverse objects in space and time, and to attempt to make it the centre of work by itself, is to introduce a principle of radiation rather than one of concentration.[4]

Returning to the contemporary context within which we might analyse Dewey's understanding of education, we have seen interesting developments over the last number of years to which Dewey's philosophy is applicable. In the post-crash situation, education has seen a renewed emphasis on mathematics in Ireland, with the introduction of an extra 25 points for Leaving Certificate students who take the higher-level paper. In line with this, there has been a stark rise in demand for college courses in STEM (science, technology, engineering, medicine) as these fields are more likely to lead to employability. This is fully understandable, even laudable, but we also need to ask ourselves questions, as Dewey did, regarding how we

3    Ibid.
4    Ibid.

should view education, what its wider goal is, and how are ethical models approached in the classroom in an evolving multicultural context.

As it stands, although there is a renewed emphasis on STEM in Irish education, we still teach other subjects, like history, English, literature, art, drama, etc. Why not abandon all of these subjects and focus on producing waves of scientific geniuses, ready to transform Ireland into a hotbed of innovation and technological advancement? Because we also acknowledge, like Dewey, that education is about more than this: it is about raising a generation of value-laden social entrepreneurs ready to tackle not just the economic and scientific challenges that life will present, but also to build a better society. Education is about science, but also social progression. In furtherance of that end, ethics becomes a vital part of education, as does religious education. This is not because religious ideals have the final word on social or ethical issues, but rather because historically this has been the sole domain of religions. Religions and ethical systems were essentially one and the same until very recently, around the eighteenth century, when the first secular ethical systems emerged, such as Jeremy Bentham and John Stuart Mill's utilitarianism: what is good is what provides the greatest happiness to the greatest number.[5] Even still, many ethical systems are based on religious ideals or have been taken from religious ideals and 'secularized', for example modern interpretations of Hegel or Thomas Aquinas by philosophers such as Alisdair MacIntyre.[6]

So for education to 'do its job', as it were, in the Deweyian representation of education as a vehicle for social progress, ethics and, as a consequence, religious ethics/religious studies must play a strong role: in a sense, it is not all about STEM (Science, Technology, Engineering, Maths). Debates regarding climate change and the very ideological and grand questions of how humanity ought to utilize our technological manipulation

---

5    J. Bentham, *The Principles of Morals and Legislation* (New York: Prometheus Books, 1988, originally published 1780), 2; also, J. S. Mill, *Utilitarianism* (London: Dover, 2007, originally published 1861).

6    See A. MacIntyre, *After Virtue: A Study in Moral Theory* (London: Duckworth, 1981) and *Dependent Rational Animals: Why Human Beings Need Virtues* (Illinois: Open Court, 1999).

of our environment are a case in point. Our scientific and engineering innovations have undoubtedly led to great social 'goods', but does purely scientific and engineering-based education offer enough time to consider whether we should engage in certain activities? This is a complex issue which I do not have time to discuss here, and of course there is no easy way of finding a balance between production and preservation, but raising a generation of engineers and scientists might easily lead to a lack of critical thinking skills in these industries, resulting in a short-sighted boom in technology, innovation and engineering, without any consideration of the social, environmental and ethical implications of such endeavours. This is a wider and more important echoing of urban planning – we can build lots and lots of affordable houses, but without amenities for social capital, such short-term economic gains (in the building and selling of homes) might be outweighed by future social problems.

I hope these examples show that ethical philosophy and the philosophy of education are not all 'pie in the sky'. It is encouraging to see that however marginal, this is being recognized, for example in Irish president Michael D. Higgins' ethics initiative and the outgoing minister for education's views on the matter. Former Irish Minister for Education, Ruairi Quinn, a self-described practising atheist, pressed for the introduction of education about religion and beliefs, a non-denominational approach to religious education which he acknowledged was important for education as social progression. As the theologian Hans Küng famously expressed, 'No peace among the nations without peace among the religions. No peace among the religions without dialogue between the religions. No dialogue between the religions without investigation of the foundation of the religion.'[7] So ethics, ethical theory, awareness of cultural differences and so forth are important elements of education; otherwise, we are left with a shell of an educational system which might be pragmatically superior in its innovation, but lacking in its appreciation of the nuance and 'humanity' of human existence. Our empathy and our understanding of fairness and equality, and so on, must also be cultivated in the educational system, and questions of whether

---

7    H. Küng, *Islam, Past Present and Future* (Oxford: Oneworld Publications, 2007), xxiii.

or not we can do something need to be supplemented with questions of whether or not we should. Notwithstanding, although I argue that ethics is a vital aspect of education, the crux of the argument I want to present is that things are not straightforward. To illustrate I will briefly draw upon some heavyweights of historical philosophy.

## Old Wisdom for a New World

In the fourth century BC, Socrates was adamant that the model of education which viewed the acquisition of knowledge as a mere process of transmission from teacher to student was deeply flawed.[8] Socrates was catalysed by this realization to develop what became known as the Socratic method of education, which involves perennially questioning fundamental assumptions and beliefs. Socrates realized that that an explicit transferral of knowledge could not be socially or indeed intellectually progressive: imagine if Einstein never challenged Newton's model of the physical universe and had just accepted what he had been told. New discoveries and advances in science and everything else often come at the expense of older models, and thus blind acceptance of knowledge being transferred will never result in change or progress. So too with ethics, though often this is even more controversial. The civil rights activists in the 1960s in the US, for example, had to challenge the pre-existing ethical model which had an established inequality between blacks and whites. There will always be strong opposition to a change in ethical models, because in order to make progress many have to accept that they have heretofore been doing things wrong. This tends not to be much of an issue when it comes to mathematical formulae, as we can accept we were 'doing it wrong' when calculating Euclidian geometry, but when it comes to ethics, we are often slow to admit that we have been acting unethically.

8    D. Lawton and P. Gordon, *A History of Western Educational Ideas* (London: Woburn, 2002), 15.

Similar Socratic sentiments are echoed in philosophers such as Jean-Jacques Rousseau, whose work on democracy and its limitations in *The Social Contract* became perhaps the most powerful intellectual resource for leaders of the French Revolution in the late eighteenth century.[9] In his seminal work on education, *Emile*, Rousseau worried about the impact of an uncritical model of education which perpetuated social inequalities:

> In the social order where each has his own place a man must be educated for it. If such a one leave his own station he is fit for nothing else. His education is only useful when fate agrees with his parents' choice; if not, education harms the scholar, if only by the prejudices it has created. In Egypt, where the son was compelled to adopt his father's calling, education had at least a settled aim; where social grades remain fixed, but the men who form them are constantly changing, no one knows whether he is not harming his son by educating him for his own class.[10]

Yet it is very difficult for such questioning to take place in practice, because of the discomfort it brings. Unjust normative frameworks are perpetuated indefinitely because people struggle to challenge the established wisdom, and students are told what is right and what is wrong. This is why it takes so long for social progress to occur – why it took so long for racial and gender equality to be written into law, for example. It was institutionally established that non-whites and non-males were of lesser value, and this norm was not challenged but transferred from teachers to students. Now, you may think that I am worrying too much, and that, left to our own devices, education will allow for such critical reflection anyway and will not hinder social progress, but let us look at a real-world example (to demonstrate again that philosophers can relate theory to practice). To do so, I will turn to the Brazilian philosopher Paulo Freire.

9    B. Russell, *The History of Western Philosophy* (London: Routledge, 2004, originally published 1946), 636.
10   J.-J. Rousseau, *Emile: Or on Education* (New York: Basic Books, 1979, originally published 1762), 41.

## Socially Regressive Education

Freire outlined a bifurcated model of approaches to education, though, as always, this bifurcation is more of a scale than a complete dichotomy. He contrasted what he termed a 'banking model of education' – the model of education Socrates was so adamantly opposed to – and the idea of education for empowerment. Freire succinctly describes the process of the banking concept of education: 'In banking education an educator replaces self-expression with a "deposit" that a student is expected to "capitalize". The more efficiently he does this, the better educated he is considered.'[11] This degree of uncritical education is a dangerous thing in Freire's view, given that it may lead to subversive acceptance of doctrines which only serve the interests of oppressors: 'The capability of banking education to minimize or annul the students' creative power and to stimulate their credulity serves the interests of the oppressors ...'[12] Freire, in this passage, suggests that education has been used to ensure the submission of the masses.

During Freire's lifetime, education had a marked influence in Latin America, contributing to a tumultuous and oppressive social landscape. The intellectual marketplace was not seen as a centre for free-thinkers to flourish, but rather as a kind of leverage point in the ideology-laden Cold War. Theodore W. Schultz, chairman of the economics department of the University of Chicago during the 1950s, for example, felt that the United States was not doing enough to combat the intellectual war with Marxism. He is reported to have said, 'The United States must take stock of its economic programmes abroad ... we want [the poor countries] to work out their economic salvation by relating themselves to us and by using our way of achieving their economic development.'[13] Cuba soon became a communist country and was in a tactically compromising position for the US (apparent later in the Cuban missile crises of 1969). Other countries

---

11    P. Freire, *The Politics of Education: Culture, Power and Liberation* (New York: Bergin and Garvey, 1985).

12    P. Freire, *Pedagogy of the Oppressed* (London: Penguin, 1970), 54.

13    N. Klien, *The Shock Doctrine* (London: Penguin, 2007), 59.

on the continent were also flirting with the concept. Consequently, the US did not want to lose the Latin American Southern cone to the ideals of communism.

The solution to this problem, from the American capitalist perspective, was quite simple; educate Latin Americans with US ideals: 'The U.S. government would pay to send Chilean students to study economics at ... the University of Chicago.'[14] Chicago's economics department was by no means ideologically neutral; it was steeped in the doctrine of extreme *laissez-faire* capitalism, advocated by the influential Chicago economist Milton Friedman, who was ardently opposed to the price- and wage-fixing of Franklin D. Roosevelt's 'New Deal.'[15] This program of 'investment' was later expanded from Chile to other countries in Latin America. Consequently, many Latin Americans returned home with a quality education from one of the world's foremost economic departments, many to PhD level. They took up jobs propagating Friedman's economic theory in Latin American universities and as government advisors. After a period of a few decades, the United States had eventually succeeded in transforming much of Latin America into an economic experiment through banking education. This economic and educational manipulation, coupled with support from military dictators such as Augusto Pinochet in Chile during the 1970s, led to the widespread implementation of extreme free-market capitalism. The results were calamitous for the Latin American people, with inflation and unemployment exponentially increasing – in Chile, for example, inflation reached 375 per cent in 1974, and unemployment reached 20 per cent (it had been just 3 per cent under the previous regime).[16] Similarly drastic figures were seen across Latin America.

It is this experience of education which contextualizes Freire's views. It is thus understandable that he became highly critical of the banking model. He insightfully illustrates how such a model of education can be a form of slavery – evident in the brief discussion of the Latin American context above:

14    Ibid. 60.
15    Ibid. 56.
16    Ibid. 79–83.

In the banking concept of education, knowledge is a gift bestowed by those who consider themselves knowledgeable upon those whom they consider know nothing. Projecting an absolute ignorance onto others, a characteristic of the ideology of oppression, negates education and knowledge as processes of inquiry. The teacher presents himself [*sic*] to his students as their necessary opposite; by considering their ignorance absolute, he [*sic*] justifies his own existence. The students, alienated like the slave in the Hegelian dialectic, accept their ignorance as justifying the teacher's existence – but, unlike the slave, they never discover that they educate the teacher.[17]

The 'economic slavery' made possible through use of the banking model of education is clearly evident in the Latin American context from which Freire's ideas emerged. The misery caused by such economic ideals and manipulative educational practices can easily be interpreted as having influenced Freire's castigation of the banking model. Similar problems will occur in uncritical acceptance of ethical models, which is why I am arguing in this essay that whilst ethics is an important element of education as a vehicle for social progress, we must be very careful in how it is approached.

## Teaching How to Think, Not What to Think

I am an optimist. I believe that on the whole and in general, we are getting better, that is, becoming more ethical. Such optimism is, of course, often called into question when we are exposed to examples of violence and blatant disregard for human life and the quality of human life. But progress has been made and many moral problems have essentially been solved: slavery and gender equality, for instance, are no longer moral questions. As Noam Chomsky observes, this is not to say that gender inequality or slavery no longer exist; rather, the meaning is that, in general, a consensus has been reached with regard to these questions.[18] Senseless violence and unjust

---

17  P. Freire, *Pedagogy of the Oppressed*, 53.

18  N. Chomsky, *Understanding Power: The Indispensable Chomsky*, ed. P. Michel and J. Schoeffel (London: Vintage Books, 2003), 356.

economic policies still occur, but doesn't more outrage ensue now than in previous generations? Look, too, to the establishment of a human rights charter, the Geneva conventions and indeed the United Nations – however flawed these endeavours may seem to some, they represent points where humanity has tried to establish a moral consensus or work towards one.

Things are far from having been resolved though, so how can education be a vehicle for this progress to continue? Eventually, we will need to rely on the children we are teaching to point out the moral failings of our generation in the same way that we can now point out how our ancestors were wrong about slavery, women's rights, and other questions. This might be an uncomfortable process, as our successive generations ascend into public leadership, political life, the academy, or wherever else, and knock us off our high moral horses. If we really wish to facilitate social progression, then we cannot teach in ethics classes what is or isn't right from our perspective, because that would hinder this progression. Teachers need to be careful not to allow their ethical views to seep into their practice. Of course, there are questions which are uncontroversial – for example, that racism is bad – but there are a lot of unsettled moral questions such as those regarding abortion and religious freedom. Furthermore, many teachers feel that they have the 'right' answer on such issues and feel they can promote such views in the same manner as uncontroversial questions. They feel they have a duty to transfer their views on religious freedom or abortion in the same way that they feel they have a duty to transfer the more established moral norms of racial equality. This is not just bad practice; it is offensive to the very essence of what education should be about. Indeed Socrates, all the way back in Ancient Greece, recognized the perils of transferring knowledge and values from teacher to student. Education should not be transferral of information, especially when it comes to moral values.

## Conclusion

Education and teaching can be patronizing at the best of times. They are too often geared towards rote learning, the aim of which is to succeed in school and earn a place at university. We take as a given that the information we teach is correct, without thinking too much about whether we are teaching the next Einsteins or Newtons. Who is to say that our students won't revolutionize the math theory we currently teach in schools? When it comes to ethics, it is even more likely that our society is 'doing it wrong' and that it will be the generation of students we are teaching who will (hopefully) point this out to us in the future. In order for this to occur, education should provide a training ground of sorts for students to hone their critical, rational, and ethical capacities. Students should be able to explore (rather than being told) how ethical decisions are made, and what considerations should be taken into account. Empathy, rational argument, ideals, and previous models of normative ethics should take the place of learning what is and isn't right. In this sense, we must consider the need to teach children *how* to think, and not what to think, as an imperative.

## Bibliography

Bentham, J., *The Principles of Morals and Legislation* (New York: Prometheus Books, 1988, originally published 1861).

Chomsky, N., *Understanding Power: The Indispensable Chomsky*, ed. P. Michel and J. Schoeffel (London: Vintage Books, 2003).

Dewey, J., 'My Pedagogical Creed', *The School Journal* 54 (3) (1897), 77–80.

Freire, P., *Pedagogy of the Oppressed* (London: Penguin, 1970).

Freire, P., *The Politics of Education: Culture, Power and Liberation* (New York: Bergin and Garvey, 1985).

Harley, N.. 'Seven Schools in Latest Trojan Horse Scandal', *The Telegraph* (21/11/2014), <http://www.telegraph.co.uk/education/11244547/Seven-schools-in-latest-Trojan-Horse-scandal.html>, accessed 20 December 2017.

Klein, N., *The Shock Doctrine* (London: Penguin, 2007).

Küng, H., *Islam, Past Present and Future* (Oxford: Oneworld Publications, 2007).

Lawton, D., and Gordon, P., *The History of Western Educational Ideas* (London: Woburn, 2002).

MacIntyre, A., *After Virtue: A Study in Moral Theory* (London: Duckworth, 1981).

MacIntyre, A., *Dependent Rational Animals: Why Human Beings Need Virtues* (Illinois: Open Court, 1999).

Mill, J. S., *Utilitarianism* (London: Dover, 2007, originally published 1861).

Rousseau, J.-J., *Emile*, trans. Barbara Foxley (London: Dent, 1974, originally published 1762).

Russell, B., *A History of Western Philosophy* (London: Routledge, 1946).

Wintour, P., 'Trojan Horse Inquiry: A Coordinated Agenda to Impose Hardline Sunni Islam', *The Guardian* (17/7/2014), < https://www.theguardian.com/uk-news/2014/jul/17/birmingham-schools-inquiry-hardline-sunni-islam-trojan-horse>, accessed 20 December 2017.

MARY IVERS

# 9   Education: Building Confidence, Changing Identities and Creating Possibilities for Flourishing

## Introduction

> Development, the possibility of 'flourishing' in one's community and culture, and access to the means to do so, is not simply a gift to be meted out by a gracious benefactor; it is both a right and a moral obligation. Development should be driven by well-informed citizens that insist on their governments implementing sound policies grounded in normative imperatives of justice, equality and dignity.[1]

At the Irish launch of the European Year of Development 2015, the President of Ireland, Michael D. Higgins, referred to the need to revise our use and understanding of the term 'development'. He spoke about the need to move away from its use as a referent to the 'developing world', a concept that divides the 'developed' from the 'developing'. Such thinking endangers us, and our society; it separates and sets these worlds in opposition to each other and provides the potential for superiority and condescension. It assumes, it ignores and it forgets that there are development needs closer to home.

President Higgins referred to the United Nations negotiations on an agenda for developing post-Millennium Development Goals (MDGs).[2] He spoke about the universality of the new agenda, not targeted, as the

---

1    M. D. Higgins, 22 January 2015, <http://www.president.ie/en/media-library/speeches/speech-by-president-michael-d.-higgins-at-the-irish-launch-of-the-european>, accessed 29 January 2018.

2    <http://www.un.org/en/ecosoc/about/mdg.shtml>, accessed 29 January 2018.

MDGs were, at poorer countries only, but at all nations. He referred particularly to the need for concerted action in tackling inequalities, and to citizens' responsibility to ensure that governments' decisions are based on the needs of all of the people, including the marginalized and vulnerable, to develop, flourish and be transformed. Moreover, the president called for citizens to contribute to the creation of the 'right atmosphere' for such development and transformation.

The sentiments expressed by the president resonate with anyone who has an interest in education, community psychology, well-being, inequalities, justice, liberation and positive strengths-based approaches to change. These areas acknowledge the significant and myriad influences on our lives and the nested ecological systems and power imbalances within which our multi-faceted beings develop.[3] They further recognize that society, the collective citizenry, has a responsibility to take action, to create the right atmosphere for development, and, importantly, that responsibility for development is not apportioned to the individual alone, but also to wider society.

My background in health and positive psychology and my experience both as a non-traditional student and as an educator in an institution that has placed great emphasis on the values of justice, leadership and service have led to my interest in the creation of the right atmosphere to support the possibility of flourishing. This has been further supported by the findings of my research with cancer survivors, which highlighted the benefits of scaffolding people as they move hopefully towards improving their quality of life in the face of life-threatening trauma.[4]

The Irish president's appeal gives hope for changes in policy development and improvements in practice in an array of areas that affect the

3    P. Freire. *Pedagogy of Hope: Reliving Pedagogy of the Oppressed*, trans. R. B. Barr (New York: Continuum, 1994). See also U. Bronfenbrenner and P. A. Morris, 'The Bio-ecological Model of Human Development', in Handbook of *Child Psychology: Theoretical Models of Human Development*. (Hoboken, NJ: John Wiley, 2006).

4    M. E. Ivers, B. A. Dooley, and U. Bates, *Development, Implementation and Evaluation of a Multidisciplinary Cancer Rehabilitation Programme: The CANSURVIVOR Project: Meeting Post-treatment Cancer Survivors' Needs* (Dublin: Health Services Executive, 2009).

lives of our citizens. For this paper, the president's speech has prompted me to explore a number of questions in the context of education and inequalities: when we talk about transformation, what is transformed? What does it mean to flourish? What is the 'right atmosphere' for such development? What follows is an exploration and linking of some concepts that I believe are important in contributing to the conversation on education and inequality.

## Education and Inequality

One of the principal settings for transformation, tackling inequalities and flourishing is the education system. Nelson Mandela is credited with saying that 'Education is the most powerful weapon which you can use to change the world'.[5] Educators all over the world will testify to this. Most societies have a formal education system from early childhood, in which school and college curricula are designed to impart knowledge and skills. Most also aim to provide a setting where human potential can develop. Not all would agree that these systems work well to provide students with the wherewithal to enable them meet their basic needs as adults and develop competencies to operate in the world, bringing about change in their local communities and wider worlds. Education systems, like other systems, are not perfect. In many ways, they do not cater very well to or for those who are marginalized or vulnerable, those who have experienced difficulties with the traditional education pathway. We know that many individuals encounter obstacles along their formal educational journey that result in them prematurely exiting the system. Numerous individuals never re-enter formal education, despite efforts to widen participation to non-traditional, vulnerable and marginalized groups.

For those who do return, much of the focus has been on three domains: barriers to access, the difficulties faced by students as they negotiate the

---

5 &lt;http://www.un.org/en/globalissues/briefingpapers/efa/quotes.shtml&gt;, accessed 29 January 2018.

system and the concept of transformational learning. Recognizing the reality of barriers to access, education systems have been developing policies that explicitly make efforts to be inclusive. Fleming and Finnegan found that in Ireland such policies and initiatives, along with the resourcing of access offices in higher education institutions, have been quite successful in supporting a small number of non-traditional students to gain entry to college, but in order to achieve social equality via education, much more needs to be done.[6]

The policy of widening participation in education is philosophically and politically controversial in terms of whether it really reduces inequality in society. Burke notes that such policies are driven by an effort to redress under-representation of some social groups in the education system and is tied to socio-economic inequalities.[7] Mavelli also questions and deconstructs the motivation behind the drive for widening participation, particularly in higher education, and asserts that such policies are driven by capitalist and economic forces that, in effect, reinforce inequality.[8]

There is a dilemma then in terms of policy development. One argument is that societal efforts and policy development on widening participation are motivated by the idea that everyone has a right to higher education to enable them to contribute in a competitive economy and to benefit them individually in terms of economic status. In this way, knowledge and skills become a commodity that implicitly benefit society and reduce inequality. Mavelli argues that such initiatives have created new inequalities and that even the language used has resulted in a pathologizing of those who are outside the norm. The use of terms such as 'non-traditional' and 'socially excluded' are examples of this. Furthermore, the use of terms such as 'lack of

6    T. Fleming and F. Finnegan, *Non-Traditional Students in Irish Higher Education: A Research Report* (University of Wrocloc, Polan: RANLHE, 2011), available at: <http://www.ranlhe.dsw.edu.pl/>, accessed 29 January 2018. See also K. Lynch, 'Neo-liberalism, Marketisation and Higher Education: Equality Considerations', in *HEA, Report on Conference Proceedings: Achieving Equity of Access to Higher Education* (Dublin: HEA, 2005), 9–21.

7    P. J. Burke, *The Right to Higher Education: Beyond Widening Participation* (London: Routledge, 2012).

8    L. Mavelli, 'Widening Participation, the Instrumentalization of Knowledge and the Reproduction of Inequality', *Teaching in Higher Education* 19 (8) (2014), 860–9.

participation' in reference to certain individuals and social groups suggests that they have deliberately chosen to not participate and have a 'motivational deficiency'.[9] The implication is that the use of such language results in a way of thinking that serves to absolve the social system of any culpability in the social exclusion of such individuals.

Mavelli puts forward an alternate motivation for the development of widening participation policies, namely that education is about transformation of the self. He refers to Foucault, noting that knowledge entails a process of enlightenment and fulfilment resulting in transcendence and informed and critical citizens. He suggests that a widening-participation approach that takes this view of knowledge and education would truly result in equality.[10]

Looked at from the individual's perspective, there are many motives for re-entering the education system. They may be motivated by the drive for knowledge and skills, a better economic prospect, the desire to develop or to gain recognition, the hope of future opportunities and possibilities, and/or a wish to be transformed and have the prospect of flourishing.[11]

## What Is Being Transformed?

Amidst the current debates on what constitutes transformative learning, Merriam and Bierma ask this very pertinent question: what is being transformed?[12] They note that the process of transformative learning is about change both on an individual level and on a societal level. They loosely categorize transformative learning into three theoretical approaches: 1)

---

9   Ibid. 865.
10  Ibid.
11  T. Fleming and F. Finnegan, 'A Critical Journey toward Lifelong Learning: Including Nontraditional Students in University', in *Higher Education in Ireland: Practices, Policies and Possibilities* (Basingstoke, UK: Palgrave McMillan, 2014), 146.
12  S. B. Merriam and L. L. Bierema, *Adult Learning: Linking Theory and Practice* (San Francisco, CA: John Wiley and Sons, 2013).

Mezirow's emphasis on rational cognitive change; 2) the beyond-rational focus, including subconscious, spiritual, and emotional processes, posited by such as Dirkx; and 3) the Freirean social action approach that challenges inequalities and oppression in society.[13] Looking at these together, we see a reciprocal ecological model of transformation emerging, with changes taking place within the individual at conscious and unconscious levels and this happening within the wider environmental context with all its influences.

Most educators familiar with transformational learning see it as a process that changes the way people view the world. The empowerment of citizens via transformative education focuses on the contribution they can make as active citizens because of the impact of education on their worldview. Much of the emphasis explaining this outcome focuses on the impact that gaining new knowledge has on the person. They become enlightened by learning to think critically and reflect on their current beliefs about the world and by exposure to alternative viewpoints. Transforming one's worldview cannot happen without profound changes taking place within the person, particularly in terms of their view of themselves and their relationship to the world.

Stevens-Long and colleagues explain that transformation as an outcome refers to deep and lasting change, a change that involves development and growth that is obvious and that fundamentally changes and empowers the person in their thoughts, emotions and actions.[14] It is about the internal psychic processes and external behaviours that are a part of the transformative experience. For Illeris, transformative learning means changes in 'elements of the learner's self'.[15] He brings together the concepts of transformative learning and identity and highlights the necessity of 'strong self-perception and confidence' and the competence to 'manage

---

13    Ibid.
14    J. Stevens-Long, S. A. Schapiro and C. McClintock, 'Passionate Scholars: Transformative Learning in Doctoral Education', *Adult Education Quarterly* 62 (2) (2012), 180–98.
15    K. Illeris, *Transformative Learning and Identity* (London: Routledge, 2013), xiii.

one's life course in a way one can answer for and be content with'.[16] The idea that education transforms the person, the 'self', falls into the domain of what are often called the soft outcomes.[17]

One of the critical changes relates to our confidence to operate in the world – the idea of agency, a belief in having personal control or power to act that becomes enhanced as transformative experiences support our changing concepts of self. These changes enable the changed worldview; they allow the person, as a changing self, to see the world differently and to operate differently in and on that world.

While we display and experience different selves in differing contexts, these are related by a coherent self-concept.[18] Our self-concept includes our memories about ourselves, our evaluation of ourselves, our beliefs about our abilities, values and motives, our possible future selves and our beliefs about what others think of us.[19] We define ourselves in terms of group membership and in terms of our unique traits and relationships so our many perceptions of 'self' involve different forms of social and personal identities.[20] Honneth's views on developing an identity, a self, and gaining recognition as a unique individual depends on modes of relating to the self that rely on the connection between the social and personal worlds.[21] These ways of relating are self-confidence, self-respect and self-esteem and are key components of our self-concept. Development of these ways of relating to self are formed in special relationships, usually in childhood, and contribute to the awareness of one's uniqueness, sense of identity, a

16    Ibid. 1.
17    R. Lloyd and F. O'Sullivan, *Measuring Soft Outcomes and Distance Travelled: A Methodology for Developing a Guidance Document* (London: Department of Work and Pensions, 2003).
18    Ibid. 122–5.
19    R. J. Gerrig, P. G. Zimbardo, F. Svartdal, T. Brennan, R. Donaldson, and T. Archer, *Psychology and Life* (Boston, MA: Pearson, 2012), 484.
20    M. A. Hogg and G. Vaughan, *Social Psychology: An Introduction* (Harlow: Pearson Education, 2002), 125.
21    A. Honneth, *The Struggle for Recognition: The Moral Grammar of Social Conflicts* (Cambridge, MA: The MIT Press, 1995).

positive image of one's abilities, autonomy, respect and gaining recognition for one's contribution to the world.[22]

Seligman makes a very important point when he notes that public policy develops on foot of what we can measure.[23] For example, we measure Gross Domestic Product (GDP) in relation to income, and Global Burden of Disease (GBD) in relation to health. In societies driven by capitalist and economic forces, 'contribution to the world' tends to be measured in terms of productivity. Soft outcomes are rarely measured. Experienced adult educators tell us that raised self-esteem and confidence are known outcomes for those who participate in a learning experience, but there are few studies focusing on such outcomes.

Research carried out by Schoenholz-Read found that students reported that not only had their learning changed their worldview, but they also felt changed emotionally, had more patience, empathy, and self-confidence.[24] In 2002, Preston and Hammond collected the views of 2,729 further education tutors on the wider benefits of learning rather than the qualification that might be gained. There was overwhelming consensus that students benefited in terms of improved self-esteem.[25] In 2004, Janssen conducted a study of 2,000 adult learners taking a wide range of non-accredited courses at the Mary Ward Centre for Adult Learning in Central London.[26] The study aimed to gain insight into students' own views on the benefits of their learning and the difference it made in their lives. They reported psychological, social and career benefits, but for them the first and primary personal gain was enhanced self-confidence. These findings are supported

22    Ibid.
23    M. E. Seligman, *Flourish: A Visionary New Understanding of Happiness and Well-being* (New York: Simon & Schuster, 2012).
24    J. Schoenholz-Read, Interim Report on Student Development and Diversity Study (Unpublished manuscript. Santa Barbara, CA: Fielding Graduate Institute, 2000).
25    J. Preston and C. Hammond, *The Wider Benefits of Learning: Practitioners Views* (Institute of Education, University of London, Centre for Research on the Wider Benefits of Learning, Research Reports, March 2002).
26    O. Janssen, 'The Impact of Learning', *Adults Learning*, 2004, 15 (9), 24–6.

by the research conducted by Stevens-Long and colleagues in 2012.[27] They found that, as well as changes in cognitive development, students reported personal development changes including increased tolerance, confidence and positive emotions.

More recently, Honneth's themes of recognition, respect, confidence and self-esteem emerged as outcomes in a European-wide study of non-traditional learners in higher education.[28] The researchers reported that Irish learners were motivated to enter the education system because of a 'desire for recognition that was rooted in a perceived lack or undeveloped capability which was often rooted in the experience of disrespect in work or school'.[29] This research reports on the increased self-confidence and self-esteem that resulted from going back to education. The study participants used the key terms 'self-confidence', 'esteem' and 'respect' time and again as they spoke of the occurrence of profound development and transformation.

On 12 March 2015, a lone (single) parent wrote an open letter to the Irish government about her struggle to make ends meet. In her letter, one of the issues she raised was the fact that she had entered the third-level education system. Unfortunately, her circumstances prohibited her from continuing and she found herself in a situation in which she was forced to drop out of college after two years and this had devastating effects. She could have chosen any number of effects to list, but what she said was very

---

27  Stevens-Long, Schapiro, and McClintock, '"Passionate Scholars": Transformative Learning in Doctoral Education', *Adult Education Quarterly* 62 (2), 180–98.

28  T. Fleming, 'Alex Honneth and the Struggle for Recognition: Implications for Transformative Learning', in A. Nicolaides and D. Holt (eds), *Spaces of Transformation and Transformation of Space: Proceedings of the XI International Transformative Learning Conference* (New York: Teachers, College, Columbia University, 2014), 318–24. See also T. Fleming and F. Finnegan, 'Critical Theory and Non-traditional Students' Experience in Irish Higher Education', in *Student Voices on Inequalities in European Higher Education: Challenges for Theory, Policy and Practice in a Time of Change* (London: Routledge, 2014), 51.

29  Ibid. 321.

profound. For her, the experience of dropping out 'totally shattered my confidence and hopes'.[30]

This consequence is important. Mavelli says that the journey in higher education transforms the person and provides knowledge to 'articulate a different vision of the future'.[31] It provides the individual with hope. This ties in with Freire's views on hope and liberation and his view that the task of the progressive educator is 'to unveil opportunities for hope'.[32] Hope is a positive human strength consisting of cognitive and motivational components, including agentic and goal-directed thinking.[33] It reflects a person's views of their capacity to 'clearly conceptualise goals, develop the specific strategies to reach those goals and initiate and sustain the motivation for using those strategies'.[34] Those who have higher levels of hope are more confident and have stronger belief in their personal or self-efficacy. Agency is about personal control and mastery beliefs, that is, beliefs in one's personal ability to be effective and having confidence to operate in the world. It is strongly linked to empowerment, the process of increasing capacity to participate meaningfully in shaping one's future.[35] Empowerment as an outcome involves the development of a sense of agency in moving towards self-determined goals, contributing towards a positive sense of identity and raising the prospect of operating meaningfully in the world and flourishing.[36]

---

30    <http://www.thejournal.ie/readme/letter-lone-parent-1968003–Mar2015/>, accessed 29 January 2018.

31    Mavelli et al., 'Widening Participation, the Instrumentalization of Knowledge and the Reproduction of Inequality', 868.

32    P. Freire, 'Pedagogy of Hope: Reliving Pedagogy of the Oppressed', trans. R. B. Barr (New York: Continuum, 1994).

33    C. R. Snyder (ed.), *Handbook of Hope: Theory, Measures, and Applications* (New York: Academic Press, 2000).

34    S. Lopez, C. R. Snyder, J. Magyar-Moe, L. Edwards, J. Pedrotti et al., 'Strategies for Accentuating Hope', in P. A. Linley and S. Joseph (eds), *Positive Psychology in Practice* (Hoboken, NJ: Wiley, 2004), 388–404 (388).

35    J. Pettit, *Empowerment and Participation: Bridging the Gap Between Understanding and Practice* (New York: United Nations Headquarters, 2012).

36    P. Howard, J. Butcher, and L. Egan, 'Transformative Education: Pathways to Identity, Independence and Hope', *Gateways: International Journal of Community Research and Engagement*, 3 (2010), 88–103.

## Flourishing

Flourishing is a relatively new concept in the literature. It has emerged as a construct in the fields of positive psychology and educational philosophy and is related to the ideas of subjective well-being and happiness. According to Seligman and other prominent positive psychologists, the key components of flourishing are high positive emotions, engagement and meaning, along with self-determination, resilience, positive relationships and a sense of accomplishment.[37]

There are a growing number of educational philosophers focusing on this concept and advocating that children should be educated to live flourishing lives, irrespective of their contribution to the economy.[38] According to Wolbert and her colleagues 'Flourishing should be regarded as an ideal aim of education'.[39] They recently set out to distinguish flourishing from concepts such as happiness and subjective well-being and propose the term 'flourishing' is a better translation of the Aristotelian concept *eudaimonia*, (most often translated as 'happiness'). They believe it to be much more than 'happiness' and set out some key criteria to help our understanding.

Human flourishing involves the worthwhile pursuit of an Aristotelian morally good and enjoyable life and it refers to the actualizing of human potential and optimal performance. This is in part dependent on the

---

37   Seligman, *Flourish: A Visionary New Understanding of Happiness and Well-being* (New York: Simon & Schuster, 2012. See also F. A. Huppert and T. T. So, 'Flourishing across Europe: Application of a New Conceptual Framework for Defining Well-being', *Social Indicators Research* 110 (3) (2013), 837–61; M. Gaffney, *Flourishing* (London: Penguin, 2011).

38   D. J. De Ruyter, 'Pottering in the Garden? On Human Flourishing and Education', *British Journal of Educational Studies* 52 (4) (2004), 377–89. See also M. C. Nussbaum, *Not for Profit: Why Democracy Needs the Humanities* (Princeton, NJ: Princeton University Press, 2012); M. Reiss and J. White. *An Aims-based Curriculum: The Significance of Human Flourishing for Schools* (London: IOE Press, 2013).

39   L. S. Wolbert, D. J. de Ruyter, and A. Schinkel, 'Formal Criteria for the Concept of Human Flourishing: The First Step in Defending Flourishing as an Ideal Aim of Education', *Ethics and Education* 10 (1) (2015), 118–29 (118).

capabilities, the opportunities and the possibilities that people have open to them. To achieve this goal, a process of continuous development is required, so flourishing is a dynamic state. It includes the development of human capacities that are good for us, such as regulation of emotions and building social relationships. It draws on De Ruyter's view that human flourishing involves the need for individuals to become 'reflective actors', 'practically wise human beings' engaged in 'virtuous activities'.[40] There is also the very practical recognition that we need the external goods necessary for us to live well.[41]

This is not about striving for perfection. Wolbert et al. paint a realistic rather than idealized picture in which people are aiming for the ideal of self-actualization, but acknowledge the circumstances of life itself and its inevitable conflicts and struggles, along with the recognition and acceptance that we are not perfect in our capabilities, nor always successful in our endeavours.

If we support the view that flourishing is an ideal aim of education then education policies and systems should be equipping people to 'contribute to society in a meaningful way and get the best chance of leading a flourishing life'.[42] Creating the right atmosphere to support such change should be the aspiration of all education systems for all students at all levels, shouldn't it?

## Creating the Right Atmosphere

Considering the value of the soft outcomes discussed earlier, we must attend to the development of the right atmosphere for such development. In the context of addressing inequalities in education, what do we need to do to support individuals to develop confidence and hope and provide possibilities for flourishing?

40   De Ruyter, 'Pottering in the Garden?', 385.
41   Wolbert et al., 'Formal Criteria for the Cconcept of Human Flourishing', 121.
42   Ibid. 126.

Articulating explicit outcomes that go beyond the capitalist agenda, developing our theories and encouraging research would be a good start. This can happen best in conjunction with policy development and provision of the necessary supports. Seligman believes that the goals of governments should be to engender flourishing.[43] At the beginning of the new millennium an Irish government white paper on adult and community education visualized adult education as enabling people to grow in self-confidence and social awareness to the point of being agents of change in society.[44] Such a vision is aspirational without articulating relevant explicit and measurable outcomes and resourcing their attainment. Seventeen years later, we are not much further along.

Support is needed to identify and develop an understanding of the factors conducive to the development of self-confidence, changing identities, increasing hope and promoting the possibility of flourishing, particularly with non-traditional, marginalized and vulnerable people. This needs to be accompanied by the development of practices that create and support the right atmosphere for achieving our aim.

We have some clues as to how to proceed. We know that a lack of confidence due to low self-esteem is a documented barrier to learning and that confidence builds up slowly and enables progression.[45] Those who have been marginalized and are vulnerable may have very low confidence levels and are in an unequal situation compared to other adults in our society when it comes to participating in the life of their community. James and Nightingale refer to some education providers focusing on self-esteem in the context of retention and achievement, but note the lack of research in the area. They highlight the idea that the promotion of positive self-esteem and confidence should be embedded in the practice of teaching and learning and refer to personal development courses as an educational

---

43   Seligman, *Flourish*.

44   Department of Education, *Adult and Community Education* (white paper) (Dublin: Stationary Office, 2000), 29.

45   Learning and Skills Council, *Successful Participation for All: Widening Adult Participation Strategy* (2003). See also V. McGivney, 'Fixing or Changing the Pattern', *NIACE* (Coventry: Learning and Skills Council, 2001), <http://www.niace.org.uk>, accessed 29 January 2018.

example in providing an atmosphere to flourish. They refer to courses specifically designed to boost self-esteem and confidence using strategies such as small group work, opportunities for positive feedback and open discussions about confidence and self-esteem. They also crucially note that good teaching and learning strategies encourage the growth of confidence and self-esteem using learner-centred approaches, providing appropriate support and respecting and valuing learners.[46]

We know that not much attention is given to constructs that cannot be measured. With the recent focus on well-being, there has been a concerted effort to develop measures of the elements of flourishing, so there is some hope that policies will follow. There have been some recent developments in this regard and there is growing interest in the research carried out by Huppert and So from the University of Cambridge on levels of flourishing in the European Union.[47]

West and colleagues point to the need to look at the nature of relationships in education, while Fleming encourages us to re-focus our attention on the processes of teaching, being mindful that mutual recognition between teacher and learner facilitates identity development.[48] Fleming proposes a transformation theory that includes 'the interpersonal process of support and recognition that build self-confidence, self-respect and self-esteem'.[49] In such a praxis, learning becomes less about function, competency, behavioural outcomes and economics and more communicative, social and transformative.[50]

Van Dinther and colleagues conducted a review of factors affecting our efficacy beliefs about our ability and power to operate in the world and they

46  K. James and C. Nightingale, 'Self-esteem, Confidence and Adult Learning: Briefing Sheet', *NIACE* (2005). Retrieved from <http://www.niace.org.uk>, accessed 29 January 2018.
47  Huppert and So, 'Flourishing across Europe'.
48  L. West, T. Fleming, and F. Finnegan, 'Connecting Bourdieu, Winnicott, and Honneth: Understanding the Experiences of Non-traditional Learners through an Interdisciplinary Lens', *Studies in the Education of Adults* 45 (2) (2013), 119–34. See also Fleming, 'Alex Honneth and the Struggle for Recognition' (2014).
49  Ibid. 324
50  Fleming, 'Alex Honneth and the Struggle for Recognition'.

found that practical mastery experiences are vital in strengthening efficacy beliefs.[51] In the higher education context, they concluded that a focus on mastery and strengths rather than a focus on mistakes and failure is called for across all levels of our education system. They also suggest that practical experiences in and of themselves are not sufficient, but that appropriate support in goal-setting, self-regulation and self-reflection are potentially important.[52] This suggests the idea of scaffolding, which clearly comes back to the nature of the relationships between educators and students.

## Conclusion

The chapter began with the agenda for developing post-Millennium Development Goals. The outcome of these negotiations was agreement on seventeen sustainable development goals for 2030, launched at the Transforming our World summit in September 2015.[53] The most relevant goal for this discussion, and one that will receive attention over the next thirteen years is the fourth goal, to 'Ensure inclusive and equitable quality education and promote lifelong learning opportunities for all'.[54]

We know that education is central to the development of an inclusive, equal and fair society and has intrinsic and instrumental value.[55] Learning communities and cultures grounded in the normative imperatives of justice, equality and dignity would shift our educational emphasis towards supporting the transformation of self and the development of the soft outcomes of self-confidence and self-esteem, in an atmosphere of strengths-based and caring supportive approaches that unveil opportunities for hope and

---

51 M. van Dinther, F. Dochy, and M. Segers, 'Factors Affecting Students' Self-efficacy in Higher Education', *Educational Research Review* 6 (2) (2011), 95–108.

52 Ibid.

53 <https://sustainabledevelopment.un.org/>, accessed 29 January 2018.

54 Ibid.

55 Nussbaum, *Not for Profit*.

provide possibilities for flourishing. However, while there is recognition of these positive outcomes of education, they are rarely planned outcomes.

In a society where there is a will to provide access to the possibility of flourishing, we need, as President Higgins pointed out, sound policies.[56] The ideas of transformation of the self, enlightenment, informed and critical citizens, speak to the need for policies that orient our education systems towards a focus on creating an atmosphere in which students can flourish.[57] The ideas of human flourishing link very well with the alternative motivations for widening participation in education set out by Mavelli and outlined earlier in this chapter.[58]

There are many difficulties to advancing the idea that a focus on building confidence and self-esteem would become a formal, planned outcome of our education systems, including the basic problems of defining and measuring the concepts themselves. There is a pressing need for research and clarity about what we hope to achieve. However, we don't have to wait for clear definitions and measures before we can begin creating atmospheres that provide opportunities to flourish.

## Bibliography

Biggeri, M., 'Education Policy for Agency and Participation', in C. S. Hart, M. Biggeri and B. Babic (eds), *Agency and Participation in Childhood and Youth: International Applications of the Capability Approach in Schools and Beyond* (London: A&C Black, 2014).

Brock, S. E., 'Learning and Transformation', in *Exploring Learning and Teaching in Higher Education* (Berlin, Heidelberg: Springer-Verlag, 2015), 233–50.

56    James and Nightingale, 'Self-esteem, Confidence and Adult Learning'.

57    M. Biggeri, 'Education Policy for Agency and Participation', in C. S. Hart, M. Biggeri and B. Babic (eds), *Agency and Participation in Childhood and Youth: International Applications of the Capability Approach in Schools and Beyond* (London: A&C Black, 2014), 44–62.

58    Mavelli et al., 'Widening Participation, the Instrumentalization of Knowledge and the Reproduction of Inequality'.

Bronfenbrenner, U., and Morris, P. A., *The Bio-ecological Model of Human Development*, in W. Damon and R. M. Lerner (eds), *Handbook of Child Psychology: Theoretical Models of Human Development* (Hoboken, New Jersey: John Wiley, 2006), 793–828.

Burke, P. J., *The Right to Higher Education: Beyond Widening Participation* (London: Routledge, 2012).

De Ruyter, D. J., 'Pottering in the Garden? On Human Flourishing and Education', *British Journal of Educational Studies* 52 (4) (2004), 377–89.

Department of Education, *Adult and Community Education* (white paper) (Dublin: Stationary Office, 2000), 29.

Dirkx, J. M., 'Nurturing Soul Work: A Jungian Approach to Transformative Learning', in *The Handbook of Transformative Learning: Theory, Research, and Practice* (San Francisco, CA: Jossey-Bass, 2012), 116–30.

Eldred, J., Ward, J., Snowden, K., and Dutton, Y., *Catching Confidence: Guidance for Tutors* (NIACE, 2006) < http://www.learningandwork.org.uk/resource/ catching-confidence/>, accessed 29 January 2018.

Fleming, T., 'Alex Honneth and the Struggle for Recognition: Implications for Transformative Learning. Spaces of Transformation and Transformation of Space', in *Proceedings of the XI International Transformative Learning Conference* (New York: Teachers' College, Columbia University, 2014), 318–24.

Fleming, T., and Finnegan, F., 'A Critical Journey Toward Lifelong Learning: Including Nontraditional Students in University', in *Higher Education in Ireland: Practices, Policies and Possibilities* (Basingstoke, UK: Palgrave McMillan, 2014), 146.

Fleming, T., and Finnegan, F., 'Critical Theory and Non-traditional Students' Experience in Irish Higher Education', in *Student Voices on Inequalities in European Higher Education: Challenges for Theory, Policy and Practice in a Time of Change* (London: Routledge 2014), 51.

Fleming, T., and Finnegan, F., *Non-Traditional Students in Irish Higher Education: A Research Report* (University of Wroclaw, Poland: RANLHE, 2011).

Freire, P., *Pedagogy of Hope: Reliving Pedagogy of the Oppressed*, trans. R. B. Barr (New York: Continuum, 1994).

Gaffney, M., *Flourishing* (UK: Penguin, 2011).

Gerrig, R. J., Zimbardo, P. G., Svartdal, F., Brennan, T., Donaldson, R., and Archer, T., *Psychology and Life* (Boston, MA: Pearson, 2012), 484.

Grant, C. A., 'Cultivating Flourishing Lives a Robust Social Justice Vision of Education', *American Educational Research Journal* 49 (5) (2012), 910–34.

Hogg, M. A., and Vaughan, G., *Social Psychology: An Introduction* (Harlow: Pearson Education, 2002), 125.

Honneth, A., *The Struggle for Recognition: The Moral Grammar of Social Conflicts* (Cambridge, MA: The MIT Press, 1995).

Howard, P., Butcher, J., and Egan, L., 'Transformative Education: Pathways to Identity, Independence and Hope', *Gateways: International Journal of Community Research and Engagement* 3 (2010), 88–103.

Huppert, F. A., and So, T. T., 'Flourishing across Europe: Application of a New Conceptual Framework for Defining Well-being', *Social Indicators Research* 110 (3) (2013), 837–61.

Illeris, K., *Transformative Learning and Identity* (London: Routledge, 2013), xiii.

Ivers, M. E., Dooley, B. A., and Bates, U., *Development, Implementation and Evaluation of a Multidisciplinary Cancer Rehabilitation Programme: The CANSURVIVOR Project: Meeting Post-treatment Cancer Survivors' Needs* (Dublin: Health Services Executive, 2009).

James, K., and Nightingale, C., 'Self-esteem, Confidence and Adult Learning: Briefing Sheet' (*NIACE*, 2005 retrieved from <www.niace.org.uk>, accessed 29 January 2018).

Janssen, O., 'The Impact of Learning', *Adults Learning* 15 (9) (2004), 24–6.

Learning and Skills Council, *Successful Participation for All: Widening Adult Participation Strategy* (Coventry, Learning and Skills Council 2003).

Lopez, S., Snyder, C. R., Magyar-Moe, J., Edwards, L., Pedrotti, J. et al., 'Strategies for Accentuating Hope', in P. A. Linley and S. Joseph (eds), *Positive Psychology in Practice* (Hoboken, NJ: Wiley, 2004), 388–404.

Lloyd, R., and O'Sullivan, F., *Measuring Soft Outcomes and Distance Travelled: A Methodology for Developing a Guidance Document* (London: Department of Work and Pensions, 2003).

Lynch, K., 'Neo-liberalism, Marketisation and Higher Education: Equality Considerations', in *HEA, Report on Conference Proceedings: Achieving Equity of Access to Higher Education* (Dublin: HEA, 2005), 9–21.

McGivney, V., 'Fixing or Changing the Pattern', *NIACE* (2001), <http://www.niace.org.uk>, accessed 29 January 2018.

Mavelli, L., 'Widening Participation, the Instrumentalization of Knowledge and the Reproduction of Inequality', *Teaching in Higher Education* 19 (8) (2014), 860–9.

Merriam, S. B., and Bierema, L. L., *Adult Learning: Linking Theory and Practice* (San Francisco, CA: John Wiley and Sons, 2013).

Nussbaum, M. C., *Not for Profit: Why Democracy Needs the Humanities* (Princeton NJ: Princeton University Press, 2012).

Pettit, J., *Empowerment and Participation: Bridging the Gap between Understanding and Practice* (New York: United Nations Headquarters, 2012).

Preston, J., and Hammond, C., *The Wider Benefits of Learning: Practitioners Views* (Institute of Education, University of London: Centre for Research on the Wider Benefits of Learning, Research Reports, March 2002).

Schoenholz-Read, J., Interim Report on Student Development and Diversity Study (Santa Barbara, CA: Fielding Graduate Institute, unpublished manuscript, 2000).

Seligman, M. E., *Flourish: A Visionary New Understanding of Happiness and Well-being* (New York: Simon and Schuster, 2012).

Snyder, C. R. (ed.), *Handbook of Hope: Theory, Measures, and Applications* (New York: Academic Press, 2000).

Stevens-Long, J., Schapiro, S. A., and McClintock, C. 'Passionate Scholars: Transformative Learning in Doctoral Education', *Adult Education Quarterly* 62 (2) (2012), 180–98.

Rahimparvar, S. F. V., Hamzehkhani, M., Geranmayeh, M., and Rahimi, R., 'Effect of Educational Software on Self-efficacy of Pregnant Women to Cope with Labor: A Randomized Controlled Trial', *Archives of Gynecology and Obstetrics* 286 (1) (2012), 63–70.

Reiss, M., and White, J., *An Aims-based Curriculum: The Significance of Human Flourishing for Schools* (London: IOE Press, 2013).

Van Dinther, M., Dochy, F., and Segers, M., 'Factors Affecting Students' Self-efficacy in Higher Education', *Educational Research Review* 6 (2) (2011), 95–108.

Webb, D., 'Paulo Freire and "the Need for a Kind of Education in Hope"', *Cambridge Journal of Education* 40 (4) (2010), 327–39.

West, L., Fleming, T., and Finnegan, F., 'Connecting Bourdieu, Winnicott, and Honneth: Understanding the Experiences of Non-traditional Learners through an Interdisciplinary Lens', *Studies in the Education of Adults* 45 (2) (2013), 119–34.

Wolbert, L. S., de Ruyter, D. J., and Schinkel, A., 'Formal Criteria for the Concept of Human Flourishing: The First Step in Defending Flourishing as an Ideal Aim of Education', *Ethics and Education* 10 (1) (2015), 118–29.

EUGENE CURRAN

## 10 A Method in Search of a Model: Examining the Relationship between the Thought of Maria Montessori and Bernard Lonergan, Applied to Adult Education

## Introduction

When it comes to transformation and justice and the way we learn and come to know, two authors that have significantly advanced these issues are Bernard Lonergan and Maria Montessori. If one is seeking to evolve, or more accurately describe, a new model of education, such an undertaking requires a strong foundation. Few authors have equalled Bernard Lonergan's painstakingly detailed account of the processes of human knowing and his reflections on the requirements necessary to facilitate people in their process of coming to know. His writings are, and remain, amongst the most clearly thought out and delineated (if not the most easily comprehended or enunciated) on the subject of human insight. In the field of educational practitioners, however, few are as widely known or have influenced as many lives as Maria Montessori.

Lonergan's output was immense, his collected works running into over twenty volumes. Yet it is the density not of his books but, rather, of his thought that makes easy summaries impossible. He seeks all possible clarity in his thought. A work such as the present one can only hope to skim the surface and cannot hope to justify Lonergan's assumptions in any depth. His work has become 'classic'[1] and, that being so, we must accept David Tracy's contention that a

---

1    This is not the place to go into a discussion of what constitutes a classic in philosophical thought but further insight into this is found in D. Tracy, *The Analogical Mind* (New York: Crossroad, 1989).

classic text's fate is that only its constant reinterpretation by later, finite, historical, temporal beings who will risk asking its questions and listening, critically and tactfully, to its responses, can actualise the event of understanding beyond its fixation in a text. Every classic lives as a classic only if it finds readers willing to be provoked by its claim to attention.[2]

In the same way, there are many educational theorists other than Montessori and they too may have a great deal to say, but the principle justification for the choice of Montessori is that, in their own field, *The Formation of Man* and *The Absorbent Mind* are classics of educational practice. Montessori, as we will see, did not limit her attentions to children, but, to date, little work has been done in applying her insights on education to the education and formation of adults. While her written output doesn't match Lonergan's, we can nonetheless hardly hope to do justice to the scope of her vision in such a confined space, but I believe that both Lonergan's insights and methods and Montessori's model of the formation environment have major contributions to make to the work of transformative adult education today and the shaping of a responsible, just and caring society.

I have spent a good deal of time setting out the framework for this chapter and its aims, but, as Lonergan himself notes, 'nothing disorientates a reader more than a failure to state clearly what a book is not about'.[3]

## Lonergan's Method: Insight

The basis of Lonergan's great work, *Insight*, is that people come to knowledge through moments of insight and that they come to insight through a process of knowing. In Lonergan's view, insight

1.  comes as a release to the tension of inquiry
2.  comes suddenly and unexpectedly
3.  is a function not of outer circumstances but of inner conditions

---

2    Ibid. 102.
3    Lonergan, *Insight*, 12.

4. pivots between the concrete and the abstract and
5. passes into the habitual texture of one's mind.[4]

While Lonergan's theory may seem dense and conceptual in the extreme, it is always firmly rooted in the concrete. As (4) above states, it pivots between the concrete and the abstract and the instrument which mediates between the two is imagination. We grasp first not the theory but an image which enables us to grasp the theory. In understanding his contentions, certain further aspects must be borne in mind:

1. The release of the tension of inquiry is not 'ex nihilo' but springs from the human desire to know. It stems not from the input of knowledge but from the seeker's predisposition to know and understand. Driven by that desire, the seeker can, and will, make many sacrifices in order to come to that moment of understanding and clarity.
2. It is creative and cannot be programmed; if it could be, then 'discoveries would be mere conclusions'.[5]

   > A teacher cannot undertake to make a pupil understand. All (s)he can do is present the sensible elements in the issue in a suggestive order and with a proper distribution of emphasis. It is up to the pupils themselves to reach understanding and they do so in varying measures of ease and rapidity.[6]

3. It is the internal, not external, conditions which are central. Many can share common external environments of learning, but not all will come to the concomitant understanding. The example he gives is of Archimedes; many frequented the baths of Syracuse, but only he had the 'Eureka' moment of insight.
4. People will come to insight as they search for answers to concrete questions. These are not merely practical or empirical questions, but, rather, questions which relate to the circumstances of their lives. They may give answers to questions posed by an outside agent, but true insight will come only when the 'outside' questions find an echo in

4    Ibid. 28.
5    Ibid. 29.
6    Ibid. 29

the person's own inner world of inquiry. Nevertheless, the process will involve a movement from the immediate and concrete to the mediated and theoretical; in order to progress through his or her own issue, the seeker turns to the conclusions and formulations of the insights of others.

5.  Insights (our own and others) become part of our habit of thinking and acting. What was unsolvable becomes easy and resolvable. The great insights of our past (personal or communal) become the commonplaces of our present and the building blocks of our future discoveries.

It is important to note that such insights may be individual or what Lonergan calls 'single unified sets'[7] – that is to say, a collection of insights which are connected intrinsically and which may serve the same function. Insights, either individual or as unified sets, form the bases of constructed processes of thought, which he divides into two types: systematic and non-systematic. Lonergan's own distinction between the two (systematic and non-systematic processes) may serve us well; he cites the situation of astronomers who can publish the exact times of the eclipses of past and future centuries (a systematic process) while meteorologists need a constant supply of fresh and accurate information to tell us about tomorrow's weather (a non-systematic process).[8]

Of systematic processes, Lonergan observes that, other things being equal

1.  the whole of a systematic process and its every event possess but a single intelligibility that corresponds to a single insight or set of unified insights;
2.  any situation can be deduced from any other without explicit consideration of intervening situations;
3.  the investigation of such processes is marked not only by a notable facility in ascertaining and checking abundant and significant data but

---

7   Ibid. 71.
8   Ibid. 74.

also by a supreme moment when all data fall into a single perspective (and) sweeping deductions become possible.[9]

In contrast, in non-systematic processes,

1. There will be no single unifying insight and thus understanding will be multiple and such insights as are involved will not have a unifying theme;
2. Because different parts of the process are understood differently, there can be no single combination of selected laws that hold for the whole process;
3. Such non-systematic process may be deducible in all its events. In essence, this maintains that, given the fulfilment of necessary conditions (full information, complete knowledge, the absence of extraneous interference, correct insights into the basic situation and the deduced situations, sufficient skill and no restriction on the amount of time available), the occurrence and dimensions of the next significantly different situation can be deduced;
4. Non-systematic processes exhibit coincidental aggregates; that is to say,
   a) the members of the aggregate have some unity based on spatial juxtaposition or temporal succession or both;
   b) there is no corresponding unity on the level of insight or intelligible relation.
   This means that one must be aware of the difference between coincidentals and insights.
5. In non-systematic processes, the difficulty of investigating their nature increases with the number and diversity of their several distinct and unrelated intelligibilities.[10]

As he himself might say, let us now pause to take our bearings. It seems vital that, in the education/formation process one can distinguish between systematic and non-systematic processes. In order to arrive at insight, there

9    Ibid. 71.
10   Ibid. 71

must be an understanding of the nature of the particular process and the fulfilment of its criteria. In his words, 'systematic process is monotonous but non-systematic process can be the womb of novelty'.[11] By monotonous, Lonergan means repetitive; positing 'a functional relation on which the relations between all appropriate subsequent measurements should converge as on a limit'.[12] Yet now the question arises: if non-systematic processes require the fulfilment of such criteria as complete knowledge, sufficient skill, the absence of extraneous interference and correct insight, etc., who can ever hope to know anything or reach any conclusions? Such criteria can never be met until the processes of time stop.

In response to this, Lonergan posits first the necessity for canons of empirical method, of which he outlines six.[13] These are:

1.  *Selection*: This is insight into the data of sensible experience. It is not some kind of scientific passivity but a conscious choice to be attentive to sensations with a specific purpose. Such an ability to perceive and be 'specifically attentive' comes with the development, practice and exercise of the attitude of scientific observation.

2.  *Operations*: This refers to the accumulation of such insights and we summarize it as being the canon which accepts the existence, operation and interaction of such laws as govern human activity. One needs to be aware of how one law can presuppose, depend on or lead to others and of the constant interaction between such laws and our human actions; as laws influence our actions, so our actions may lead to reconsideration and reformulation of these laws. Thus, this canon requires attentiveness to the processes and implications of analysis.

3.  *Relevance*: This is focused on the process of understanding itself and operates at the level of pure rather than applied science. As Lonergan points out,[14] the same data can provide a starting point for different

11   Ibid. 75.
12   Ibid. 87.
13   These are given in expanded form in *Insight*, Chapter 3.
14   Lonergan, *Insight*, 100.

types of insight.[15] One must then be clear as to which type is, or should be, active and how this would differ from others. Equally, it ties in with John Henry Newman's contention that all aspects of knowledge are linked.[16] This being so, one must choose to be clear about those methods to which one will be attentive.

4. *Parsimony*: This canon requires one to acknowledge the limitations of one's knowledge; but, as Lonergan observes, it is the wise person who knows what he does not know. Yet it also requires that one acknowledge what, within the limits of accepted laws and probability, one does know. It hinges on the verification of the formulations of explanation of the data.

5. *Complete Explanation*: This is a sticking point for many as it requires that we account for all data. Given the limits of human existence (that we are bounded by time, space and our individual experience and make-up), how can we hope to meet the demands of complete explanation? What is sought is not an absolute and total explanation for all time, but an explanation that is as complete as is possible at this time, within the parameters and constraints of human knowledge and existence. This is what Lonergan calls 'the virtually unconditioned'.[17] For the moment, however, suffice it to say that incomplete explanation need not, of itself, negate any process; it highlights its limits and the limits of its application.

6. *Statistical Residue*: This is best understood as the canon which states that that which cannot be explained by the current process must be explained by some other process(es) and the limitations of the current process must be acknowledged. It is this canon which calls for

---

15  Although it is far beyond the scope of this chapter, it is at this point that one should pay attention to the insights of Howard Gardner in his book on different forms of intelligence. If people have and exercise different intelligences then the formation environment needs must take cognizance of and facilitate this. See H. Gardner, *Multiple Intelligences* (New York: Basic Books, 2006).

16  Cardinal J. H. Newman, *The Idea of a University* (University of Notre Dame Press, 1982), especially section 9.

17  Lonergan, *Insight*, 305.

enquiry into that which cannot be explained by our knowledge as it is and urges us to further research and clarity.

Finally, a note on biases: Lonergan enumerates four biases; that of the dramatic subject; of the individual egoist; of the member of a group and of intellectual capacity. Such biases must be acknowledged both by the subject and by the 'observer'. The method calls for honest acknowledgement of biases and the ramifications of such biases.[18]

## The Process of Coming to Understanding

What then might describe the process by which the individual comes to knowledge and understanding? It is important to note that Lonergan's focus is not on 'knowledge' in itself, but on the process of 'coming to know', which is to say that 'it is not that an individual performing the listed acts really does know but merely that I perform them and that by "knowing" I mean no more than such performance'.[19] The 'listed acts' he mentions are sensing, perceiving, imagining, inquiring, understanding, formulating, reflecting, grasping the unconditioned and affirming.

Lonergan's concern is not with the product (what is known), nor solely with the subject (the one who knows), but with the person in the conscious process of coming to know. Consciousness is thus understood not as some sort of inward look or the process of knowing something. Rather, the person performs the act of knowing and becomes aware of how they perform this act and the interconnectedness of the various elements of the process. What is to be known is the real and the true, but it must be noted that Lonergan does not posit some absolute status of 'real' or 'true' in the process of knowing, but, rather, the 'virtually unconditioned', by which he means that although the result may be conditioned under certain

18    Further elucidation on biases can be found in *Insight*, Chapter 7, 244–67.
19    Lonergan, *Insight*, 344.

circumstances, those conditions have either been fulfilled, are negligible or are not yet known. An awareness of conditions which have not been met would mean that the result could no longer be considered true or real. In Lonergan's words, 'absolute objectivity is simply a property of the unconditioned; and the unconditioned, as such, says nothing about space and time'.[20] In a world which is limited by space and time, the true and real is that which is 'virtually unconditioned'.

This objectivity rests solely on the 'unrestricted, detached, disinterested desire to know', which is a recurring theme in *Insight*.[21] It is explicated more fully in *Method in Theology*, in which he observes, 'Method is not a set of rules to be followed meticulously by a dolt. It is a framework for collaborative creativity'.[22]

## The Transcendental Method

Lonergan calls his method 'the Transcendental Method' since 'the results envisaged are not confined categorically to some particular field or subject but regard any result that could be intended by the completely open transcendental notions'.[23] This method is concerned with 'meeting the exigencies and exploiting the opportunities presented' not by some particular area of knowledge, but 'by the human mind itself'.[24] Transcendence is taken to be 'a development in human knowledge relevant to a development in human being'.[25] Accepting that human beings and society are in a constant process

---

20   Ibid. 404.
21   Ibid. 407.
22   B. Lonergan, *Method in Theology* (Toronto: University Press, 1971), xi.
23   Ibid. 14.
24   Ibid.
25   Lonergan, *Insight*, 659.

of change and development, he sees that the human person has to 'grasp and affirm, accept and execute [their] own developing'.[26]

The transcendental method involves making specific the transcendental precepts which we shall seek to clarify below. Underpinning all of these is Lonergan's stated belief that we achieve authenticity in self-transcendence: 'One can live in a world, have a horizon, just in the measure that one is not locked up in oneself'.[27] The transcendental method is, itself, a way of achieving, or striving towards, this end, for now our focus is 'not what appears to me, not what I imagine, not what I think, not what I wish, not what I would be inclined to say, not what seems to me, but what is so'.[28] In this, Lonergan is speaking of the 'virtually unconditioned', which is to say that, though conditioned, the conditions are known and, being known, have been met.

The transcendental precepts; the description of each level is taken from Lonergan's own words (the italics are mine):

1.   Be Attentive.
     This refers to the initial level of sensory and life *experience*. The focus here is on the existent and the world of experience. From the myriad events which occur daily, even momentarily, one chooses those to which one's attention will be paid and which are significant. This is the *empirical level* on which we sense, perceive, imagine, feel, speak and move.

2.   Be Intelligent
     This is the level of intelligibility where one seeks to begin to make sense of the sensory data received. It is the level of *understanding*, the process of sorting through and expressing what we have experienced. It is the *intellectual level* on which we inquire, come to understand, express what we have understood, work out the presuppositions and implications of our expression.

26   Ibid.
27   Lonergan, *Method*, 104.
28   Ibid.

3.  Be Reasonable
    This is level where one focuses on the truth (or, more accurately, on what is true) and where one exercises *judgement*. It is the *rational level* on which we reflect, marshal the evidence, pass judgement on the truth or falsity, certainty or probability, of a statement or position. It is at this level that one exercises discernment, distinguishing between the true and the false, the apparent truth and the real truth.

4.  Be Responsible
    This is the level of the good, where one exercises wisdom and *decides* on a response or a course of action. It is, therefore, the level of *responsibility* on which we are concerned with ourselves, our own operations, our goals and so deliberate about possible courses of action, evaluate them, decide and carry out our decisions.[29]

## The Human Good

Before moving to a brief initial reflection on the implications of Lonergan's theory and method, some last areas need to be examined, namely the relationship between the individual and the group, and the relationship between the intellect and the emotions. Lonergan does not envisage the one who seeks knowledge as a person alone. Rather, one is linked to all those who seek, have sought and will seek the true and the good. Nor is the one who seeks to know some form of disembodied intellect; it is a whole person who, as such, is in relationship with others and with the world in all its forms. A central aspect of his thought is the recognition that with maturity comes the move from the immediate world of the child (where things simply 'are' in direct relation to the child) to the world of meaning mediated in many ways to the adult. Part of the duty and work of the adult is to reflect on the mediated meanings, discern what is true and good and accordingly act responsibly.

29   Ibid.

With regard to the human good, Lonergan asserts that it is 'at once individual and social'.[30] He outlines his ideas under three major headings:

1.  individuals in their potentialities and actuations;
2.  co-operating groups;
3.  ends.

Given the extent of the requirements of Lonergan's method – that one explore all aspects of any subject in the process of coming to know it – this can itself provide a model for a different type of 'coming to know', wherein it is not necessary that all the work be done by one individual. Instead, teams of 'seekers', committed to helping one another in the learning process, could work together without the competitiveness which seems to be endemic to the present educational system. While Lonergan is concerned more with the method which underlies all processes of coming to know than with any particular model, there are some pointers for achieving this goal in his writings.

## Models and Methods

### Initial Deductions

The above considerations highlight some significant aspects of adult education/formation. I can only touch on them here, but they underpin so much of the work undertaken at All Hallows College and third-level education in general:

a)  adults 'learn' best when they come to insight themselves;
b)  since all knowledge is linked, one can, and should, begin from where one is;

---

30    Ibid. 47.

c)   part of the process of 'coming to know' is to come to know ourselves as knowers and to know the means by which we come to know;

d)   a major part of that process will be facing of our own biases and prejudices;

e)   what is essential is not the data but an understanding of the method by which one comes to an awareness of what is true and good and what the consequent actions might be;

f)   such 'coming to understanding and knowledge' is not solely an individual process and is linked with how humans interact in groups, especially those with common purpose.

## Every Method Needs a Model

Lonergan ends *Insight* with a powerful comment. Speaking of Special Transcendent Knowledge (and having just made one point 'in the thirtieth place'!), he speaks of the one who seeks such knowledge (whom, throughout, Lonergan has referred to as male, though nothing in his writing suggests that such searching is limited to men):

> Nor will he labour alone in the purification of his own mind, for the realisation of the solution and its development in each of us is principally the work of God who illuminates our intellects to understand what we had not understood and to grasp as unconditioned what we had reputed error, who breaks the bonds of our habitual unwillingness to be utterly genuine in intelligent and critical reflection, by inspiring the hope that reinforces the detached, disinterested, unrestricted desire to know by infusing the charity, the love, that bestows on intelligence the fullness of life.[31]

This is a clear statement of his conclusions, but he was not concerned with suggesting a model in which this method could be carried out. I am told that he himself used the classical 'Chalk and Talk' when teaching, yet he envisaged his method not as some academic exercise, but as a process of conversion. Lonergan suggests:

31   Lonergan, *Insight*, 751.

the method is intended to guide you toward an ever-expanding awareness of your own knowing, choosing and loving and of how you operate in and through these operations to achieve certain goals.[32]

If such an aspiration remained only that, or remained accessible only to a select few, then a great deal would be lost. Furthermore, it would remain an interesting insight, but it would have little effect on the processes of education and formation. I propose that Maria Montessori provides a model for Lonergan's method of transformative education for personal and communal ethical responsibility.

## Montessori's Model of Education

In *The Absorbent Mind*, Montessori, speaking in and to a Europe still ravaged by the destruction of the Second World War, begins ironically:

> I do not doubt that philosophy and religion can bring to the task [educating humanity] an immense contribution but how numerous are the philosophers in this ultra-civilised world! How many have there not been in the past and how many more will there not be in the future. Noble ideals and high standards we have always had. They form a great part of what we teach. Yet warfare and strife show no signs of abating. And if education is always to be conceived along the same antiquated lines of a mere transmission of knowledge there is little to be hoped from it in the bettering of [humanity's] future.[33]

Although Montessori is associated, in the popular consciousness, with kindergarten or pre-school children, her concern, especially in *The Absorbent Mind*, is with education itself and not with any particular stages of human intellectual development. While she uses the appellation 'The Montessori

---

32    J. Flanagan, *Quest for Self-Knowledge* (Toronto: University Press, 1997), 262.
33    M. Montessori, *The Absorbent Mind* (New York: Henry Holt and Company, 1995), 4.

Method', she did not see it as a method at all,[34] unlike, for example, the Froebel Method, which is concerned only with children below school-going age. As she observes:

> No secondary teacher worries about the methods employed in pre-primary schools, still less about those employed in crèches. Each stage is clearly defined and the methods, which nowadays are constantly on the increase, are always limited to schools of one or the other of these well-defined categories.[35]

It was her basic belief that the human person has 'periods' of sensitivity to learning; times at which, by nature, the person is open to knowledge of particular kinds. She observes that this is most true of language – children in all countries and cultures learn their mother tongue at the same developmental stage and, in *The Absorbent Mind*, she offers a schema to show this development.[36] The child, unlike the adult, does not learn everything through 'attention, volition and intelligence'.[37] Such sensitivity both to their own inner drives and to the external environment, while not conscious or reflective, leads the child to absorb, through practice and repetition, what they need to survive in their own world. When such developments become manifest outwardly, they are termed 'characteristics'.[38] Using language as an example again, she notes:

> no language that one may wish to add to the mother-tongue can become a characteristic and none will be so sure a possession as the first ... further, if this foreign language is not kept in continuous practice it is easily forgotten.[39]

At about the age of three, however, this unconscious creator (the child) becomes the conscious worker[40] and from then on, the individual becomes

---

34    M. Montessori, *The Formation of Man* (Madras: Kalakshetra Publication, 1976), 8.
35    Ibid. 6.
36    Montessori, *The Absorbent Mind*, Table 8, 'Development of Language from Its Nebulous Stage'.
37    Montessori, *Formation*, 84.
38    Ibid. 83.
39    Ibid.
40    Montessori, *The Absorbent Mind*, 165.

more and more self-conscious and reflective, although this consciousness will not be clearly developed until the late teen and early adult years. For Montessori, the 'teacher' is referred to as the 'guide', but this needs to be clearly understood; the role of the 'guide' is not, in any way, to interfere with the child's learning processes, either through encouragement or discouragement. Rather, the 'guide' is like one who accompanies travellers; their main function is, through preparation of the environment, to facilitate the child's own learning. It is the child who makes the choices and discerns what they will next interact with. It is this that is most novel about Montessori's thinking; the 'guide' is there principally as a facilitator of the child's own learning processes and should not allow their own prejudices or concerns to influence the child, either in a positive or a negative fashion. This is, in truth, the antithesis of what we earlier described as the Seminary Model. Montessori's belief is that the child's absorbent mind will discern what the child needs to know.

While her books develop this theme and look at specific areas of childhood formation, it is, in fact, in the context of a Montessori school that one can see these principles in action.[41] Lest it be thought that Montessori's theories were built on wistful thinking, it should be kept in mind that her contentions are borne out by the writings of many psychologists dealing with human development, most especially theorists such as Erik Erikson, Jean Piaget, Lawrence Kohlberg, James Fowler and Robert Kegan.

## Montessori and Lonergan: Initial Points of Contact

Montessori is an acknowledged expert, then, in the area of education and child development, but in what ways is her thought similar to Lonergan's, such that her model might be a useful carrier for his method?

---

41   I am particularly grateful to Ms Kathy Minardi of the Aidan Montessori School of Washington, DC, and Ms Jacquie Bergen of the Near North Montessori in Chicago for allowing me to spend a day as a participant observer in the classes of their respective schools, watching and interacting with pupils and teachers as they went about their day's work. I am grateful also to Phyllis Wallbank for sharing her memories and experiences of her Gatehouse School in London.

*Insight*

Like Lonergan, Montessori holds that lasting knowledge comes from the release of the tension of inquiry and that it comes suddenly and unexpectedly as a result of the interaction between the concrete and the abstract. To this end, the child is the recognized subject of their own education and allowed to follow their inclinations and interests:

> The child's first instinct is to carry out all [their] actions by [themselves] without anyone helping [them] and [their] first conscious bid for independence is made when [they] defend [themselves] against those who try to do the action for [them].[42]

In the Montessori schools, the child is allowed to choose the area that interests him or her and to spend the time needed on it. Help is given when requested, but not offered. I was fortunate to spend a day in a Montessori class and learn the dynamics of teaching and learning in this particular context.

Though, as a teacher, I could observe, but not assist the younger students, it was different with the next older group, as the students were encouraged to bring their completed work to me or to explain what they were doing or what interested them. Yet, it was still the children who decided, in the main, on their work and who assisted one another. As they explained their work to me, they became the teachers and I the student. What is learned in one area then 'enters the habitual texture of the mind' (Lonergan) and becomes the basis for the next stage of exploration and enquiry. So, for example, the practice of pouring water and cleaning tables forms the basis for the hand movements needed for cursive writing. Once again, we see how the commonplace is transfigured. The minutiae of the child's environment and daily life become the means by which knowledge is reached and the child is informed, shaped and transformed.

*Coming to Knowledge and Understanding*

Like Lonergan, Montessori believes that the most important thing is not 'what is known' (the data), but 'the process of knowing' itself. The child learns the methods behind the process.

42 Montessori, *The Absorbent Mind*, 176.

They say that in this [three- to six-year-old] period of life the child begins to imitate. This, in itself, is no new idea, for children have always been said to imitate their elders ... Today one realises that, before one can imitate, one must first of all understand.[43]

It would be true to say that what I term as the 'Seminary Model' or what Paulo Freire named as the 'Banking Model' depends, essentially, on *mimesis*, the pupils repeating what they have learnt.[44] It has led also to the focus on the need for the teacher to be the best possible in his or her field, to have amassed data on the subject being taught. In the Montessori school, Elektra, who was seven, solemnly instructed me in the use of an abacus (a counting device), something that had not been part of my own schooling. I watched Nathan and Tom identify the countries of Southern Asia – something still beyond me!

## The Montessori Model and the Lonergan Method

### *The Canons of the Method*

1.  Selection
    The participant learns to choose what they will learn and to what they will pay attention. Only when requested or if there is lack of clarity about what to move to next does one hear the guide offer suggestions. Students learn further that, to master this 'discipline', whatever it may be, they must be attentive to what they are doing.
2.  Operations
    Through the practice of a discipline, they learn how it is dependent on other areas of knowledge which they have practised and how there are

---

43   Ibid. 158.
44   P. Freire, *Pedagogy of the Oppressed*, trans. M. Bergman Ramos (London: Penguin, 1996, new revised edn).

certain laws which govern human activity, for example, how physical activity prepares them for cursive writing.

3. Relevance

The student learns that the same activity can be the starting point for many different disciplines and types of insight.

4. Parsimony

As well as learning what he or she knows, the student also discovers the limitations of his or her knowledge, which can lead to the following two canons.

5. Complete Explanation

Linked with the next canon, this is what inspires the student to their next area of investigation. If their information is insufficient to explain what they need to know, then they feel impelled to examine another area of research and practice.

6. Statistical Residue

Their exploration allows the students to identify for themselves the further questions which need to be asked in order to understand the particular discipline more fully.

## The Transcendental Method

Like Lonergan, Montessori posits that there are three stages, or, more accurately, types, of obedience. In the first stage, the child is dependent, not solely on the actions and decisions of others, but also on the development of his or her own powers: '(s)he may succeed in obeying once but [then] cannot do it the next time'.[45] This is not always wilful but, sometimes, the child's own capacities fail or falter. In the second stage, the child's powers are consolidated and the child can 'absorb another person's wishes and express them in [the child's] own behaviour'.[46] In the final stage, the child becomes aware of something (in the child's case, the teacher's personality, knowledge or wisdom) which is superior to his or her own limited abil-

45   Ibid. 259.
46   Ibid. 260.

ity; the child obeys and co-operates because he or she is aware of a higher order of things than the purely personal.

Yet, to avoid courting approval, the 'guide' expresses neither personal approval nor disapproval, but comments on the merits of the work undertaken. In terms of the Transcendental Method, Montessori recognizes that it is the internal conditions which are the most significant and that the purpose of the external environment is to encourage and facilitate the child's own explorations. She explores the effects of obstacles to development – those which act as blockages and those which act as spurs to further exploration. If we examine the Montessori Model in the context of the Transcendental Method, we see the following:

## Be Attentive

The student first learns to explore their actual environment and to use their sense perceptions to learn. Thus, much emphasis is placed on objects, colours, activity and, where possible, the involvement of all the senses. In this way, they learn to operate at the empirical level. The environment itself acts as guide and stimulus to the child's questioning and concerns. The function of the 'teacher' is to prepare that environment and provide the material stimuli, not to direct the child's learning.

## Be Intelligent

The physical environment (and apparatus) having provided a key, the child seeks understanding of the operations involved in the activity and learns to operate at an intellectual level. Such intelligent grasping of the operation is often the result of practice, repetition or application. This may follow directly on the period of attention or may be separated from it by a space of time. This is the level at which the child discovers for him- or herself the method behind the learning process and learns to apply it in other practices of the discipline and, gradually, to move to other applications in other arenas.

*Be Reasonable*

Here the child learns to exercise judgement and rationality and to work out appropriate solutions, while discarding those which (s)he deems are not applicable. This is often the moment of insight, when, without conscious effort, the child makes the connections that make the experience comprehensible. Here, the child moves from the world of the concrete and immediate to the world of the conceptual. At this level, too, the child learns to make connections with other areas that he or she has explored.

It is important to note that, at this stage, Montessori is careful to emphasize what is positive: there are no real failures; each setback can be seen as a learning experience. Such input as comes from the teacher is in the form of affirmation of what the child has discovered, but care is taken not to couch it in language of approval or disapproval.

*Be Responsible*

At this level, the child learns to decide and to act. This involves both a decision about what to do with the information (there are no formal examinations) and also what to move to next. Equally importantly, the child learns to pass on to those others, who are exploring the same area, what he or she has already learnt – should those others seek their participation. As Montessori herself is said to have observed, every room with a teacher and thirty pupils is, in fact, a room with thirty-one teachers. One can observe easily how students are 'transfigured' in this way into the agents of their own formation.

## Conclusion

This last issue (the children as teachers to one another) leads to a consideration of Montessori's understanding of the environment as model of society. She states her belief that 'the human being is a united whole but this unity has to be built up and formed by active experiences in the real world'.[47] The children learn their own discipline through interaction with others, 'obtaining discipline by giving freedom'.[48] The children in the Montessori room seem to be the living embodiment of Lonergan's third level of human interaction in society. Liberty, exercised through orientation or conversion and dependent on true personal relations, leads to terminal values. Activity and rest, interaction and independent work and skills involving different and combined aspects of the person are all integrated into the 'work day'.

The 'class-room' or, as she preferred, 'children's houses', serves as a stimulus to learning. One of the most impressive moments in the Aidan school was watching a young boy of three, who had just spent half an hour busily washing a table, neatly and conscientiously clean everything and replace it so that his classmates could also use the materials. There was no need for the teacher to remind him of his duties.

Montessori herself imagined high schools and universities operating along the outlines she had traced,[49] but, in the west at any rate, this has not happened. Yet, in such an environment, we 'may get answers to questions [we] never thought of asking [but ought to have asked]'.[50]

## Bibliography

Buchmann, M., 'Improving Education by Talking; Argument or Conversation', *Teachers College Record* 86 (3) (1985), 43–5.
Freire, P., *Pedagogy of the Oppressed*, trans. M. Bergman Ramos (London: Penguin, 1996, new revised edn).
Flanagan, J., *Quest for Self-Knowledge* (Toronto: University Press, 1997).

47   Ibid. 203.
48   Ibid. 202.
49   Montessori, *The Formation of Man*, 5.
50   M. Buchmann, 'Improving Education by Talking; Argument or Conversation', *Teachers College Record* 86 (3) (Spring 1985), 43–5.

Lonergan, B. J., *Insight* (CA: Philosophical Library, 1967).
Lonergan, B. J., *Method in Theology* (Toronto: University of Toronto Press, 1990).
Montessori, M., *The Absorbent Mind* (New York: Henry Holt and Company, 1995).
Montessori, M., *The Formation of Man* (Madras: Kalakshetra Publication, 1976).
Newman, J. H., Cardinal, *The Idea of a University* (Notre Dame, IN: University of Notre Dame Press, 1982).
Tracy, D., *The Analogical Mind* (New York: Crossroad, 1989).

GRÁINNE DOHERTY

# 11 Catholic Social Thought: A Pedagogical Model for Justice-Based Education

## Introduction

The estimated 1 million asylum seekers who have fled to Europe by sea in the past year are among the more than 60 million people now displaced by war or repression – the highest figure since the Second World War. The heart-rending reality of people fleeing oppression and tyranny is only one of the deeply disturbing global situations radically re-shaping the world: the world's population is only now beginning to be convinced by what scientists and environmentalists have been pointing out for years – human activity is intimately connected with the warming-up of our planet, the rapid depletion of natural resources, the loss of biodiversity, etc. Greenhouse gases are at their highest in 800,000 years, while global greenhouse gas emissions have increased by almost 80 per cent since 1970. Ecosystems which support a rich diversity of life forms and which took millions of years to perfect are breaking apart. The number of people on the planet is set to rise to 9.7 billion in 2050, with population growth concentrated in some of the world's poorest countries. Already one in nine people suffer from chronic undernourishment in our current population of just over 7 billion. Situated within this worldwide context is Ireland, struggling with – among many other issues – a housing crisis, unemployment, and high rates of suicide among the nation's young people.[1]

---

[1] Information from this section was gleaned primarily from the following: <http://www.worldhunger.org/2015–world-hunger-and-poverty-facts-and-statistics/#hunger-number>; <https://www.weforum.org/events/

Many third-level students today – who have grown up with much of the reality just outlined – are searching for ways to respond to such issues. They will be expected to be the agents of change which the generations of the past century have often failed to be. Many of them are pursuing educational opportunities and careers that will enable them to be such agents of change. The challenge is not to find such future leaders; rather, the challenge is to ensure that the third-level institutes they are attending are places which live out, promote and bear witness to the value system needed for such radical leadership. What would help educational institutes embody such a value system?

Many educationalists currently practising in the Irish higher educational system would have been exposed to the pedagogical approach of Paulo Freire during their initial training and it is often to such a methodology that an essay such as this automatically turns when addressing the topic of global educational change. Freire's presentation of the dynamic of power/powerlessness inherent in any human organization has been fundamental to much of the understanding needed for systemic or structural change in a variety of situations.

While this chapter will refer to some aspects of Freire's pedagogy, it will rather be to one of the great influences on his thought – the tradition of social teaching within the Catholic tradition – that it will turn in order to present one approach that could significantly help in the creation and flourishing of a value system needed for third-level education in Ireland today. The Catholic bishops of the United States define Catholic social teaching as 'the tradition of thought in which the Church seeks to advance justice in the world by engaging social, cultural, political, and economic realities in our day'.[2] This vision for a just society is rooted in the Scriptures and in the lived experience of the Christian community as it responded to situations of oppression and discrimination throughout its history.

---

world-economic-forum-annual-meeting-2016/>; <http://www.conserve-energy-future.com/15–current-environmental-problems.php>; all accessed 29 January 2018.

2    <http://www.usccb.org/sdwp/projects/socialteaching/excerpt.shtml>, accessed 29 January 2018.

# Catholic Social Teaching

This chapter argues that Catholic social teaching (CST) has much to offer any discussion on the role, nature and methodology of third-level education in Ireland today. Beginning by briefly outlining the foundations and history of CST and by presenting two of its central principles – the dignity of the human person and the common good – the chapter looks at the role of education – particularly higher education – and illustrates how these principles are essential to any pedagogy that aims to change society for the better. The research illustrates how CST's understanding of education both affirms and challenges the current practice and vision for higher education as presented by the *National Strategy for Higher Education to 2030 Report*, also known as the Hunt Report. (As this report extends to 130 pages and offers a broad vision of tertiary education in Ireland for the next thirteen years, this essay is limited by space to briefly addressing only a few of the report's ideas.) The chapter concludes by arguing that although CST has firm foundations in the Scriptures and Catholic tradition, its method and concepts have the potential to speak to *all* who view education as something that is transformative for both the individual and society.

Throughout the Gospels, Jesus is constantly referred to and presented as *rabbi* (teacher). In one of the earliest accounts of his 'teaching in the synagogues', Jesus marks out the key elements of such teaching. He declares that:

> The Spirit of the Lord is upon me,
> Because he has anointed me
> To proclaim good news to the poor.
> He has sent me to proclaim freedom for the prisoners
> And recovery of sight for the blind,
> To set the oppressed free
> To proclaim the year of the Lord's favour. (Lk 4:18–19)

With these words, Jesus aligned his voice to a radical prophetic tradition that consisted of holding out a vision of personal and societal liberation and transformation. The named prophets of his Jewish history were known for their courage in taking a counter-cultural stance by looking critically at the society in which they lived, examining it in the light of their religious tradition and proclaiming how current practices were against the wishes of God in relation to all creation. They spoke out, therefore, against social injustice, religious and political abuses, a relationship of greed with regard to the earth's resources and the mistreatment and oppression of the vulnerable. In doing so, the Jewish prophets criticized the wealthy and powerful and sought to re-establish God's vision of equality, justice and dignity for all. One well-known quotation from the prophet Amos (eighth century BCE) will suffice to illustrate the nature of the prophetic justice tradition found throughout the Scriptures.

> There are those who oppress the innocent and take bribes
>     and deprive the poor of justice in the courts.
> Therefore the prudent keep quiet in such times,
>     for the times are evil.
> Seek good, not evil,
>     that you may live.
> Then the LORD God Almighty will be with you,
>     just as you say he is ...
> 'I hate, I despise your religious festivals;
>     your assemblies are a stench to me.
> Even though you bring me burnt offerings and grain offerings,
>     I will not accept them.
> Though you bring choice fellowship offerings,
>     I will have no regard for them.
> Away with the noise of your songs!
>     I will not listen to the music of your harps.
> But let justice roll on like a river,
>     righteousness like a never-failing stream! ...'[3] (Amos 5:12b-14, 21–14)

---

3    The term 'Righteousness' was a way to describe how God acted in the world (e.g., Jer 9:23–24). 'Righteousness' as used in the Scriptures describes what is meant to be in right relationship with God, and consequently how to be in right relationship with others in and through community. It is often simplistically understood as 'justice' – but not in the legalistic sense, or understood as something that can be reduced to a series of rights; rather as a covenantal promise to be freed from everything that is oppressive and to have fullness of life in every aspect of one's life.

Such prophetic proclamations on the reality of oppression and injustice in society have continued to be voiced strongly throughout the history of the Catholic Church and have become formalized into a body of thought found in a variety of official Church documents, generally accepted to begin with Pope Leo XIII's 1891 encyclical on work called *Rerum Novarum* and continuing up to the present, with Pope Francis' encyclical on the environment, *Laudato Si*. These documents develop the tradition of bringing to light situations of oppression in the society of the day, particularly in the context of political, economic and environmental issues. CST affirms the imperative call to 'read the signs of the times' (cf. Matt 16:4)[4] and to challenge and transform modern society in the light of Gospel values and ideals. In the wake of and the momentum of Vatican II and the influence of liberation theology, the bishops' synodal document, 'Justice in the World', encapsulates the centrality and essence of such teaching when it observes that 'action on behalf of justice and participation in the transformation of the world fully appear to us as a constitutive dimension of preaching the Gospel'.[5] It goes on to say that this requires the liberation of the human race from *every* oppressive situation.

CST is often referred to the Catholic Church's 'best kept secret'. This is evident in the large amounts of people who remain unfamiliar with its principle ideas and practices – this unfortunately is often as true of the ordained, as of the laity.[6]

---

4    This well-known phrase is found initially in Pope John XXIII's *Pacem in Terris* (1963), but is possibly most associated with *Gaudium et Spes* ('The Church in the Modern World', n. 4) from the close of Vatican II in 1965: 'To carry out such a task, the Church has always had the duty of scrutinizing the signs of the times and of interpreting them in the light of the Gospel. Thus, in language intelligible to each generation, she can respond to the perennial questions which men ask about this present life and the life to come, and about the relationship of the one to the other. We must therefore recognize and understand the world in which we live, its explanations, its longings, and its often dramatic characteristics.'

5    'Justice in the World', n. 6

6    There are many reasons why Catholic social teaching is often unknown. However, they do include the fact that the teaching is sometimes very complex and often resists a 'one-size-fits-all' style of application when it comes to evaluating different

In addition, the Church has often been criticized for reserving the practice of its justice principles for society at large and failing to apply them to a wide range of issues of injustice within the institution of the Church itself. Despite these limitations, however, CST has been fundamental to much of the work undertaken by lay, professed and ordained Catholics throughout the world on a vast array of social justice issues. It has also found very particular expression through the theologies of liberation and feminism. Unlike with other official Catholic Church documents, many of the writings from the CST tradition are addressed to a much broader audience than just Catholics due to the global dimension of the social issues involved. For this reason and because the values outlined by CST have a broader appeal than perhaps some of the Church's other confessional claims, they can speak to a wide spectrum of people from various religious traditions and none. What is known as the 'Golden Rule' – 'Do unto others as you would have them do unto you' – which is central to CST, is also found in a similar form in many other faith practices and secular values.[7] As such, proposing the 'Golden Rule' aspect of Catholic thought as a lens through which higher education in Ireland can be re-envisaged and practised is a lens that should appeal across the whole of the third-level curriculum.

Much has already been written on the various principles and thought that comprise this social teaching. Suffice to say that the whole body of thought is built primarily on two separate, but interwoven ideas: (i) the dignity of the human person, and (ii) the common good. These are the ideas on which much of this essay will be based.

---

situations; also, it often fails to get deserved attention by the media – this is in stark contrast to the Catholic Church's teachings on sexual morality regarding such issues as contraception, abortion, sexual orientation and so forth.

7   Cf: <http://www.uri.org/kids/act_pass_golden.htm>, accessed 29 January 2018; <http://www.thegoldenrule.net/quotes.htm>, accessed 29 January 2018. A. Sen, 'The Contemporary Relevance of Buddha', *Ethics and International Affairs* 28 (1) (2014), 15–27.

## Dignity of Each Person

The inherent dignity of each person is the cornerstone of CST. Each person is uniquely gifted, special and incomparable. This dignity exists regardless of any other factor, such as age, race, sexual orientation or gender and can be anticipated in the fullness of life promised by Jesus Christ (Jn 10:10). The Catholic Church understands that such fullness of life envisages a person who is freed from every type of oppression to live out her/his unique potential and deep giftedness that is within. This involves all aspects of the person, including the material, the spiritual, the social and the political. It is essential to the dignity of the person that s/he be recognized as and allowed to be an acting subject rather than an object (with identity being gauged by her/his level of usefulness to others). A person's dignity is given its fullest expression in and through relationship with others. Rather than the uniqueness of a person resulting in some expression of individualism and separatism, it leads instead to a pursuit of a type of societal living that acclaims everyone as equal and interdependent and which is marked by inclusivity, participation and a lack of hierarchical ordering. The common good is often erroneously reduced to some form of limited democratic principle, such as 'the greatest good for the greatest number', but, as the bishops of England and Wales observe, it is much more radical than that: 'Because we are interdependent, the common good is more like a multiplication sum, where if any one number is zero then the total is always zero. If anyone is left out and deprived of what is essential, then the common good has been betrayed.'[8] In other words, the common good ought to involve

8    The Bishops' Conference of England and Wales, *Choosing the Common Good*, n. 8. Perhaps the most famous expression of the common good is the opening lines of Vatican II's *Gaudium et Spes*: 'The joys and the hopes, the griefs and the anxieties of the men [*sic*] of this age, especially those who are poor or in any way afflicted, these are the joys and hopes, the griefs and anxieties of the followers of Christ. Indeed, nothing genuinely human fails to raise an echo in their hearts. For theirs is a community composed of men [*sic*]. United in Christ, they are led by the Holy Spirit in their journey to the Kingdom of their Father and they have welcomed the news of salvation which is meant for every man [*sic*]. That is why this community realizes that

every person and every person can contribute to the common good of all, no matter what their personal circumstances may be. Transformative education can assist in empowering learners to understand the common good for all and how they can enhance and sustain the dignity of all in a diverse society.

It is within this framework of recognizing and acclaiming the unique dignity of each person and working to ensure that this dignity is also acknowledged and affirmed at the macro-societal level – be that at community, national or international level – that Catholic bishops from all over the world declared unambiguously the nature and role of education:

> But education demands a renewal of heart, a renewal based on the recognition of sin in its individual and social manifestations. It will also inculcate a truly and entirely human way of life in justice, love and simplicity. It will likewise awaken a critical sense, which will lead us to reflect on the society in which we live and on its values; it will make people ready to renounce these values when they cease to promote justice for all people. In the developing countries, the principal aim of this education for justice consists in an attempt to awaken consciences to a knowledge of the concrete situation and in a call to secure a total improvement; by these means the transformation of the world has already begun.[9]

Despite many educational theories that have argued otherwise down through the centuries, education is still often perceived as something passive – a body of knowledge that is passed on almost unchanging from one generation to the next. With strong echoes of Paulo Freire's critical pedagogy, CST posits that education is rather an agent of transformation – a transformation of both the individual and the society in which s/he lives. Situating oneself and practising within this praxis-driven

---

it is truly linked with mankind and its history by the deepest of bonds.' *Gaudium et Spes*, n. 1.

9    'Justice in the World', n. 51, 1971. The content and ethos of this statement is reminiscent of Paulo Freire's statement that 'Education either functions as an instrument which is used to facilitate integration of the younger generation into the logic of the present system and bring about conformity or it becomes the practice of freedom, the means by which men and women deal critically and creatively with reality and discover how to participate in the transformation of their world.'

and transformation-oriented model of education has implications for both student *and* teacher.

According to CST, therefore, educators are – like the prophets of the Jewish Scriptures – responsible for awakening and sustaining in their students a critical engagement with the world, resulting in an ongoing praxis-based working towards a society rooted in the Gospel values of participation, inclusivity and justice. In the same way as Jesus consistently lived out and bore witness to the radically transforming values he proclaimed, so the teacher also has to bear witness to the belief that education is a dynamic – concerned as much with learning the ability to critique, evaluate and address the presence of injustice and powerlessness as it is with the learning of concepts. Enabling this to happen means that everything the educator does must be rooted in such an approach. S/he is called therefore to ensure the centrality of such belief in the ongoing daily reality of the drawing-up of curriculum and learning outcomes, in methods of assessment, in departmental and inter-departmental planning and in and through classroom teaching.

Whatever values are given primary expression within the curriculum and classroom are those that will be absorbed by student and teacher alike and consequently continue to be given expression. Values, once internalized, encourage and often impel people to act and make choices – either deliberately or inadvertently. These values are the barometer by which the inherent worth and significance of everything is judged. The recently published *National Strategy for Higher Education to 2030* confirms this essence of education as replicating the dominant values of any learning context when it acknowledges that 'through education, we find our place in the world, understand that world, and pass on our understanding and our values to others'.[10] Finding 'our place' in the world is an interesting

---

10   *National Strategy for Higher Education to 2030* (Dublin: Department of Education and Skills, 2011, also known as the Hunt Report), 30. The Hunt Report was published on 11 January 2011 after being commissioned by the then Minister for Education Batt O'Keeffe almost two years previously. The brief of the expert group was to formulate a national strategy for higher education and the team was chaired by economist, stockbroker and banker Dr Colin Hunt.

suggestion about the role of education. Surely, finding our place must mean that we are treated equally, feel included in the process of education, recognize that we all learn differently and have the resources needed in order to flourish in 'our place' in the world. The role of education ought to be about passing on particular values that enhance every person and create a better society in which each person lives and interacts.

## The Role of Education

It is not necessary, therefore, to question whether education involves the passing-on of values; as every major ideology in history has explored in relation to education, it is more important to reflect on the *type* of values that are being passed on. After stating the above, the *National Strategy* proceeds to state that one of the key purposes of education is that it 'contributes to economic development and to the quality of life that economic development makes possible'.[11] Throughout the report, the direct and primary connection between economic development and every aspect of higher education's mission – teaching, research and/or outreach to the wider community – is highlighted. In language eerily reminiscent of Freire's concept of banking education, the *National Strategy* report closely aligns the aims and objectives of higher education in Ireland with those of the government and the national plan for economic development.

Despite the appearance and rhetoric of autonomy, the country's universities are required to be fully accountable to the government for the achievement of the latter's national objectives in the economic and social spheres. They may be forced to focus more on aligning themselves with what ensures governmental financial support rather than with the pursuit of knowledge that fosters the ability to critique and challenge such priorities and values when necessary. Over forty years prior to the publication of

11    Ibid.

the *National Strategy*, the Catholic bishops of the world warned how easy it is for education to become the means by which people are drawn into a position of conformity with the status quo. They warned that the close aligning of educational institutions with political and economic power often leads to the former finding themselves compromised to 'allow the formation only of people desired by that order, that is to say, people in its image, not new people but a copy of people as they are'.[12]

It is precisely due to the ease with which values can be compromised and usurped by the more dominant agenda for its own ends that CST insists on a *praxis* methodology of action rooted in ongoing critical reflection. The social doctrine of the Catholic Church is one whose whole identity is realized by putting its values into practice in and through daily living. Again, the roots of this are clearly evident throughout the Scriptures, as the following quotations demonstrate:

> And what does the Lord require of you? To act justly and to love mercy and to walk humbly with your God. (Micah 6:8)

> But be doers of the word, and not hearers only, deceiving yourselves. (Jas 1:22)

> Let us stop just saying we love people, let us really love them, and show it by our actions. (1 Jn 3:18)

Belgian priest – and later cardinal – Joseph Cardijn (1882–1967), observed in 1896 with regard to putting values into action that 'in order to act well, it is necessary to see and judge well'. Out of such thinking, Cardijn founded the Young Christian Workers, an international movement that enables young people to value the dignity and worth of each person and to challenge social exclusion and injustice using the 'See, Judge, Act' method. This method is now used widely in the Catholic Church at all levels and, in particular, in the very many forms of its educational practices. When talking of the imperative in working for social justice, John XXIII stated that:

---

12    Synod of Bishops, 'Justice in the World' (1971), n. 50, <https://www1.villanova.edu/content/dam/villanova/.../JusticeIntheWorld1971.pdf>, accessed 29 January 2018.

> It is not enough merely to formulate a social doctrine. It must be translated into
> reality. And this is particularly true of the Church's social doctrine ... There are three
> stages which should normally be followed in the reduction of social principles into
> practice. First, one reviews the concrete situation; secondly, one forms a judgment
> on it in the light of these same principles; thirdly, one decides what in the circum-
> stances can and should be done to implement these principles. These are the three
> stages that are usually expressed in the three terms: look, judge, act ... Knowledge
> acquired in this way does not remain merely abstract, but is seen as something that
> must be translated into action.[13]

The necessity of putting values learned in academia into action has been at
the core of changes occurring in third-level education in very many parts
of the world over the past couple of decades, often taking the form of what
is called 'service learning'. The *National Strategy* repeatedly outlines the
importance of outreach and places it as one of three interconnected core
roles of higher education – devoting a whole chapter to 'engagement with
the wider society'. Referencing the American IT and science-based organization, Education, Training and Research (ETR), the report talks of service
learning as 'a teaching and learning strategy that integrates meaningful
community service with instruction and reflection, to enrich the learning
experience, teach civic responsibility and strengthen communities'.[14]

There are many interpretations of what form this service learning may
take and how it may be interpreted by any particular educational institute. It
is not the existence of service learning *per se* that must be examined but the
particular interpretation and shape it may take and the values it expresses.
Service learning is often portrayed by higher education programmes as
something transforming and radical. However, research shows that very
often this is far from the actual reality. The type of service learning that
takes place often fails to cater for any form of critical reflection which would
challenge students in their thinking; as a result, students often complete an
outreach programme with existing prejudices and stereotypes reinforced.

13    John XXIII, *Mater et Magistra* (1961), nn. 226, 236, 237, <http://w2.vatican.va/
      content/john-xxiii/en/.../hf_j-xxiii_enc_15051961_mater.html>, accessed 29 January
      2018.
14    *National Strategy for Higher Education to 2030*, 29, which references ETR Associates,
      *What Is Service Learning?*, <http://www.servicelearning.org>, accessed 29 January
      2018.

As already stated, the synod of Catholic bishops stated that an educational curriculum's default position is often one of creating people in its own image rather than one of transformation. Bringing students off campus and into the local community may not be the transformative pedagogy it initially appears to be as many service-learning programmes fail to engage with the kind of pedagogical experiences that best develop a student's orientation towards justice. As the bishops noted in 'Justice in the World', education is essentially a dynamic process that challenges students to look closely at the society in which they live and conscientize themselves to the existence of injustice, to examine the causes of such injustice – which also involves reflecting on their own biases and assumptions – and to provide and enact possible solutions. In order to achieve such transformative educational practice, the type of service learning that emerges out of CST is most often one rooted in social analysis, called the Pastoral Cycle (or Circle).

## The Pastoral Cycle (or Circle)

The Pastoral Cycle (or Circle) is a multi-disciplinary process used by many groups involved in working for a more equal and inclusive society. It is constructed around the key aspects mentioned above: 'See, Judge and Act'.[15] It recognizes that inherent in every societal structure, there is injustice. According to this method, injustice is caused by two separate yet interwoven factors: (i) unjust actions and attitudes of individuals, and (ii) organizations are themselves unjust in what they actually do and/or the very way they are designed. This second form is termed structural injustice or – within the Catholic social justice tradition – structural sin, for example, an individual

---

15    There are many different forms of the Pastoral Cycle, but all are built strongly on the three elements 'See, Judge and Act'. Two key sources in this discussion – and from which much of the information in this section is taken – are S. Healy and B. Reynolds, *Social Analysis in the Light of the Gospel* (Dublin: Folens and Co. Ltd, 1983); and J. Holland and P. Henriot, *Social Analysis: Linking Faith and Justice* (Washington: Orbis Books, 1983).

may not be personally racist, but that does not mean that racism does not exist in many of the organizations with which s/he engages or of which s/he is a significant part.[16] Structures are not inanimate or impersonal; every organization, no matter how large, is composed of individuals – all of whom, to differing degrees, influence its overall ethos and practice.

As an educational tool within third-level education, the Pastoral Cycle/ Circle encourages students to look critically at the situation in which they find themselves on an outreach placement, noting what their initial observations are – and it challenges them to become aware of their own particular standpoint in relation to such observations. Working from the belief that

16    The concept of 'structural sin' emerged from Latin American liberation theology in the 1960s and 1970s as a way to describe the dehumanizing conditions experienced by the continent's poor. In their attempts to understand and combat widespread poverty, early liberation theologians interpreted Marxist models of structuralist economic analysis through a Christian theological lens. Using the term/theological concept of 'structural sin' puts a name on conditions of oppression which fail to be adequately explained or addressed by narrowing such suffering to the sinfulness of individuals. Such structures influence and form the contexts in which individuals decide to act in many situations. The terms 'structural sin' and 'social sin' are often used interchangeably and have now moved beyond the parameters of economic poverty to include sexism and racism. The concept has been adopted by official Catholic teaching, notably in John Paul II's *Reconciliatio et Paenitentia*, 1984 (<http://w2.vatican.va/content/.../hf_jp-ii_exh_02121984_reconciliatio-et-paenitentia.html>, accessed 29 January 2018), and *Sollicitudo Rei Socialis*, 1987 (<http://w2.vatican.va/content/john...ii/.../hf_jp-ii_enc_30121987_sollicitudo-rei-socialis.html>, accessed 29 January 2018). In talking of the causes and nature of the Cold War in the latter, John Paul states: 'It is important to note therefore that a world which is divided into blocs, sustained by rigid ideologies, and in which instead of interdependence and solidarity different forms of imperialism hold sway, can only be a world subject to structures of sin. The sum total of the negative factors working against a true awareness of the universal common good, and the need to further it, gives the impression of creating, in persons and institutions, an obstacle which is difficult to overcome. ... [It] is not out of place to speak of "structures of sin", which ... are rooted in personal sin, and thus always linked to the concrete acts of individuals who introduce these structures, consolidate them and make them difficult to remove. And thus they grow stronger, spread, and become the source of other sins, and so influence people's behaviour.' *Sollicitudo Rei Socialis*, n. 36.

the causes of any structural injustice are multi-faceted and complex, issues that have been noticed and experienced by the student are then examined – either individually or in a group – from a variety of lenses, such as the *political* (where is power situated?), the *economic* (the use, development and distribution of resources); the *social* (the demographic of groupings and the relationships between them) and the *cultural* (the control and articulation of values and beliefs at play within the issues involved). Through each of these lenses, the student is faced with three separate, yet related questions with regard to the issues being explored:

1. Who makes the decisions?
2. Who benefits from those decisions?
3. Who pays for those decisions?

Such reflective engagement with their placements almost invariably leads students to an increased awareness and understanding of the complex and multi-faceted nature of many societal issues. It also helps them become much more effective, innovative and knowledgeable when seeking out and enacting solutions for such issues.

As previously stated, the *National Strategy* report talks of the value of student engagement with the college's local community and talks of service learning as one way of facilitating such engagement.

In language similar to that of CST's understanding of education quoted above, the report quotes former United States Commissioner of Education Ernest Boyer (1928–95) – a man who advocated strongly for community education placements for students – and former president of Harvard University Derek Bok (b. 1930) when it states that:

> Teachers in higher education 'need to stimulate active not passive learning, and to encourage students to be critical, creative thinkers, with the capacity to go on learning after their college days are over.' They need to 'create a process of active learning by posing problems, challenging student answers, and encouraging (students) to apply the information and concepts in assigned readings to a variety of new situations.'[17]

17   *National Strategy for Higher Education*, 53 (cf. footnotes 64 and 65 of the report).

Despite the similar language, however, the model of service learning subsequently outlined to facilitate such critical thinking seems to be in marked contrast to that envisaged by CST outlined above. Two ways in which they markedly differ are:

1.   The locus of learning, and
2.   The role of questioning.

(i) *The locus of learning*: While stating that the relationship between the third-level institute and the community must be reciprocal – through 'inward and outward flows of knowledge, staff, students and ideas between each institution and its external community'[18] – much of the report's vision of outreach and community engagement actually seems to lean towards the more traditional approach of situating the starting point of the expertise being present in the academy rather than in the community. The report not only highlights the need and capacity of higher education to engage more intensely than before with the wider community; it also states how this is to be done: by providing (a) 'intellectual leadership' and (b) 'authoritative opinion'. It mentions that academia has a 'great number of people who can make very valuable contributions to the community and to wider civic life in many different ways'.[19] While such servicing of community needs is to be applauded, there seems to be little, if any, envisaging in the *National Strategy* of a reciprocal contribution by the community that might lead to academia's own self-examination in the pursuit of a more justice-based practice of teaching and learning. In stressing engagement with the community as a 'core mission element' of Irish higher education, and as a means by which the transformative potential of education can be unlocked, the report ironically fails to specifically include engagement within the educational institutes themselves.[20] Despite language to the contrary, this one-way movement of knowledge, skills and expertise seems to permeate the vision of the report. So, while there may be some sharing of ideas and

18   Ibid. 13.
19   Ibid.
20   Ibid.77.

vision, such service learning is far removed from the critical pedagogy and conscientization methodology implicit in the Pastoral Cycle of CST.

(ii) *The locus of questioning*: Integral to the 'See-Judge-Act' methodology of CST in general, and of the Pastoral Cycle in particular, is the imperative to ask 'Why?' and to keep on asking 'Why? – specifically, 'Why are things the way they are?'

Despite educational training in Bloom's taxonomy on the role and variety of questioning in the classroom, the main use of questioning seems to be initiated by the teacher in order to examine knowledge that has already been presented. The focus tends to be on the answer – generally fact-based – and therefore prioritizes short-term memory skills. However, knowledge, as the Pastoral Cycle demonstrates, only occurs through questions being asked; if questions are not asked, learning does not happen. The essence of praxis education is a recognition that answers are multifaceted and dynamic and, as such, have to be continuously re-examined and re-considered. In highlighting the necessity of question-based learning, Bowker states that questioning:

> Involves speculating about possibilities both real and unreal, given and hypothetical. To question is an immensely creative act because questioning requires that an object be not just as it is. If every object were just as it is, then questions would serve no purpose, for the only answer we could give would be to point at the object and say, 'But here is your answer.' On the contrary, questions are designed to probe, to find something that is not already there, to discover relationships and possibilities that are not given.[21]

Deep questions challenge student and teacher alike to move beyond the obvious and quantifiable and deal instead with complexity and the hidden.

As already stated, educators are challenged to live out the type of learning they wish to draw out in their students. Therefore, with regards to the importance of developing the ability to intelligently question, teachers

---

21  M. H. Bowker, 'Teaching Students to Ask Questions Instead of Answering Them', *NEA: Thought and Action* 26 (Fall 2010), 127–34, <https://sites.udel.edu/.../bowker-2010–teaching-students-to-ask-questions-16echtl.pdf>, accessed 29 January 2018.

have to engage seriously in continuously investigating and re-imagining their own specific discipline, rather than being merely the interpreters of other people's writings.

The *National Strategy* report's emphasis on research and ongoing training of teachers could be a useful aid to this, if allowed to be truly critically based. The current prominence given to the drawing-up and adherence to learning outcomes in education at all levels, while important in many respects, does, however, lead more to a factual, knowledge-based pedagogy than a questioning one. This is due to the fact that such target-setting and goal attainment greatly limit the freedom of the teacher to follow questions raised by the students in the course of any module. Such questions should function as an intrinsic yet dynamic element of both teaching and learning and, as such, would hopefully – if necessary – change the direction of the planned curriculum. Service learning rooted in a CST approach to critical enquiry challenges – and reminds – student *and* teacher that the key to figuring out solutions to problems of social injustice is often found by asking smart questions.

When societal and individual change is mentioned in the report, it is often primarily articulated in terms of economic development. This is confirmed by three Trinity College academics, Loxley, Seery and Walsh. They observe that although the report is still in its infancy and therefore it is too early for any comprehensive critique, many of its recommendations seem to be rooted in a vision that is essentially economic and they point out that the political goals of national economic growth and the aims and objectives of Irish higher education seem to be intrinsically linked. They argue that one of the primary reasons the *National Strategy* strongly recommends the broadening of access to higher education in Ireland is to provide a skilled workforce for the economy and question the use of the term 'human capital' in the document.[22] 'Human capital' is a concept which emerged out of

22    A. Loxley, A. Seery, and J. Walsh (eds), *Higher Education in Ireland: Practices, Policies and Possibilities* (Basingstoke: Palgrave Macmillan, 2014). See in particular the chapter by A. Loxley in the collection, entitled 'From Seaweed and Peat to Pills and Very Small Things: Knowledge Production and Higher Education in the Irish Context' (55–85).

the world of economics and which refers to capital produced by investing in certain values. Such assets as a person's knowledge and skills – and even one's personal, prestigious connections – can all be used to create economic value for the individual, her/his employer, a company or the community at large.[23] The close connection between the national economy and higher education is also evident in the report's emphasizing the importance of technology. It talks positively of the rich and varied contributions that continue to be made in the area of the humanities and social sciences, but it is to the areas of Science, Technology, Engineering and Mathematics (STEM) that the report leans. The contribution of higher education in Ireland to the country's continued increase in employment rates and economic revival is, it envisages, in and through the STEM subjects. As such, financial support – either from the state or from industry – will be more available when it is clear that such areas advance the national economic plan.

While much of this funding and development of technology is to be welcomed, the CST principle of the dignity of the human person is an inviolable reminder that economics and technology must always be at the service of the person and not the other way round. As previously stated, CST is often said to have originated in 1891, when Pope Leo XIII addressed the horrors that were occurring as a result of the Industrial Revolution – primarily, the exploitation of the human being for economic gain and the increasing gap between the wealth of a small group of elites and the widespread poverty of the majority. Against the backdrop of the development of both capitalism and communism, due to which the value of the human person was being increasingly disregarded and devalued, CST constantly reminded the world of the dignity of the person and the true nature and role of work, that is, the person is *always* the subject in relation to both money and work, never the object. This thinking is still spoken to the increasingly capitalist and globalized modern world of today. Focusing on the person as an acting subject in relation to work highlights the fact that any vision of

---

23    Cf. *National Strategy for Higher Education to 2030*, 10. As part of its vision for higher education in Ireland, the report states that 'if Ireland is to achieve its ambitions for recovery and development within an innovation-driven economy, it is essential to create and enhance human capital by expanding participation in higher education'.

her/his development – at personal, local, national or international level – could never be reduced to mere economic development. Such thinking is clearly summarized in the following two quotes:

> Development cannot be limited to mere economic growth. In order to be authentic, it must be complete: integral, that is, it has to promote the good of every person and the whole of the person. As an eminent specialist has very rightly and emphatically declared: 'We do not believe in separating the economic from the human, nor development from the civilizations in which it exists. What we hold important is the human person, each person and each group of people ...'[24]

> True development cannot consist in the simple accumulation of wealth and in the greater availability of goods and services, if this is gained at the expense of the development of the masses, and without due consideration for the social, cultural and spiritual dimensions of the human being.[25]

Higher-level education, in its development of human capital and in its working alongside the government's plan for economic development and growth, would do well to reflect on three questions posed by the American bishops:

- What does the economy do for people?
- What does it do to people?
- And how do people participate in it?[26]

The American bishops, in asking these questions, are concerned that the economy is not helping everyone to achieve their full potential. Many do not benefit from the prosperity that a more compassionate marketplace could deliver, if regulated more fairly. The bishops are rightly concerned that the economy might only be allowing a few to realize their potential.

24  Paul VI, *Populorum Progressio* (1967), n. 14, <http://w2.vatican.va/content/paul-vi/en/.../hf_p-vi_enc_26031967_populorum.html>, accessed 29 January 2018.
25  John Paul II, *Sollicitudo Rei Socialis*, n. 9.
26  United States Conference of Catholic Bishops. *Economic Justice for All: Pastoral Letter on Catholic Social Teaching and the U.S. Economy* (Washington, DC, 1986), n. 1.

The above questions pose challenges for many people to participate in the economy so that they can all flourish rather than to serve the needs of a few who run and manage the economy. The economic migration crisis around the world, and particularly in the Mediterranean area, highlights the huge imbalances in the global marketplace. Millions of people are forced to leave their economically deprived communities to find essential resources to sustain themselves and their families. Linked to economic sustainability for all is ecology.

## Ecology

Any discussion in this area must include what Thomas Berry refers to as 'the earth deficit', as opposed to the more narrow and traditional understanding of economic deficit in purely monetary terms. As should be obvious from the problems outlined at the beginning of this paper, issues of social justice are complex and interconnected. It is necessary, therefore, to interweave into any vision of third-level education an assessment of its operations in terms of sustainable development. Such a reminder of the broader ecological context in which third-level institutes operate is largely absent in the strategy report. By referring to ecology and the integrity of creation as the 'ultimate pro-life issue', the Filipino bishops hold up a valuable reminder to keep extending beyond a constricted, anthropocentric worldview in all aspects of life.[27] The CST principles of a preferential option for the poor, as well as the integrity of creation, should be a challenge to all – staff, students and guests – to work towards a lighter carbon footprint without undue impact on the quality of education being offered. Most obviously, this would involve a deep commitment to resource conservation – from the use of paper to the use of energy sources, such as heating and lighting.

27    Filipino Bishops, *What Is Happening to Our Beautiful Land?* (1988), <http://www. catholicsocialteaching.org.uk/.../What-is-Happening-to-our-Beautiful-Land.pdf>, accessed 29 January 2018.

Addressing 'the earth deficit' would also challenge decision-making about the extensive everyday use of plastics and disposable cups and plates, as well as having implications for the sourcing and purchasing of everything from food to photocopiers.

Recognizing the ecological interconnectedness of the whole of creation also demands serious discernment by the management of higher education institutes in relation to the sourcing of financial support. As the significant movement from state sponsorship to sponsorship by industry and the private sector increases, there needs to be strong judgement of an institute's chosen value system, which will underpin all financial donations. What may be compromised in intellectual and ethical freedom by educational institutes becoming increasingly dependent on corporate sponsorship? Ecological awareness in the running of such institutes is gradually becoming more widespread, but still has a significant way to go before being fully integrated in the Irish higher education system.

## Conclusion

In summary, third-level education is in an unprecedented period of change and this change is set only to increase in both form and pace as the *National Strategy* continues to be implemented. As such, a holistic and ethical understanding of the human person is fundamental to any discussion of its ultimate purpose and direction. Only within the context of such an anthropology can decisions be made that ensure a third-level education system that caters for all aspects of the human person and of the society in which s/he is situated – all aspects that recognize and celebrate the spiritual as well as the cognitive, the cultural as well as the economic. This chapter has argued that the principles of Catholic social teaching – in particular, the core concepts of the dignity of each person and a responsibility for the common good – can help in the development of such an education. Two short quotations will facilitate a final reflection on the role and nature of teaching within education. The Congregation for Catholic Education suggests that:

> Teaching has an extraordinary moral depth and is one of the human being's most excellent and creative activities, for the teacher does not write on inanimate material but on the very spirits of human beings.[28]

And Pope Benedict prompts:

> Let us feel a common responsibility towards present and future generations, especially in the task of training them to be people of peace and builders of peace ... Let us pool our spiritual, moral and material resources for the great goal of educating young people in justice and peace.[29]

These statements illustrate the role of a transformative education that educates for justice, which is fundamental to peace and which respects the creative abilities of every learner in that transformative process. This is a holistic learning that embraces the very spirit of what it is to be authentically human.

# Bibliography

## *Books and Journal Articles*

Ayers, W., *Teaching Toward Freedom: Moral Commitment and Ethical Action in the Classroom* (Boston: Beacon Press, 2005).
Ayers, W., Hunt, J. A., and Quinn, T. (eds), *Teaching for Social Justice: A Democracy and Education Reader* (New York: The New Press, 1988).
Bishops' Conference of England and Wales, *Choosing the Common Good* (Stoke-on-Trent: Alive Publishing, 2010).

---

28 Congregation for Catholic Education, *The Catholic School on the Threshold of the Third Millennium* (1997), <http://www.vatican.va/roman.../rc_con_ccatheduc_doc_27041998_school2000_en.html>, accessed 29 January 2018.

29 Benedict XVI, World Day of Peace address, *Educating young people in justice and peace* (2012), n. 6, <https://w2.vatican.va/.../messages/peace/.../hf_ben-xvi_mes_20111208_xlv-world-day>, accessed 29 January 2018.

Deberri, E. P., Hug, J. E., Henriot, P. J., Schultheis, and M. J., *Catholic Social Teaching: Our Best Kept Secret* (New York: Orbis Books, 2003, 4th edn, revised).

Dorr, D., *Option for the Poor and for the Earth: Catholic Social Teaching (20th Anniversary Edition)* (Maryknoll, NY: Orbis Books, 2012).

Freire, P., *Pedagogy of the Oppressed (30th Anniversary Edition)*, trans. M. Bergman Ramos, introduction by D. Macedo (New York: Bloomsbury Press, 2000).

Healy, S., and Reynolds, B., *Social Analysis in the Light of the Gospel* (Dublin: Folens, 1983).

Healy, S., and Reynolds, B., *Values, Catholic Social Thought and Public Policy* (Dublin: CORI Justice, 2007).

Higher Education Authority, *National Strategy for Higher Education to 2030* (Dublin: Department of Education and Skills, 2011).

Himes, K. R. (ed.), *Modern Catholic Social Teaching: Commentaries and Interpretations* (Washington, DC: Georgetown University Press, 2005).

Holland, J., and Henriot, P., SJ, *Social Analysis: Linking Faith and Justice* (Maryknoll, New York: Orbis Books, 1983).

Loxley, A., Seery, A., and Walsh, J., *Higher Education in Ireland: Practices, Policies and Possibilities* (Basingstoke: Palgrave Macmillan, 2014).

Massaro, T., *Living Justice: Catholic Social Teaching in Action Second Classroom Edition* (Lanham, MD: Rowman and Littlefield Publishers Inc., 2012).

O'Brien, D., and Shannon, T. A., *Catholic Social Thought: The Documentary Heritage* (Maryknoll, NY: Orbis Books, 2010).

Pontifical Council for Justice and Peace, *Compendium of the Social Doctrine of the Church* (USCCB, 2005).

United States Conference of Catholic Bishops. *Economic Justice for All: Pastoral Letter on Catholic Social Teaching and the U.S. Economy* (Washington, DC, 1986).

Sen, A., 'The Contemporary Relevance of Buddha', *Ethics and International Affairs* 28 (1) (2014), 15–27.

## Websites

Association of Catholic Colleges and Universities (Accunet) <http://www.accunet. org>, accessed 29 January 2018 > Services and Projects > Peace and Justice Initiatives.

Benedict XVI, 'Educating Young People in Justice and Peace', World Day of Peace address (2012), <https://w2.vatican.va/.../messages/peace/.../hf_ben-xvi_ mes_20111208_xlv-world-day>, accessed 29 January 2018.

Bowker, M. H., 'Teaching Students to Ask Questions Instead of Answering Them', *NEA: Thought and Action* 26 (Fall 2010), 127–34, <https://sites.udel.edu/.../bowker-2010–teaching-students-to-ask-questions-16echtl.pdf>, accessed 29 January 2018.

Congregation for Catholic Education, *The Catholic School on the Threshold of the Third Millennium* (1997), <http://www.vatican.va/roman.../rc_con_ccatheduc_doc_27041998_school2000_en.html>, accessed January 2018.

Conserve Energy Future <http://www.conserve-energy-future.com/15–current-environmental-problems.php>, accessed 29 January 2018.

Filipino Bishops, *What Is Happening to Our Beautiful Land?* (1988), <http://www.catholicsocialteaching.org.uk/.../What-is-Happening-to-our-Beautiful-Land.pdf>, accessed 29 January 2018.

John Paul II, *Reconciliatio et Paenitentia* (2 December 1984), <http://w2.vatican.va/content/.../hf_jp-ii_exh_02121984_reconciliatio-et-paenitentia.html>, accessed 29 January 2018.

John Paul II, *Sollicitudo Rei Socialis* (30 December 1987), <http://w2.vatican.va/content/john...ii/.../hf_jp-ii_enc_30121987_sollicitudo-rei-socialis.html>, accessed 29 January 2018.

John XXIII, *Mater et Magistra* (15 May 1961), <http://w2.vatican.va/content/john-xxiii/en/.../hf_j-xxiii_enc_15051961_mater.html>, accessed 29 January 2018.

John XXIII, *Pacem in Terris* (1963), <http://w2.vatican.va/content/john-xxiii/en/.../hf_j-xxiii_enc_11041963_pacem.html>, accessed 29 January 2018.

*National Strategy for Higher Education to 2030 Implementation Plan*, June 2011, <http://www.hea.ie/en/policy/national-strategy/implementation>, accessed 29 January 2018.

Paul VI, *Gaudium et spes* (1965), <http://www.vatican.va/archive/hist.../vat-ii_const_19651207_gaudium-et-spes_en.html>, accessed 29 January 2018.

Service Learning <http://www.servicelearning.org>, accessed 29 January 2018.

Synod of Bishops, 'Justice in the World' (1971), <https://www1.villanova.edu/content/dam/villanova/.../JusticeIntheWorld1971.pdf>, accessed 29 January 2018.

United States Conference of Catholic Bishops <http://www.usccb.org/sdwp/projects/socialteaching/excerpt.shtml>, accessed 29 January 2018.

World Economic Forum <https://www.weforum.org/events/world-economic-forum-annual-meeting-2016/>, accessed 29 January 2018.

World Hunger <http://www.worldhunger.org/2015–world-hunger-and-poverty-facts-and-statistics/#hunger-number>, accessed 29 January 2018.

PART III

# Transformation and Service

CORA LAMBERT

## 12    Community-Based Service Learning at All Hallows College: A Case Study

## Introduction

This chapter offers the perspective of an educator responsible for the sourcing, monitoring and evaluation of community-based service learning among undergraduate and postgraduate students. For the purposes of this chapter, I will focus on the learning experiences of a cohort of undergraduate students studying for a level 8 BA degree in Theology and English Literature or Psychology or Philosophy at All Hallows College, Dublin. The principles and practices of community-based service learning will be discussed and the various perspectives of community organizations and students on the programme will be explored. The challenges and opportunities of integrating academic learning with community-based service will be examined. Transformative education has to be linked to lived experience for it to be worthwhile and for it to be of meaningful service. John Dewey, one of the most influential educational thinkers of the last century, made this point when he wrote: 'I assume that amid all uncertainties there is one permanent frame of reference; namely the organic connection between education and personal experience.'[1] Dewey further stated that 'All genuine education comes through experience ... not all experiences are genuinely educative'.[2] Dewey concurred with and developed Ernest L. Boyer's concept that 'Scholarship has to prove its worth not on its own terms, but by

---

1    J. Dewey, *Experience and Education* (New York: First Touchstone Edition, 1938, 1997).
2    Ibid.

service to the nation and the world.'[3] These quotations contain the insights on which my argument about community-based service learning is based.

## Community-Based Service Learning and Higher Education Policy in Ireland

The *National Strategy for Higher Education to 2030*[4] accords a central role to higher education in equipping graduates with generic skills and competencies such as critical thinking, problem-solving capacity, and entrepreneurship. Kerins posits that higher education has two roles: the dominant and ancillary. The dominant role is economic and is aimed at helping students prepare for the work world and the economy. The ancillary role is social and focuses on the wider needs of society.[5] All Hallows College has attempted to build its programmes of study centred on developing three core values: social justice, leadership and service (All Hallows College Aisling Plan 2013–17), with community-based service learning identified as a key learning strategy.

Founded in 1842 by Fr John Hand, All Hallows College has been under Vincentian administration since 1892. The initial undertaking was to train priests for missions abroad. For more than 100 years, newly ordained priests went from All Hallows to minister in parishes across the English-speaking world. By the 1980s, it was becoming apparent that this annual supply of candidates for ordained ministry was in terminal decline.[6]

Thus, the year 1982 saw a new phase in the history of the college, when it moved from being a seminary to being an 'Institute for Mission and

3 O. Handlin, cited in E. L. Boyer, 'The Scholarship of Engagement', *Bulletin of the American Academy of Arts and Sciences* 49 (7) (1996), 33.
4 C. Hunt, *National Strategy for Higher Education to 2030: Report of tthe Strategy Group* (Dublin: Department of Education, 2011).
5 A. Kerins, *An Adventure in Service-learning: Developing Knowledge, Values and Responsibility* (London and New York: Routledge, 2010).
6 D. Balfe and J. J. Spring, 'Poverty Reduction – A Vincentian Initiative in Higher Education: The All Hallows Experience', in M. Tavanti (ed.), *Vincentian Heritage: What Would Vincent do? Vincentian Higher Education and Poverty Reduction* (Chicago: DePaul University Vincentian Studies Institute, 2008), 127–38.

Ministry'. A new course, designed for deacons who provided a synthesis of spiritual, intellectual and emotional formation for seminarians, became the catalyst that led to the opening of the doors of the college to laymen and lay women.[7] A decade later, All Hallows was offering undergraduate and postgraduate programmes, validated by the National Council for Education Awards (NCEA). Undergraduate programmes comprise a joint major degree in Theology, combined with either Psychology, Philosophy or English Literature. Postgraduate programmes include Leadership and Pastoral Care, Management in the Community and Voluntary Sector, Social Justice and Public Policy, and Applied Christian Spirituality. With an emphasis on pastoral leadership, pastoral care and human development, most of the students envisaged a future in pastoral ministry.[8] In that context, reflective engagement in pastoral activities in the community was a critical component of the All Hallows model of education.

## Concepts and Practice

Definitions of learning in the community are variously referred to in the literature as: service learning, civic engagement, community-based service learning, community field placement, etc. In All Hallows College, the term 'pastoral field placement' is used. For the purpose of this chapter, Barbara Jacoby's definition will be used because it expresses well what pastoral field placements are:

> Pastoral field placements ... are a form of experiential education in which students engage in activities that address human and community needs together with structured opportunities intentionally designed to promote student learning and development.[9]

7    K. Rafferty, 'All Hallows 1982–1995, a Time of Transition', *All Hallows Studies* (Summer 2006), 143–62.
8    Balfe and Spring, 'Poverty Reduction'.
9    B. K. Bushouse, 'Community Non-profit Organisations and Service-Learning: Resource Constraints to Building Partnerships with Universities', *Michigan Journal of Community Service Learning*, vol. 12 (Fall 2005), 32–40.

The contribution of service-learning pedagogy and practice is to develop students as 'expert learners' – that is, as people who are able to approach new situations flexibly, are skilled at acquiring new knowledge quickly and efficiently, and are able to learn throughout their lifetimes.[10]

David Kolb introduced a cycle of experiential learning which comprises four elements: concrete experience; observations and reflections; formulation of abstract concepts and generalization; and testing implications of concepts on new situations. Kolb asserts that learning occurs and good practice develops when students engage in all four stages of the cycle; in reality, this is a continuing process which may proceed in any order.[11]

## Experience of Community-Based Service Learning

At All Hallows College, our students are diverse in age, nationality, and socio-economic backgrounds. All second-year undergraduate students in All Hallows College are required to study a module called Pastoral Education, comprised of three components:

1.  Pastoral field placement;
2.  Pastoral reflection group; and
3.  Social analysis.

Thesethree components provide the students with the skills to engage critically with structures they experience in society. In fourth year, Pastoral Education is an elective module. This module also consists of the pastoral field placement and the reflection group, but it also has a new component

---

10   M. Singham, *The Achievement Gap in U.S. Education: Canaries in the Mine* (Lanham: Rowman and Littlefield Education, 2005).

11   D. Kolb, 'Experiential Learning Cycle' (adapted), *Experiential Learning: Experience as a Source of Learning and Development* (Englewood Cliffs, New Jersey: Prentice Hall, 1984), xx.

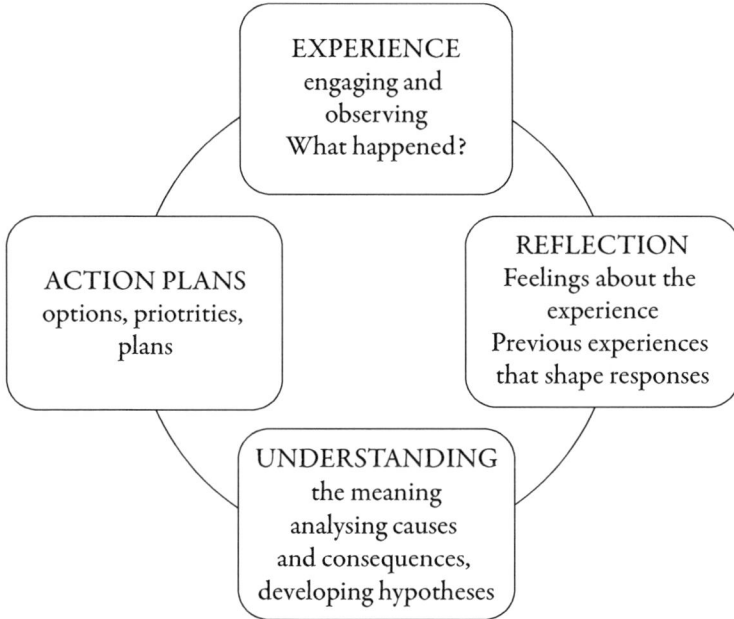

Figure 12.1: David Kolb Experiential Learning Cycle (adapted)[12]

for which students undertake a social analysis study of an aspect of their pastoral field placement.

Student service in the community includes teaching at primary and secondary level, pupil support in afterschool homework clubs, and supporting clients in community organizations, hospitals, and nursing homes. Harvey writes that the reasons that students chose a particular pastoral field placement in which to gain experience included to get an insight into a profession or type of work, to see how the theory they were learning on their course was applicable in the workplace and to supplement their learning with practical experience.[13]

12    Ibid.
13    B. L. Harvey, *Learning through Work Placements and Beyond* (Sheffield: Organisation Forum, Report for HECSU and the Higher Education Academy's work placements, 2006).

The impact of student engagement on community organizations will be examined later in the chapter. For now, let us use the rubric provided by Enos and Morton, for considering student learning experiences, which range from transactional (i.e. instrumental, task-oriented, project-based activities) to transformative (i.e. deeper and sustained commitment between partners, in which there is an expectation of change).[14] Community organizations and schools provided a sustained commitment to accommodating All Hallows students every year; however, these relationships remained at the project-based, transactional level.

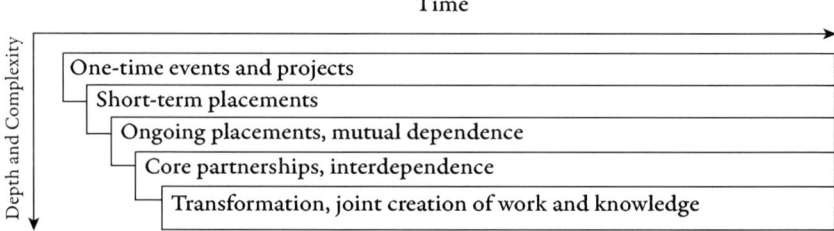

Figure 12.2:  A Framework for Development of Campus-Community Partnerships
Source: Enos, S., & Morton, K. (2003). Developing a theory and practice of campus-community partnerships. In B. Jacoby & Associates (Eds.), *Building partnerships for service-learning*. San Francisco: John Wiley & Sons, Inc.


## Preparing Students for Service in the Community


As already noted, All Hallows College's education provision is the faculty of arts – the education provided is formative and does not guide students towards specific professions. Our students typically choose postgraduate

---

14    B. K. Bushouse, 'Community Non-profit Organisations and Service-Learning: Resource Constraints to Building Partnerships with Universities', *Michigan Journal of Community Service Learning*, vol. 12 (Fall 2005), 30.

programmes to educate them for specific professions. However, through Pastoral Education modules (mandatory in the BA programmes and in many MA programmes), students are given the opportunity to gain pastoral experience in an area of their choice. Preparation for pastoral field placements in the community starts in the first year of the degree programme, when all students undertake a module called Pastoral Education One, the aim of which is to introduce students to the basic principles, attitudes and skills necessary for effective pastoral care. At the start of the second year of their degree programme, before the pastoral placements begin, students are prepared for pastoral field placement, trained in child protection, and sign a code of conduct relating to their professional behaviour while on their pastoral field placement. Students are given a portfolio that includes a learning agreement, a time record, a mid-year review and a final evaluation for assessment. In the early stages of their pastoral field placement, each student creates a learning contract, which outlines the student's academic goals and objectives in the pastoral field placement, the activities they would be participating in to accomplish those goals, and verification of these activities and achievements.

## Supervision, Mentoring and Evaluation

All organizations that took our students on pastoral field placements provided a staff member who introduced our students to their organization, giving them an outline of its aims, objectives and ethos, service user needs and how the staff responds to them. Throughout the pastoral field placement, the supervisors supported and mentored the students on pastoral field placement. They also provided a written review of the students' learning at the end of the first semester and a written evaluation of the students' placement learning. For many students, typically those who were in an education setting, the activities they engaged in remained the same throughout the pastoral field placement; for those in community organizations, students were sometimes given further responsibilities as the placement progressed.

Harvey writes that greater responsibility also came about through progression and also because of unplanned events – for example, having to cover for staff absences and changes in staffing levels.[15]


## Assessment


The evaluation of pastoral field placements was undertaken by community supervisors and students; each completed evaluations for review at the end of the first semester, and a final evaluation upon completion of the placement, using a Likert scaled evaluation form. Students were evaluated in the following areas – skills and competencies gained through the pastoral field placement, their development of pastoral and professional identity, and their ability to make connections between academic learning and experience in the community. Students completed a self-review and self-evaluation using the same scale.


## Reflection and Analysis


Maria Slowey et al. suggest that the importance of reflecting on experience is underscored in the *National Strategy*, which accords a central role to higher education in equipping graduates with generic skills and competencies, such as critical thinking, problem-solving capacity, and entrepreneurship.[16]

L. B. Anderson outlined the role of reflection in the learning process when he asserted that the quality of reflective thought brought by the

---

15   Harvey, *Learning through Work Placements and Beyond*.
16   M. Slowey et al., *Voices of Academics in Irish Higher Education: Perspectives on Professional Development* (Dublin: AISHE, 2014).

learner is of greater significance to the eventual learning outcomes than the nature of the experience itself.[17] S. Ash and P. Clayton offer a developed reflection framework,[18] based on the work of G. Kiser,[19] in which the analysis phase is structured to include consideration of these three areas: the academic, the personal and the civic.

When engaged in academic analysis, students examine their experiences in light of specific course concepts, exploring similarities and differences between theory and practice. In analysis from the personal perspective, students consider their feelings, assumptions, strengths, weaknesses, traits, skills, and sense of identity as they are brought to the surface and sometimes challenged by service-learning experiences. Ash and Clayton write that:

> when examining their service-learning related activities from the civic perspective, students explore decisions made and actions taken in light of consequences for the common good, consider alternative approaches and interpretations, identify elements of power and privilege, and analyse options for short-term versus long-term and sustainable change agency.[20]

To assist our students in learning through their experience in the community, weekly reflection groups, which comprised between eight and ten students and a staff facilitator, ran in tandem with field placements. D. Cone and S. Harris suggest that the process requires that students learn to 'read' their workplaces as 'texts' in which they examine the histories, power arrangements and values underlying their work organizations.[21] Student engagement in this reflective process is predicated on what Freire termed the horizontal student–teacher relationship,[22] which creates a learning environment that enables students to feel comfortable to communicate

17   L. B. Anderson, 'Experience-Based Learning', in G. Foley (ed.), *Understanding Education and Training* (Sydney: Allen and Unwin, 2000), 225–39.

18   S. Ash and P. Clayton, 'The Articulated Learning: An Approach to Guided Reflection and Assessment', *Innovative Higher Education* 29 (2) (December 2004), 137–54.

19   G. Kiser, in Ash and Clayton, 'The Articulated Learning', 141–2.

20   Ash and Clayton, 'The Articulated Learning', 141–2.

21   D. Cone and S. Harris, 'Service-Learning Practice: Developing a Theoretical Framework', *Michigan Journal of Community Service Learning* 3 (1) (1996), 31–43.

22   P. Freire, *Pedagogy of the Oppressed* (New York: Herder and Herder, 1970), Chapter 2.

openly, without fear of judgement. For some students, communicating openly can be daunting experience.

In our study, a second-year undergraduate student opined, 'I'm not really a sharing person, but I could see the group blossomed through the process'. This result recalls P. Hondagneu-Sotelo and S. Raskoff, who write that:

> If students bring their assumptions unchallenged to their reflection on those experiences, they not only close the door to potentially powerful new perspectives, they also allow those experiences to reinforce their stereotypes and prejudices.[23]

Another student reported that her experience in the reflection group 'opened my understanding of human nature and different viewpoints and cultures', while another admitted that 'in the past I was quick to act without reflecting, now I have tools to allow me see situations differently'.

These quotations indicate the value of looking at group reflection on experiences which if unchallenged negate the possibility of new experiences and/or reinforce stereotypes and prejudices. The reflection process enabled and empowered the students to view experiences from different perspectives than before.

## Theological Reflection

Pastoral leadership and identity evolve through pastoral reflection groups and theological reflection on the students' experiences while on pastoral field placement. Theological reflection is the process of bringing the influence of Gospel values to bear directly on the student experience of their pastoral field placement. Through weekly pastoral reflection groups, students have the opportunity to analyse their experience in the community and reflect on it through the Gospel. Students are encouraged to investigate

---

23    P. Hondagneu-Sotelo and S. Raskoff, in Ash and Clayton, 'The Articulated Learning', 139.

their experience in a systematic and analytical way. Students are presented with the question: 'How do I understand or make sense of this incident theologically?' Public discourse, Church and Gospel teachings are the resources students use in conversation about the personal, academic, and societal issues arising from their pastoral field placement experiences.

Paulo Freire claims that 'knowledge emerges only through invention and reinvention, through the restless, impatient, continuing, hopeful inquiry human beings pursue in the works, with the world, and with each other'.[24]

Kolb's work[25] (see Figure 12.1) continues to be recognized as one of the significant steps forward in the scholarly understanding of experiential learning; his association of experience with reflection has stood the test of time. In addition to the academic, personal and civic dimensions of reflection and analysis, All Hallows College has trained students in the art of theological reflection as a way of helping them to link faith, action and social issues in their daily lives.

This process helps students to develop critical judgement about situations, events and structures. Stephen Pattison commended a model for theological reflection, which he entitles the 'critical conversation'.[26] Pattison's model centres on the basic idea that the student should imagine him- or herself as being involved in a three-way conversation between:

(a)  His or her own ideas, beliefs, feelings, perceptions and assumptions;
(b)  The beliefs, assumptions and perceptions provided by the Christian tradition (including the Bible); and
(c)  The contemporary situation which is being examined.[27]

Building on Pattison's model, J. Eyler, D. E. Giles and A. Schmiede suggest that the process of critical reflection is that which brings about

---

24  P. Freire, in Cone and Harris, 'Service-Learning Practice', 31–43.
25  D. Kolb, 'Experiential Learning Cycle' (adapted), xx.
26  S. Pattison and J. Woodward, '"Some Straw for Bricks": A Basic Introduction to Theological Reflection', in J. Woodward, S. Pattison, and J. Patton (eds), *The Blackwell Reader in Pastoral and Practical Theology* (Oxford: Blackwell, 2000), 135–45.
27  Ibid. 139.

transformation. It is the link between theory and practice – and it gives meaning between service in action and the understanding of learning. They write:

> It is critical reflection that provides the transformative link between the action of serving and the ideas and understanding of learning.[28]

In relation to theological reflection, Killen and de Beer's framework for theological reflection[29] provides a number of parallels with Kolb's Cycle as a way of making meaning: focusing on some aspect of experience; describing that experience to identify the heart of the matter; exploring the heart of the matter in conversation with the wisdom of Christian heritage; and identifying from this conversation new truths and meanings for living (Killen, 2001).[30]

Table 12.1: The Movement toward Insight and Framework for Theological Reflection[31]

| Movement | Framework |
|---|---|
| 1. When we enter our experience, we encounter our feelings. | 1. Focusing on some aspect of experience. |
| 2. When we pay attention to those feelings, images arise | 2. Describing that experience to identify the heart of the matter |
| 3. Considering and questioning those images may spark insight. | 3. Exploring the heart of the matter in conversation with the wisdom of the wisdom of the Christian heritage |
| 4. Insight leads, if we are willing and ready, to action. | 4. Identifying from this conversation new truths and meanings for living. |

28   J. Eyler, D. E. Giles and A. Schmiede, in Ash and Clayton 'The Articulated Learning', 139.
29   P. Killen and J. de Beer, *The Art of Theological Reflection* (US: Crossroad Publishers, 1994), 74.
30   P. Killen, 'Gracious Play, Discipline, Insight and the Common Good', in *Teaching Theology and Religion* (US: John Wiley and Sons, 2001), vol. 4, 1.
31   Killen and de Beer, *The Art of Theological Reflection*, 74.

From our case study, a student reported that his experience in pastoral reflection group gave 'an increased confidence in my ability to reflect on my own experiences, and that of others that I will carry as a life skill', while another commented, 'we addressed difficult subjects. I got insight into other peoples' problems and I am less judgemental'.

Students of all denominations and none can engage in theological reflection. For students who do not have a religious faith or who are determining their position on faith, the wisdom of their other discipline (the words of a song or a poem, the perception of psychology or the insight of philosophy) helped to create meaning. Schön saw 'reflection' as 'a continual interweaving of thinking and doing' and he described the 'reflective practitioner' as one who 'reflects on the understandings which have been implicit in [one's] action, which [one] surfaces, criticizes, restructures, and embodies in further action'.[32]

Schön provides us with a possible definition of 'reflection'. He makes the point that critical reflection, in particular theological reflection, gives meaning to our perceptions. He stresses that reflection can take place, regardless of whether or not one is a member of any denomination. The core argument is that reflection on our experiences can help us to gain new insights and thus helps in our transformative learning.


## Benefits and Challenges of Community-Based Service Learning for Students


For students on placement, the benefits included the experience of some form of teamwork. They were frequently required to work with people from different age groups, backgrounds and life experiences, and they realized that they had to make the effort to fit in and be a part of the team. Some

---

32    D. Schön, *The Reflective Practitioner: How Professionals Think in Action* (US: Basic Books Inc., 1983), 281.

students made links between academic subjects and their placements, while others were unable to make connections. In many cases, the placement experience helped inform the students' future intentions. This occurred in the following ways: previous ideas and plans regarding career choices were confirmed, new areas of interest were opened up, specific areas of work were rejected, and future career plans were changed completely.

## Benefits and Challenges for Community-Based Organizations

Without community organizations, there would be no service learning. If service learning is to meet its goals of improving student learning, preparing students for civic involvement, and addressing community needs, then it is critical for service-learning practitioners and administrators to pay closer attention to the role of community in this endeavour.[33]

Bushouse concurs and writes:

> If a community organisation finds that it is a net loser in the partnership, then service-learning has not achieved its most basic aim of mutual benefits for students, universities and community partners.[34]

Worrall tells us that it must also be noted that 'community organisations take risks in these partnerships, especially when they divert time away from core, funded activities'.[35] Some of the benefits identified by the community organizations we surveyed in our case study for the purposes of this chapter include:

- Expertise relevant to particular service from volunteering perspective;
- Increase in resources;

33  K. Wolf-Wendell, 'Community-centered Service Learning: Moving from Doing for to Doing With', *American Behavioral Scientist* 43 (5) (February 2000), 767–80.
34  Bushouse, 'Community Non-profit Organisations and Service-Learning', 32–40.
35  L. Worral, 'Asking the Community: A Case Study of Community Partner Perspectives', *Michigan Journal of Community Service Learning* 14 (1) (2007).

- Works well if well managed;
- Giving students experience of the sector, encouraging them to consider it as a career option.

The challenges of engaging with students for community-based service learning may include:

- Consistency of service provision of the organization can be affected;
- Unclear expectations of the organization/supervisor;
- Students not taking initiative/lacking motivation/can't take feedback;
- Increased supervision and administration required;
- Student apathy, connected to lack of professional focus;
- Lack of appreciation of the personal and professional value of their engagement in the community.

## Benefits and Challenges of Co-ordinating and Administrating CBSL for the University Context

The following list outlines the advantages and challenges that presented themselves in the All Hallows College third-level education context:

- Relationship-building;
- Brand All Hallows College significant;
- Supported the college;
- Raising awareness/PR;
- Extended the brand awareness of All Hallows beyond the parish community;
- Alumni network – maintained connection with the college;
- Value in the ongoing contribution to the organizations by the students;
- Pre-recession there was an acknowledgement of the need for CBSL;
- Community organizations found students on placement to be an additional and valuable resource; however, in the recession the volunteer market became saturated and competitive;

- Increase the likelihood of students volunteering/being employed in the sector they received the experience from;
- Valuable experience of teaching practice;
- Students experienced the world of work, and the placement experience contributed to their application for higher diplomas in teaching;
- Fewer students had been in part-time student employment with experience;
- Staff from external community projects then became aware of All Hallows College and joined the college to study/pursue postgraduate programmes;
- Perception of the college by the wider community was that it was a seminary; this perception changed to that of a college that was less focused on educating men for priesthood and more focused on inclusive education for all;
- Improved interpersonal skills through interaction with others;
- Despite AHC historical history as a seminary, the vast majority of the student body were non-ordained and studying theology in combination with other arts subjects.

The above are significant as they represent transformation in the type of learning that is taking place. Also, they reinforce the idea of theological reflection not being based totally on a specific Christian denomination. Above all, they signify that this type of learning is inclusive education for all.

## Assessment of Student by Community Organization Supervisors

Our experience shows that there are a number of variables that affect the quality and consistency of community organizations' evaluation and feedback of students. The students that have thus far gone on placement have been assessed by their supervisors through evaluation forms that use a Likert scale to measure their competency and proficiency in various areas. These have been completed at the end of semesters one and two.

One of the challenges we have had was ensuring that community organizations had the resources required to take the time to supervise and give feedback to the student on placement. There were also difficulties ensuring the consistency and fairness of evaluation across the cohort of evaluated students in a variety of organizational contexts.

Sheridan writes that some organizations may perceive the time and costs associated with providing placements as potential barriers. Additionally, the time and effort it takes to make links with HEIs and subsequently with potential students may also act as barriers, particularly for smaller organizations. The difficulties in applying academic and administrative resources to the placement process have been exacerbated by growing full-time student numbers and reducing staff numbers in most HEIs. He says:

> The most pervasive barrier is the simplest to identify and understand: there are not enough work experience placements available to meet the growing demand from students. This has a number of effects. For community organisations, it means increased resource cost to respond to the large number of requests received. For education institutions, it means that finding work experience for students can often be time-consuming, difficult, and not always successful.[36]

Organizing successful community engagement requires considerable resources from community organizations. It needs time, money, expertise and commitment, and not all organizations can provide these. The amount of time necessary to supervise a student and set up and monitor projects or the work that students undertake may be considered too resource-intensive. Community engagement is full of potential, promise, risk and uncertainty, because it entails a willingness to change, a capacity to accommodate the other and a preparedness to be transformed in the process.[37]

However, very little research explicitly explores how the placement experience translates into academic development from the point of view of current students. Much is taken for granted; the observed maturity of undergraduates returning from a period of work placement is assumed to

---

36  I. Sheridan, *Work Placement in Third-level Programs* (Cork: CIT Press, 2011).
37  S. Bjarnason and P. Coldstream (eds), *The Idea of Engagement: Universities in Society* (London: Association of Commonwealth Universities, 2003).

carry over into a more studious or reflective approach to learning, but there is little direct evidence to be found of this in the literature.[38]

We believe that service learning needs to consider the personal and intellectual growth of both the student and the community. Dewey made a similar point when he wrote:

> The belief that all genuine education comes about from experience does not mean that all experiences are genuinely or equally educative. Everything depends on the experience ... as ... every experience lives on in further experiences.[39]

As mentioned before, transformative education needs to be linked to lived experience for it to be worthwhile and for it to be of meaningful service. Community-based service learning (CBSL) *is* transformative education and *is* the way forward for future learning.

## Conclusion

In this chapter, the concepts and practices of community-based service learning were discussed. The perspectives of community organizations, All Hallows College and our students were outlined. Finally, the challenges and benefits of integrating academic learning with community-based service through pastoral field placement, academic learning and theological reflection was explored in depth.

Through the evolution of All Hallows, from its long history as a seminary to its current function as a higher education institute, community-based service learning was incorporated into the All Hallows academic curriculum through pastoral education. This has been a distinctive component of the All Hallows education system. The promise of this learning is that it promotes personal, academic and civic growth and responsibility

---

38    Harvey, *Learning through work placements and beyond.*
39    J. Dewey, *Education and Experience* (New York: Kappa Delta Pi, 1938).

in the student. The challenge for the higher education institute is to combine the constituent elements – academic knowledge, field placement, and theological reflection – into an embedded and transformative learning experience.

# Bibliography

Anderson, L. B., 'Experience-Based Learning', in G. Foley (ed.), *Understanding Adult Education and Training* (Sydney: Allen & Unwin, 2000), 225–39.

Ash, S. L., and Clayton, P., 'The Articulated Learning: An Approach to Guided Reflection and Assessment', *Innovative Higher Education* 29 (2) (2004), 137–54.

Awbrey, S. M. et al., *Integrative Learning and Action a Call to Wholeness* (New York: Peter Lang, 2006).

Balfe, D., and Spring, J. J., 'Poverty Reduction – A Vincentian Initiative in Higher Education: The All Hallows Experience', in M. Tavanti (ed.), *Vincentian Heritage What Would Vincent Do? Vincentian Higher Education and Poverty Reduction* (Chicago: DePaul University Vincentian Studies Institute, 2008), 127–38.

Benefiel, M., and Holton, G., *The Soul of Supervision: Integrating Practice and Theory* (Pennsylvania: Moorhouse Publishing, 2010).

Bjarnason, S., and Coldstream, P. (eds), *The Idea of Engagement: Universities in Society* (London: Association of Commonwealth Universities, 2003).

Boland, J., 'Capturing the 'Insight' Dimension of Civic Engagement in National Framework of Qualifications' (Dublin, 2012), <http://www.campusengage.ie>, accessed 16 March 2015.

Boyer, E. L., 'The Scholarship of Engagement', *Bulletin of the American Academy of Arts and Sciences* 49 (7) (1996), 18–33.

Bringle, R. G., Hatcher, J. A., and Jones, S. G., 'Review Essay; Progress and Promise in International Service Learning', *Michigan Journal of Community Service Learning* (Spring 2011), 78–82.

Bushouse, B. K., 'Community Non-profit Organisations and Service-Learning: Resource Constraints to Building Partnerships with Universities', *Michigan Journal of Community Service Learning*, vol. 12 (Fall 2005), 32–40.

Cone, D., 'Service-Learning Practice: Developing a Theoretical Framework', *Michigan Journal of Service Learning* (1996), 31–4.

Dewey, J., *Experience and Education* (New York: First Touchstone Edition, 1997, originally published 1938).

Freire, P., *Pedagogy of the Oppressed* (New York: Herder and Herder, 1970).

Ginger-Hofman, N., and Rosing, H. (eds), *Pedagogies of Praxis Course Based Research in the Social Sciences* (Bolton: Anker Publishing Company Inc., 2007).

Harvey, B. L., *Learning through Work Placements and Beyond* (Sheffield: Organisation Forum, Report for HECSU and the Higher Education Academy's work placements, 2006).

Hunt, C., *National Strategy for Higher Education to 2030*, Report of the Strategy Group (Dublin: Department of Education, 2011).

Jacoby, B., *Civic Engagement in Higher Education Concepts and Practices* (San Francisco, CA: Jossey-Bass, 2009).

Jarvis, P., *Adult Education and Lifelong Learning* (London: RoutledgeFalmer, 2004, 3rd edn).

Kerins, A., *An Adventure in Service-Learning: Developing Knowledge, Values and Responsibility* (London and New York: Routledge, 2010).

Killen, P., 'Gracious Play, Discipline, Insight and the Common Good', in *Teaching Theology and Religion* (US: John Wiley and Sons, 2001), vol. 4, 1.

Killen, P., and de Beer, J., *The Art of Theological Reflection* (US: Crossroad Publishers, 1994).

Kolb, D. A., *Experiential Learning: Experience as a Source of Learning and Development* (Englewood Cliffs, New Jersey: Prentice Hall, 1984).

McIlrath, L., and Lyons, A., '*Driving civic engagement within higher education in Ireland: A Contextual picture of Activities from the local to the National through the evolution of a Network*' in McILrath, L., et.al., Mapping Civic Engagement within Higher Education in Ireland (report) (Dublin: AISHE and Campus Engage, 2007), 18–29.

McIlrath, L., Lyons, A., and Munck, R., *Higher Education and Civic Engagement* (New York: Palgrave Macmillan, 2012).

Moon, J. A., *Learning Journals A Handbook for Reflective Practice and Professional Development* (Oxon: Routledge, 2007, 2nd edn).

National Organization for Human Services (2014), <http://www.nationalhuman-services.org/what-is-human-services>, accessed 5 December 2014.

Pattison, S., and Woodward, J., '"Some Straw for Bricks": A Basic Introduction to Theological Reflection', in J. Woodward, S. Pattison, and J. Patton (eds), *The Blackwell Reader in Pastoral and Practical Theology* (Oxford: Blackwell, 2000), 135–45.

Rafferty, K., 'All Hallows 1982–1995, a Time of Transition', *All Hallows Studies* (Summer 2006), 143–62.

Schön, D., *The Reflective Practitioner: How Professionals Think in Action* (US: Basic Books Inc., 1983), 281.

Sheridan, I., *Work Placement in Third-Level Programs* (Cork: CIT Press, 2011).

Singham, M., *The Achievement Gap in U.S. Education: Canaries in the Mine* (Lanham: Rowman and Littlefield Education, 2005).

Slowey, M. et al., *Voices of Academics in Irish Higher Education: Perspectives on Professional Development* (Dublin: AISHE, 2014).

Stanton, T.K, 'Liberal Arts, Experiential Learning and Public Service: Necessary Ingredients for Socially Responsible Undergraduate Education', in J. K. Associates (ed.), *Combining Service and Learning 1* (Raleigh, NC: National Society for Internships and Experiential Education, 1990), 175–89.

Wolf-Wendell, K., 'Community-centered Service Learning: Moving From Doing For to Doing With', *American Behavioural Scientist* 43 (5) (February 2000), 767–80.

Worrall, L., 'Asking the Community: A Case Study of Community Partner Perspectives', *Michigan Journal of Community Service Learning* (Fall 2007), 5–17.

MARJORIE FITZPATRICK

# 13  Mentoring as a Transforming Tool in 'Holistic' Education at Third Level

## Introduction

This chapter addresses the importance of 'mentoring' as a way of supporting transformative learning in the context of higher education. This is a crucial service to the community of learning. Theories of transformational learning are presented to illustrate that there are differences in how scholars view the transformation of individuals and communities. In defining the origin of the concepts 'mentoring' and 'holistic education', it is of benefit to look at them within their historical context. The original 'mentor' appears in Homer's *Odyssey* as an old and trusted friend of Odysseus. He is appointed to look after Odysseus's estate and, more importantly, to look after Odysseus's son Telemachus. It is in the form of the mentor that Athena, goddess of wisdom, speaks at critical times throughout the epic. In Homer's *Odyssey*, according to Daloz,[1] 'mentor' serves as a guide in the Journey of Adults.

'Holistic' Education can be summed up in John Dewey's philosophy of education: 'Education is not preparation for life but rather life itself'.[2] Ron Miller suggests that:

> Holistic Education is based on the premise that each person finds identity, meaning, and purpose in life through connections to the community, to the natural world, and to spiritual values such as compassion and peace. Holistic education aims to call forth from people an intrinsic reverence for life and a passionate love of learning.

---

1    L. A. Daloz, *Mentor: Guiding the Journey of Adult Learners* (San Francisco: Jossey-Bass, 1999, 2nd edn), 20.
2    J. Dewey, *Experience and Education* (New York: Macmillan, 1938).

> This is done, not through an academic 'curriculum' that condenses the world into instructional packages, but through direct engagement with the environment. Holistic education nurtures a sense of wonder. Holistic Education, therefore, is looking at the whole person – the intellectual, social, emotional, physical, aesthetic and spiritual dimensions.[3]

This quotation summarizes very succinctly what a good education ought to achieve. A good holistic education tries to inculcate a sense of the mystery of life and the yet undiscovered potential and becoming of every learner. Much research has been carried out to illustrate that education, and holistic education in particular, is a transformational journey. Robin Ann Martin, when writing about the term 'holistic education' at its most general level, suggests that what distinguishes it from other forms of education are its goals, its attention to experiential learning and the significance that it places on relationships and primary human values within the learning environment.[4]

## Holistic Education as Transformative

Holistic education advocates a transformative approach to learning. Rather than seeing education as a process of transmission and transaction, transformative learning involves a change in the frames of reference that a person may have. This change may include points of view, habits of mind and worldview. Papastamis and Panitsides argue that traditionally theory and research in adult education have examined learning as a purely cognitive process:

---

3    R. Miller, *Journal of Holistic Education Review* (now *Encounter: Education for Meaning and Social Justice*, 2004), 1.
4    R. A. Martin, *An Analysis of Holistic Schools' Literature*, paper co-presented with Dr Scott H. Forbes at the (American Education Research Association Annual Conference, California, 2004), 9.

> Theory and research in adult education over-relied on rational and cognitive processes in describing perspective transformation, while it makes the assumption that for transformative learning to take place, cognitive, physical, emotional and spiritual dimensions are closely interrelated. When it comes to knowing and learning, linear and fragmented approaches cannot account for the perplexity of the human being.[5]

Jack Mezirow,[6] although influenced very much by the writings of Paulo Freire,[7] is generally regarded as the father of transformative learning. Freire's theory of transformative learning involves a social-cultural approach in which personal empowerment and social transformations are two inseparable processes. Mezirow goes further in his theory of transformative learning, which focuses on the process of personal transformation and empowerment.[8] In his theory, Mezirow argues that transformative learning is a form of learning through which previously uncritically assimilated beliefs, attitudes, assumptions and emotional reactions are questioned and thereby become more explicit and thoroughly validated.[9] He believes that transformations involve both changes in meaning schemes – a specific set of beliefs, biases, feelings, attitudes and knowledge and a frame of reference which offers an integrated set of meaning schemes, assumptions and expectations through which individuals filter their experiences. Mezirow points out that in adulthood individuals reassess the assumptions they acquired during childhood, often in response to disorienting dilemmas that challenge their perspective and their frame of reference for interpreting reality. A transformative learning process, for Mezirow, unravels in ten consecutive stages (see E. Houlihan, Chapter 1).

5    A. Papastamis and E. A. Panitisides, *Transformative Learning: Advocating for a Holistic Approach* (Greece: University of Macedonia, 2014), 74 <http://dx.doi.org/10.5539/res.v6n4p74>, accessed 29 January 2018.

6    J. Mezirow, *Transformative Dimensions of Adult Learning* (San Francisco, CA: Jossey-Bass, 1991), 167.

7    P. Freire, *Pedagogy of the Oppressed* (New York: Herder and Herder, 1972).

8    See Mezirow, *Transformative Dimensions of Adult Learning*, and J. Mezirow, *Learning as Transformation: Critical Perspectives on a Theory in Progress* (San Francisco, CA: Jossey-Bass, 2000), 55.

9    Ibid. 4–7.

## Adult Transformative Learning

*Andragogy*

How does transformative learning take place in adult education? In order to guide a 'mentee', a mentor should ask this core question. Malcolm Knowles can provide possible answers. The term 'andragogy' is often associated with Malcolm Knowles (1913–1997) and refers to the method and practice of teaching adult learners. According to Knowles, 'andragogy is the art and science of adult learning, thus andragogy refers to any form of adult learning'.[10] The term can thus be considered an equivalent to the term 'pedagogy'; in Greek, 'andragogy' means 'man-learning' whereas 'Pedagogy' means 'child-learning'. Alexander Kapp, a German educator originally used the term 'andragogy' in 1833.

Knowles writes that formal adult education programmes are those sponsored for the most part by established educational institutions. Although concerned mainly with informal adult education, the following outcomes apply to both informal and formal adult education:

1.  Adults should acquire a mature understanding of themselves. They should understand their needs, motivations, interests, capacities and goals. They should be able to look at themselves objectively and maturely. They should accept themselves and respect themselves for what they are, while striving earnestly to become better.
2.  Adults should develop an attitude of acceptance, love and respect towards others. This is the attitude on which all human relations depend. Adults must learn to distinguish between people and ideas, and to challenge ideas without threatening people. Ideally, this attitude will go beyond acceptance, love and respect, to empathy and the sincere desire to help others.
3.  Adults should develop a dynamic attitude toward life. They should accept the fact of change and should think of themselves as always changing. They should acquire the habit of looking at every experience as an opportunity to learn and should become skilful in learning from it.

---

10   G. Kearsley, *Andragogy* (M. Knowles) (2010), <http://tip.psychology.org>, accessed 29 January 2018.

4. Adults should learn to react to the causes, not the symptoms, of behaviour. Solutions to problems lie in their causes, not in their symptoms. We have learned to apply this lesson in the physical world but have yet to learn to apply it in human relations.

5. Adults should acquire the skills necessary to achieve the potentials of their personalities. Every person has capacities that if realized, will contribute to the well-being of himself [or herself] and of society. To achieve these potentials requires skills of many kinds- vocational, social, recreational, civic, artistic and the like. It should be a goal of education to give each individual those skills necessary for him [or her] to make full use of his [or her] capacities.

6. Adults should understand the essential values in the capital of human experience. They should be familiar with the heritage of knowledge, the great ideas, the great traditions, of the world in which they live. They should understand and respect the values that bind men together.

7. Adults should understand their society and should be skilful in directing social change. In a democracy the people participate in making decisions that affect the entire social order. It is imperative, therefore, that [everyone] know enough about government, economics, international affairs, and other aspects of the social order to be able to take part in them intelligently.[11]

For Knowles, andragogy is premised on at least four crucial assumptions about the characteristics of adult learners that are different from the assumptions about child learners on which traditional pedagogy is premised. A fifth was added later. These five assumptions offer a helpful insight into the way adults can learn and help also in how a process of informal learning or a formal programme of learning might be developed. Such a programme of learning will have elements in it that address these assumptions.

1. Self-concept: As a person matures, his/her self-concept moves from one of being a dependent personality towards one of being a self-directed human being.

2. Experience: As a person matures, he/she accumulates a growing reservoir of experience that becomes an increasing resource for learning.

3. Readiness to learn: As a person matures, his/her readiness to learn becomes oriented increasingly to the developmental tasks of his/her social roles.

4. Orientation to learning: As a person matures, his/her time perspective changes from one of postponed application of knowledge to immediacy of application,

11   M. Knowles, *The Modern Practice of Adult Education: Andragogy Versus Pedagogy* (New York: Association Press, 1950), 9–10.

and accordingly his orientation toward learning shifts from one of subject-centeredness to one of problem-centeredness.

5.   Motivation to learn: As a person matures, the motivation to learn is internal.[12]

Knowles went on to suggest that the idea of self-direction could be packaged forms of activity that could be taken by both educators and learners alike. He gives us a five-step model:

1.   Diagnosing learning needs;
2.   Formulating learning needs;
3.   Identifying human material resources for learning;
4.   Choosing and implementing appropriate learning strategies;
5.   Evaluating learning outcomes.[13]

In 1994, Brookfield develops Knowles' idea about adult learning being concerned with self-direction when he asks the question, 'What are the essential characteristics of a critical, rather than technical interpretation of self-directed learning'.[14] Brookfield answers the question regarding essential characteristics of a critical interpretation of self-directed learning by suggesting two:

1.   Self-direction should be considered the continuous exercise by the learner of authentic control over all decisions having to do with learning; and
2.   Self-direction is the ability to gain access to, and choose from, a full range of available and appropriate resources.

Malcolm Knowles, acknowledging a significantly individualistic focus in his work, wrote, 'I am just not good at political action. My strength lies

---

12   M. Knowles et al., *Andragogy in Action: Applying Modern Principles of Adult Education* (San Francisco, CA: Jossey-Bass, 1984), 12.

13   M. Knowles, *The Making of an Adult Educator: An Autobiography* (San Francisco, CA: Jossey-Bass, 1989), 57.

14   S. D. Brookfield, *Understanding and Facilitating Adult Learning: A Comprehensive Analysis of Principles and Effective Practices* (San Francisco, CA: Jossey-Bass, 1986), 60.

in creating opportunities for helping individuals become more proficient practitioners.'[15] Here, Knowles underlines the importance of providing opportunities or processes so that learners can learn in their own ways and become better at what they are already doing as practitioners. This transformative teaching and learning and mentoring is a significant part of the opportunity to become a proficient practitioner.

## Mentoring and Adult Learning

One opportunity for helping individuals become more proficient practitioners is through student mentoring. As stated already, Daloz, in his proposed definition, considers mentoring 'the process of guiding the Journey of Adult Learners'.[16] In his research, Daloz looks at how adults change and develop and suggests that 'we grow as we age, not just bigger but in some ways better'.[17] In order to become a mentor, it is important to understand not only how transformative learning takes place in adult education but also how adults learn. According to Daloz,

> One of the most influential developmental theorists was Daniel Levinson and his associates in *The Seasons of a man's life* (1978). Levinson was the first to see clearly how mentors help us through crucial times in our lives and based his research on furthering Carl Jung's work. The core of Levinson's work is that we can understand common tasks that people confront as they face the problems associated with aging.[18]

Mentoring adults is crucial to help them understand what confronts them and to accompany them in the learning cycle. With problems associated with aging, for example, the learner can continue to learn and achieve wisdom within the limits imposed on them. The mentoring relationship is a vital support in that process.

In another branch of developmental theory, often termed 'The Stage Theory', which may help mentors understand how adults learn, Robert

15    Knowles, *The Making of an Adult Educator*, 146.
16    Daloz, *Mentor*, 17.
17    Ibid. 45.
18    Ibid. 46ff.

Kegan's book *The Evolving Self* provides us with his theory.[19] His research furthers Jean Piaget's theory that we pass through distinct and qualitatively different stages in how we construct our childhood experiences. This idea gained greater sophistication as applied to adults in the work of Lawrence Kohlberg and Carol Gilligan, who proposed that we pass through different stages in life.

Erik Erikson and James Fowler also put forward theories about different stages of development in the human person. Erikson reminds us that growth is fundamentally seated in a sense of basic trust, a capacity learned in the parent's arms, but arching through a lifetime of progressive reaching-out to others. To the degree that we can find this basic trust in ourselves, sharing ourselves, giving ourselves to others and finally affirming meaning where there is only uncertainty.[20]

James Fowler, in his research and in his book *Stages of Faith: The Psychology of Human Development and the Quest for Meaning*, has constructed a sequence of faith stages – 'transformations along the journey of faith'.[21] This sequence, he contends, illustrates how we can travel through different stages in our faith development, which in turn is related to how we learn to make meaning through different stages in our life cycle.

Knowing how adult learners learn is essential for mentors but it is also equally important to understand how learning changes the learner. First of all, mentors should realize that the value of a particular development depends on its context. Secondly, growth can be understood as a series of transformations in how we make meaning. As we grow older, each new horizon demands that we form new, overarching ways of making sense of the diversity and conflict we see with increasing clarity around us. For each, we need to learn to think in whole new ways.[22]

19    R. Kegan, *The Evolving Self: Problem and Process in Human Development* (Cambridge, MA: Harvard University Press, 1982), 14.
20    E. Erikson, *Childhood and Society* (New York: Norton, 1950), 222.
21    J. Fowler, *Stages of Faith: The Psychology of Human Development and the Quest for Meaning* (New York: HarperCollins, 1981), 34ff.
22    Daloz, *Mentor*, 133.

For Mezirow, 'the central process of adult development' entails the shift toward a 'more inclusive, differentiated, permeable and integrated perspective'.[23] Thus Daloz suggests that as we grow, we develop ways of knowing that can include more information and experience, but make still finer distinctions; ways that are ever more open to new learning but integrate and pull these learnings together in more comprehensive patterns. In summary, learning changes the learner because it is a shift in perspective from viewing oneself through the eyes of others towards increasingly seeing through one's own eyes.[24]

For the mentor, also, it is important to understand that if growth means transformation and transformation means the yielding of old structures of meaning-making to new, then the ways that this takes place are to acknowledge that:

1.  We learn as much or more from the way we are taught as from the content itself;
2.  We dismantle old structures and construct new ones;
3.  We understand that there are different perspectives in the learning process;
4.  The importance of life experience is essential to learning.

The process of mentoring has much to do here with exploring these four insights. The adult learner in a professional trusting relationship has an opportunity to perhaps unlearn some of the ways in which they experienced the learning process in the past as an adult or as a child. This can be most transforming in itself for the adult in a lifelong learning context.

## Mentoring as Relationship

Parker Palmer writes that if learning is about growth and growth requires trust and agency, then teaching is about recognizing and nourishing the conditions in which trust and agency can flourish and this is the role of

---

23   Mezirow, *Transformative Dimensions of Adult Learning*, 155.
24   Daloz, *Mentor*, 137.

the mentor. It is the partnership of teacher and student that finally determines the value of an education. The mentor's art lies in the nurturing of
that partnership.[25] As Palmer tells us:

> Mentors and apprentices are partners in an ancient human dance, and one of teach-
> ing's greatest rewards is the daily chance it gives us to get back on the dance floor. It
> is the dance of the spiralling generations in which the old empower the young with
> their experience and the young empower the old with new life, reweaving the fabric
> of the human community as they touch and turn.[26]

A. T. Wong and K. Premkumar, in their work, concur with Palmer:

> mentoring is a learning process where helpful, personal, and reciprocal relation-
> ships are built while focusing on achievement; emotional support is a key element.
> Within mentoring relationships, mentees develop and learn through conversations
> with more experienced mentors who share knowledge and skills that can be incor-
> porated into their thinking and practice. By comparison, tutoring or coaching is
> provision of academic and professional assistance in a particular area with a sole
> focus on competence.[27]

They suggest that there are three models of mentoring – the apprentice,
competency and reflective models. In the apprentice model, the mentee
observes the mentor and learns. In the competency model, the mentor
gives the mentee systematic feedback about performance and progress.
In the reflective model, the mentor helps the mentee become a reflective
practitioner. This learning object subscribes to the reflective model in which
mentoring is seen as an intentional, nurturing and insightful process that
provides a powerful growth experience for both the mentor and mentee.

The mentoring relationship advocated by Wong and Premkumar
involves helping learners learn, a relationship which shifts the mentor's
role from 'sage on the stage' to the 'guide on the side'. It is important for

---

25   P. Palmer, *The Courage to Teach* (New York: Jossey-Bass Inc., 1998; 2007 10th
     anniversary edn), 247.
26   Ibid. 25.
27   A. T. Wong and K. Premkumar, *An Introduction to Mentoring Principles, Processes
     and Strategies for Facilitating Mentoring Relationships at a distance* (2007), <http://
     www.usask.ca/gmcte/drupal/?q=resources>, accessed 29 January 2018, 1ff.

the mentor and the mentee to realize that the human nature of mentoring relationships must drive the mentoring process. It is also important for both parties in the relationship to recognize that this relationship is a 'learning' relationship. This learning object has three main goals:

1.  To introduce mentoring as a learning relationship that is rooted in the principles of adult learning;
2.  To identify the key tasks and processes for enhancing the mentoring relationship;
3.  To provide examples of process tools and strategies for understanding and operationalizing the mentoring relationship.

The quality of the mentoring relationship is important in the process of learning. The mentor has to allow the mentee space for his or her own potential in the learning process. Otherwise, the relationship could descend into the mentor's presence overpowering the mentee. The balance of power is important. 'Guide on the side' is a good description of the effective relationship which allows the mentee to discover new learning for themselves.

## The Importance of the Nature of Mentoring

The role of the mentor is to engender trust, issue a challenge, provide encouragement and offer a vision for the journey. Mentoring can be a powerful growth experience for both the mentor and mentee; mentoring is a process of engagement that is most successful when carried out collaboratively. It is a reflective process that requires preparation and dedication. Mentoring helps the mentee to negotiate new identities and reconceptualize themselves both as people and as professionals in addition to learning specific skills.

## Mentoring as a Transforming Tool in Third-Level Holistic Education

Mentoring can be considered a transforming tool in third-level holistic education in two major ways: (a) by passing on skills and helping the mentee to develop these skills in order to help the learner learn and (b) by helping the mentee to reconceptualize their identity. The mentoring relationship empowers the mentee and the mentor, while at the same time helping the learner learn in a different way to how they learned as a child, which in turn has a reciprocal effect on the mentor.

## (1) BY PASSING ON SKILLS AND HELPING THE MENTEE TO DEVELOP THESE SKILLS WHICH HELP THE LEARNER LEARN

As a mentor, you use your knowledge, experience and skills to help others. By mentoring in third-level holistic education, you can help people increase their effectiveness, advance their careers and create a more productive human person. Being a mentor can be very rewarding as it has many benefits.

### Benefits of mentoring

Research carried out in Durham University in 2009 illustrates the benefits of mentoring for the mentees and for the mentors. For the mentees, mentoring:

- Provides impartial advice and encouragement;
- Develops a supportive relationship;
- Assists with problem-solving;
- Improves self-confidence;
- Offers professional development;
- Encourages reflection on practice.

For the mentor, mentoring:

- Offers an opportunity to reflect on own practice;
- Enhances job satisfaction;
- Develops professional relationship;
- Enhances peer recognition;
- Uses one's experience, making it available to a new person;
- Widens one's understanding of the organization and the way it works;

- Enables one to practise interpersonal skills;
- Provides personal satisfaction through supporting the development of others.[28]

Lois Zachary points out that mentors, in addition to their expertise and experience, need to be familiar with specific process skills that can help the mentoring process. She suggests the following strategies:

1. Asking questions that will help mentees to reflect on and articulate their own thinking.
2. Reformulating statements helps mentors to clarify their own understanding and encourage mentees to reflect on what they articulated.
3. Summarizing helps to remind the mentoring partners of what has transpired and allows both parties to check out assumptions in the process.
4. Listening for silence – Silence can indicate boredom, confusion, discomfort or embarrassment. On the other hand, some individuals just need time out to think quietly.
5. Providing feedback that is authentic and suggests future action.[29]

Zachary continues:

> Because of their experience and accumulated insights, mentors can guide a mentee's sense of the possible. By fostering reflective practice, the mentor helps the mentee to take a long view and create a vision of what might be. Reflective practice should be encouraged during and after the mentoring relationship.[30]

As a mentor, you pass on valuable skills, knowledge and insights to your mentee to help them develop their career. Mentoring can help the mentee feel more and more confident and self-supporting. Mentees can also develop

---

28   Durham University, *Survey on the Benefits of Mentoring* (UK, 2009), <https://www.dur.ac.uk/hr/mentoring/mentoringguidelines/mentoringbenefits/>, accessed 29 January 2018.
29   L. J. Zachary, *The Mentor's Guide: Facilitating Effective Learning Relationships* (San Francisco, CA: Jossey-Bass, 2000),
30   Ibid.

a clearer sense of what they want in their careers and personal lives. They will develop greater self-awareness and see the world, and themselves, as others do. For an educational organization, mentoring is a good way of efficiently transferring valuable competencies from one person to another. This expands the organization's skills base, helps to build strong teams and strong leadership.

*Ethics of mentoring*

Good mentoring has a strong ethical component. The mentor ought to bear in mind:

- The responsibility of the learner for his/her own learning;
- Respect for the learner's right to make his/her own decisions and to live as he/she chooses;
- A non-judgemental approach that treats people with respect and honesty;
- Confidentiality regarding personal issues.

The power of the mentor is significant. The mentor has influence and it is vital that the mentee is not feeling uncomfortable or intimidated by the mentor. The mentor is responsibility for ensuring that their power and influence benefits the mentee. For example, decisions taken in a session should be recorded and both parties should sign off on the items discussed and actions agreed upon. This can help to make sure the mentee is empowered to explore and achieve agreed goals.

*Skills for mentoring as a transforming tool*

Caroline Smith et al. suggest that to be an effective mentor

> you need similar skills to those used in coaching, with one big difference – you must have experience relevant to the mentee's situation. This can be technical experience, management experience, or simply life experience. The most effective mentors have the desire to help, willing to spend time helping someone else, and remain positive throughout. Mentors need to be motivated to continue developing and growing – as the mentor's own development never stops. To help others develop, a mentor must

value their own growth too. Many mentors say that mentoring helps them with their own personal development.[31]

A mentor needs to have confidence and an assured manner – that is, the mentor needs to have the ability to critique and challenge mentees in a way that is non-threatening and helps them to look at a situation from a new perspective. The effective mentor knows how to ask the right questions – the best mentors ask questions that make the mentee do the thinking. An effective mentor also listens actively and is careful to process everything the mentee is saying. It is necessary for the mentor to watch body language, maintain eye contact, and understand which topics are difficult for the mentee to discuss. Showing someone that you are listening is a valuable skill in itself. It shows that you value what the person is saying and that you will not interrupt them. This requires patience and a willingness to delay judgement.

An effective mentor provides feedback – this should be done in a way that accurately and objectively summarizes what you have heard, but also interprets things in a way that adds value for the mentee. In particular, the mentor should use feedback to show an understanding of what the mentee's thinking approach has been. This is key to helping the mentee see a situation from another perspective. Always remember that mentoring is about transferring information, competence, and experience to mentees, so that they can make good use of these, and build their confidence accordingly. As a mentor, you are there to encourage, nurture and provide support, because you've already 'walked the path' of the mentee.

Smith et al. provide guidelines for effective mentoring:

(a) Set regular mentoring meetings.
   A mentoring relationship is one of mutual trust and respect. So meet regularly, and lead by example. The mentoring conversation may be informal, but treat the overall arrangement with formality and professionalism. If possible, conduct mentoring meetings away from the mentee's working environment. A change of environment helps remove the conversation from everyday perspectives.
(b) Be honest and open.

---

31   C. Smith et al., *Management Training and Leadership Training Online*, Mind Tools. com (London: Mind Tools Ltd 1996–2015).

If you're not honest, a mentoring meeting will probably be a waste of time for both of you. Discuss current top issues or concerns. Sometimes, an honest exchange leads to a mentor and mentee deciding that they don't really like or respect each other. It's better to know up front and build from this sort of understanding, rather than have it hurt the relationship.

(c) Build sustainable improvements not quick fixes.

Use the mentoring session to exchange views and give the mentee guidance, and do not just give the mentee immediate answers to a problem. A simple answer to a problem is rarely as valuable as understanding how to approach such problems in the future.

(d) Play by the rules.

Establish some rules or a charter for the mentoring arrangements, with desired outcomes. This could be a set agenda for points to cover, or some performance goals for the mentee to pursue outside of their regular appraisal structure. (One of the key reasons that mentoring can fail is that there is a fundamental misunderstanding about what's expected from the mentor and mentee.) Most mentoring arrangements work best when they're outside of the day-to-day line management relationship between people. That does not mean that you cannot mentor the people in your team, but it's often best to have a mentoring relationship that crosses reporting lines.[32]

Finally, Smith et al. give mentors some key points to bear in mind:

(e) Mentoring is a great way to progress a person's professional and personal development and help create a more productive organization. It can also be very rewarding – for the mentor and the mentee.

(f) The mentor should treat the mentoring relationship with the respect it deserves. The mentor should focus the relationship on the mentee's needs and use the powerful skills of smart questioning, active listening, and value-added feedback to achieve the best outcomes from your mentoring.[33]

Mentoring reminds the mentor that students are individuals who are at different learning stages, have differing goals and expectations and have needs differing from those of their mentors. Spending quality time with learners is important and actually believing in the potential of every student can make a difference to all. As Daloz argues, 'if every teacher made a point

32    C. Smith et al., Management Training and Leadership Training Online.
33    C. Smith et al., Management Training and Leadership Training Online.

of spending at least some real time with at least some students, our colleges and universities might be better places for genuine learning to occur'.[34]

## (2) BY HELPING THE MENTEE TO RE-CONCEPTUALIZE THEIR IDENTITY

A second major way that mentoring can be a transforming tool in third-level holistic education is by helping the mentee to re-conceptualize their identity. In Yendol-Hoppey and Dana's *Reflective Educator's Guide to Mentoring*, we are told that:

> Mentoring requires planned, intentional reflection on the ways years of experience as a thoughtful, reflective reform-minded teacher can be captured and translated effectively to the next generation of teachers. The goal of mentoring must be to cultivate these reform-minded practices.[35]

Yendol-Hoppey and Dana are concerned with the identity of the mentor teacher and how the mentor teacher conceptualizes the mentoring role in varying ways. In other words, the mentor has to have the power to understand mentoring by discovering the unique, effective form of mentoring that lies within themselves by carefully and critically scrutinizing the ways that they conceptualize their role as *mentor*.

However, one of the roles of mentoring as a transforming tool in third-level holistic education is to re-conceptualizing the mentee's identity. In an essay by Hall and Burns, 'Identity Development and Mentoring in Doctoral Education',[36] they use theories of identity to understand mentoring relationships between the faculty members and doctoral students who are prepared as educational researchers. My experience as a mentor to research students at master's and PhD level resonates with their research.

---

34    Daloz, *Mentor*, 239.
35    D. Yendol-Hoppy and N. F. Dana, 'Reflecting on Your Mentoring Practice', in *The Reflective Educator's Guide to Mentoring* (US: Corwin Press, 2009), 6.
36    L. Hall and L. Burns, 'Identity Development and Mentoring in Doctoral Education', *Harvard Educational Review* 79 (1) (2009), 49–70.

Hall and Burns write that mentoring in doctoral education is critical to students' development as professional researchers.[37] In order for the mentee to re-conceptualize their identity and in this case the researcher identity, 'it is necessary that the mentoring relationship improves when both faculty and students take the time to recognize and discuss how each conceptualizes what it means to be a researcher and from where those understandings come'.[38] They cite Pallas, who writes, 'Doing so requires embracing epistemological diversity in both teaching and scholarship'.[39]

One of the ways mentors can help mentees to re-conceptualize their researcher identity is to encourage students to express questions and ideas that do not necessarily agree with the mentor's own ideas and questions. Secondly, the mentor, if they critically reflect on their own identity, will empower and make it safer for the mentee to do the same. Anderson and Shannon had similar ideas. They believed that good mentors should be committed to three values: first, mentors should be disposed to opening themselves to their mentees – for example, allowing their mentees to observe them in action and conveying to them the reasons behind their decisions and actions. Second, mentors should be prepared to lead their mentees incrementally over time. Third, mentors should be willing to express care and concern about the personal and professional welfare of their mentees.[40]

Hall and Burns cite Shambaugh, who suggests that in the reconceptualizing of identities, it will benefit both mentors and mentees to explore and critically discuss what it means to be a member of a particular discipline or field and thus what it means to be a researcher. Students can continue to learn the skills needed to do research while at the same time engaging in open dialogue about how they conceptualize what it is to be a researcher.[41]

37    Ibid.
38    Ibid. 61.
39    A. M. Pallas, *Indigenous Research Methodologies*, ed. B. Chilisa (University of Botswana, 2001), 9.
40    E. Anderson and A. Shannon, 'Towards a Conceptualization of Mentoring', in T. Kerry and A. Shelton Mayes (eds) *Issues in Mentoring* (Buckingham: Open University Press, 1995), 25.
41    Hall and Burns, 'Identity Development and Mentoring in Doctoral Education', *Harvard Educational Review* 79 (1) (2009), 66.

Several conclusions are drawn from Hall and Burn's research. They include: (1) students who are helped to understand, negotiate, and acquire the identity capital involved in becoming professional researchers, intentionally and systematically – by mindful mentors and more intentional curriculum designs – are more likely to benefit from doctoral training; (2) mentors who make socialization more explicit and negotiable are likely to produce more (and more successful) graduates who enrich their profession; (3) as a result of more open negotiations, students are more likely to acquire identity capital and use it to attain important opportunities, such as opportunities to co-present at conferences, co-author research and teach courses that will make them more employable.[42] Re-conceptualizing identities will not solve all problems but it will go a long way towards changing attitudes.

## Conclusion

In their work, *Transformative Learning: Advocating for a Holistic Approach*, Papastamatis and Panitsides make the argument that:

> Adult Education and learning are inherently intertwined with change, change in knowledge, understanding, attitudes, beliefs, skills and/or behaviours. Traditionally, theory and research in adult education has examined learning as a purely cognitive process, drawing on rationality and cognitivism, such as in experiential learning (Kolb, 1984), critical thinking (Brookfield, 1989), reflective practice (Schön, 1983) and transformative learning (Freire, 1972; Mezirow, 1991).[43]

They put forward the view, posited by Mezirow,[44] that instead of looking at the adult learner as andragogy and, to a large extent, as self-directing theo-

---

42   Ibid. 67

43   A. Papastamis and E. A. Panitisides, *Transformative Learning: Advocating for a Holistic Approach* (Greece: University of Macedonia, 2014), 76 <http://dx.doi.org/10.5539/res.v6n4p76>, accessed 29 January 2018.

44   J. Mezirow, 'An Overview of Transformative Learning', in P. Sutherland (ed.), *Adult Learning: Concepts and Contexts* (New York: Routledge, 2005), 24–38.

ries have done, transformative learning evolves around the cognitive process of meaning-making. This constitutes a dynamic interpretative framework for contextualizing adult learning as a powerful lever of transformation.

However, taking this concept a step further and shifting the emphasis onto more holistic approaches – perceiving the individual as a whole, consisting of mind, body and spirit –holistic education transformation which addresses the whole person, mind, body and spirit, can change our perception of how adults learn. Mentoring today can be seen as a transforming tool in third-level holistic education by building on Mezirow's theory on how the learner makes meaning. As a mentor in holistic education, there is an opportunity for the mentor to guide the learner through the interface of the mind, body and spirit, physical, emotional and spiritual dimensions. I can relate this to my own experience of mentoring third-level students in research methodology:

*Mind*: The mentor can guide the learner cognitively and pass on the skills of research.

*Body and spirit*: The mentor can guide the learner in 'learning by doing'. Learning by doing is a holistic experience in which the whole person is engaged and on which learning is grounded, making it evident that ways of learning and knowing beyond the cognitive domain are equally important. By actually physically carrying out a research method in their research the learner realizes that learning and knowing beyond the cognitive is equally important to the cognitive dimension.

*Emotions*: J. M. Dirkx assumes that learning itself is inherently an imaginative, emotional act and that significant learning is impossible without emotion.[45] He implies that it is through emotions that deeply personal meaningful connections are made in order for learning to effectively take place. As a mentor to research students, it is important to understand that as adult learners they have a wealth of life experience and different worldviews

---

45    J. M. Dirkx, 'The Power of Feelings: Emotions, Imagination and the Construction of Meaning in Adult Learning', in S. B. Merriam (ed.), *The New Update on Adult Learning Theory: New Directions for Adult and Continuing Education*, no. 89 (San Francisco, CA: Jossey-Bass, 2001), 63–72.

that have to be taken into consideration before they carry out their research. It is important, therefore, for the mentor not to underestimate the role of emotions and feelings in the process of transformational learning. *Spiritual Dimension*: Spiritual learning also has to do with meaning-making.[46] Tisdell suggests that 'spirituality revolves around personal beliefs and experience of a divine spirit or higher purpose, determining how we construct meaning and what we individually and collectively experience and attend to and honor as the "sacred" in our lives'.[47]

As a mentor to students in research methodology, it is particularly important for me to realize these concepts as the students come from all different cultures and faiths to carry out research on many topics, some of which include social justice, leadership and pastoral care, management of non-profit organizations, personal and professional development, theology etc. Mentoring can act as a transforming tool in third-level education holistic education. In the words of the mentor in *The Odyssey*: 'Reason and heart will give you words, Telemachus; and a spirit will counsel others. I should say the gods were never indifferent to your life.' Transformative education is not indifferent to the life-world of learners. Such an education celebrates and embraces all that is precious about becoming what we are all called to become fully human and alive to the wonder of the world.

## Bibliography

Anderson, E., and Shannon, A., 'Towards a Conceptualization of Mentoring', in T. Kerry and A. Shelton Mayes (eds), *Issues in Mentoring* (Buckingham: Open University Press, 1995), 25–34.

46 S. B. Merriam, R. S. Caffarella and L. M. Baumgartner, *Learning in Adulthood: A Comprehensive Guide* (San Francisco, CA: Jossey-Bass, 2007, 3rd edn), 189.
47 E. J. Tisdell, *Exploring Spirituality and Culture in Adult and Higher Education* (San Francisco, CA: Jossey-Bass, 2003), 29.

Brookfield, S. D., *Understanding and Facilitating Adult Learning: A Comprehensive Analysis of Principles and Effective Practices* (San Francisco, CA: Jossey-Bass, 1986).

Daloz, L. A., *Mentor: Guiding the Journey of Adult Learners* (San Francisco, CA: Jossey-Bass, 1999, 2nd edn).

Dewey, J., *Experience and Education* (New York: Macmillan, 1938).

Dirkx, J. M., 'The Power of Feelings: Emotions, Imagination and the Construction of Meaning in Adult Learning', in S. B. Merriam (ed.), *The New Update on Adult Learning Theory: New Directions for Adult and Continuing Education*, no. 89 (San Francisco, CA: Jossey-Bass, 2001), 63–72.

Durham University, *Survey on the Benefits of Mentoring* (UK: Durham University, 2009), <https://www.dur.ac.uk/hr/mentoring/mentoringguidelines/mentor-ingbenefits/>, accessed 29 January 2018

Erikson, E., *Childhood and Society* (New York: Norton, 1950).

Fowler, J., *Stages of Faith: The Psychology of Human Development and the Quest for Meaning* (New York: HarperCollins, 1981).

Freire, P., *Pedagogy of the Oppressed* (New York: Herder and Herder, 1972).

Hall, L., and Burns, L., 'Identity Development and Mentoring in Doctoral Education', *Harvard Educational Review* 79 (1) (2009), 49–70.

Homer, *The Odyssey* (750 BCE).

Kearsley, G., *Andragogy (M. Knowles)* (2010), <http://tip.psychology.org>, accessed 29 January 2018.

Kegan, R., *The Evolving Self: Problem and Process in Human Development* (Cambridge, MA: Harvard University Press, 1982).

Knowles, M., *The Making of an Adult Educator: An Autobiography* (San Francisco, CA: Jossey-Bass, 1989).

Knowles, M., *The Modern Practice of Adult Education: Andragogy Versus Pedagogy* (New York: Association Press, 1950).

Knowles, M. et al., *Andragogy in Action: Applying Modern Principles of Adult Education* (San Francisco, CA: Jossey-Bass, 1984).

Martin, R. A., 'An Analysis of Holistic Schools' Literature', paper co-presented with Dr Scott H. Forbes at the American Education Research Association Annual Conference, California, 2004.

Merriam, S. B., Caffarella, R. S., and Baumgartner, L. M., *Learning in Adulthood: A Comprehensive Guide* (San Francisco, CA: Jossey-Bass, 2007, 3rd edn).

Mezirow, J., *Learning as Transformation: Critical Perspectives on a Theory in Progress* (San Francisco, CA: Jossey-Bass, 2000).

Mezirow, J., 'An Overview of Transformative Learning', in P. Sutherland (ed.), *Adult Learning: Concepts and Contexts* (New York: Routledge, 2005), 24–38.

Mezirow, J., *Transformative Dimensions of Adult Learning* (San Francisco, CA: Jossey-Bass, 1991).

Miller, R., *Journal of Holistic Education Review* (Now *Encounter: Education for Meaning and Social Justice*) (2004).

Pallas, A. M. *Indigenous Research Methodologies*, ed. Bagele Chilisa (University of Botswana, 2001).

Palmer, P., *The Courage to Teach*, 10th anniversary edn (New York: Jossey-Bass Inc., 2008, originally published in 1998).

Papastamis, A., and Panitisides, E. A., *Transformative Learning: Advocating for a Holistic Approach* (Greece: University of Macedonia, 2014), <http://dx.doi.org/10.5539/res.v6n4p74>, accessed 29 January 2018.

Shambaugh, R. N., 'Reframing Doctoral Programs: A Program of Human Inquiry for Doctoral Students and Faculty Advisors', *Innovative Higher Education* 24 (4) (2000), 295–308.

Smith, C. et al., Management Training and Leadership Training Online, MindTools.com (London: Mind Tools Ltd 1996–2015).

Tisdell, E. J., *Exploring Spirituality and Culture in Adult and Higher Education* (San Francisco, CA: Jossey-Bass, 2003).

Wong, A. T., and Premkumar, K., *An Introduction to Mentoring Principles, Processes and Strategies for Facilitating Mentoring Relationships at a Distance* (2007), <http://www.usask.ca/gmcte/drupal/?q=resources>, accessed 29 January 2018.

Yendol-Hoppy, D. and Dana, N. F., 'Reflecting on Your Mentoring Practice', in *The Reflective Educator's Guide to Mentoring* (US: Corwin Press, 2007), 113–127.

Zachary, L., *The Mentor's Guide: Facilitating Effective Learning Relationships* (San Francisco, CA: Jossey-Bass, 2000).

THOMAS G. GRENHAM

## 14 Educating for Tolerance: Learning about, from and within Diverse Religions and Beliefs in the Irish Primary School, a Strategy for Transformation

## Introduction

This chapter deals with transformative education from a religious education perspective in order to promote perspective change in Ireland and beyond. The discussion is grounded in a specifically Irish perspective and the debate around religious education in Irish primary schools. Religious education provides a service to the community in that it is part of forming integrated citizens for the common good of society. Religion is a significant component of cultural change and the life-giving and beneficial transformation of contemporary Ireland and Europe. The rise of political and religious extremism across Europe is a concern for many countries. This is fuelled by fear of difference, especially reflected in the migration crisis across the Mediterranean. However, economic globalization has a significant influence in creating the space for cultural and religious change. Teaching religion has a crucial and potentially life-giving transformative role to play in schools across Europe as it can educate for tolerance, acceptance and appreciation of different cultures and religions. A strategy for transformative dialogue is proposed towards the end of this chapter.

Currently in Ireland, there is a lot of debate about the role of religion and the teaching of religion in Irish primary schools. In view of the growing and changing cultural and religious demographics of Irish society, the rethinking of religion and religious education in primary schools has become significant for parents and children. There are more children from different cultural and religious backgrounds living in Ireland. Ireland has experienced a lot of migration into the country as a consequence of economic globalization and the free movement of people, goods, services and capital across the European Union in general. Ireland is no longer a mono-cultural or mono-religious island. Some might argue whether Ireland was ever mono-cultural or mono-religious, given its diverse history. However, contemporary Ireland is diverse in a new and different way. Its society is a plural society where many cultures, religions and beliefs co-exist. Hence, there is a need for choices regarding types of education and types of schools to meet the diverse educational requirements of parents.

## Special Forum Commissioned

The Forum on Patronage and Pluralism in the Primary Sector, commissioned by former Irish Minister of Education Ruairi Quinn in 2011, has become the basis for much political and educational exploration and its subsequent recommendations (2012) are being implemented. As a consequence, the National Council for Curriculum and Assessment (NCCA) was tasked with preparing a new state religious education curriculum known as ERB and Ethics (Education about Religions and Beliefs and Ethics). At the time of writing, no decision has yet been made regarding when or how the new curriculum will be implemented in schools. This ERB and Ethics proposal is viewed by many as a complementary programme, which would exist alongside the existing religious education programmes provided by the patrons of primary schools. The majority of primary schools in Ireland are faith-based: approximately 96 per cent. Catholic faith-based schools account for approximately 92 per cent of all Irish primary schools. Opponents of the new religious education curriculum fear that it will interfere with the predominantly faith-based ethos of most schools run by Christian denominations. All primary schools in Ireland are funded by the Irish state, whatever their particular secular or religious ethos.

Introducing ERB and Ethics will be a historical initiative as all religious education up to now has been developed and delivered by the various patrons of Irish primary schools, mostly from a Christian and Catholic perspective. Such a move by the state, should it become a reality, will open the way for all children from various religious and secular backgrounds to learn about their own and other secular and religious traditions. Children can learn about life-giving values from these living and practised traditions. It has not been decided whether ERB and Ethics ought to be compulsory or whether children could opt in or out. Not all religions of the world can be addressed in this proposed new curriculum and a decision needs to be taken regarding which world religions and beliefs can be adequately covered in the new curriculum. The Irish state agency tasked with overseeing the primary curriculum and the development of ERB and Ethics is the NCCA. This agency has recently published its report subsequent to a period of consultation with all stakeholders.[1] Such an addition to the existing curriculum, or as part of a possible revised national curriculum in the future, has the potential to transform learning and teaching in this area. A weakness of ERB and Ethics is the addition of 'Ethics' to the curriculum as ethics are part of most world religions, as well as the existing religious education programmes. Clarification is warranted regarding what kind of secular ethics is being proposed and whether this will add to or complement the teaching of religious ethics when children are tasked with learning (ethics/morality) from other religions. Otherwise, secular ethics could become an isolated and exclusive subject area for some learners. Again, the question is whether this is an option or a compulsory element of the curriculum and whether children will have the right to opt in or opt out of this ethics element if they are already participating in a religious education programme which includes ethics and morality, offered by various patrons of primary schools.

However, in my view, the new ERB and Ethics recommendation, once it is clarified and the ethics component is designed to be more inclusive,

1    For further details, see NCCA (2017), *Consultation on the Proposals for a Curriculum in Education about Religions and Beliefs (ERB) and Ethics: Final Report* (Dublin: National Council for Curriculum and Assessment), <http://www.ncca.ie/en/Curriculum_and_Assessment/Early_Childhood_and_Primary_Education/Primary-Education/Primary_Developments/ERB-and-E/Developments/Consultation/Consultation-Report-February.pdf>, accessed 29 January 2018.

may further enhance an education for tolerance as a minimum and may assist in the transformation of possible dangerous and extreme sectarian and fundamentalist perspectives now seen across Europe, particularly in France, Belgium and London. This fundamentalism (both secular and religious) has been seen and experienced across Europe in the recent terror attacks and in the rise in popularity of far-right political movements across the continent and beyond. The election of Donald Trump in the USA and the ongoing developments after the Brexit vote in Britain in June 2016 are some examples of a populism which is exclusive, anti-immigrant and prejudiced against people who belong to other races and ethnic groups. A pluralist and inclusive, diverse culture is held suspect in this rising tide of dangerous, misguided populism, the likes of which has not been seen since the 1930s and 1940s.

## Culture and Catholic Schools

The role of culture and religion in shaping society and in cultural perspective change is significant and should not be underestimated or indeed manipulated or misused by political leaders and political movements. The human need of every person to be connected to a particular narrative, tradition, religion or secular belief is significant. The contemporary Irish primary school is a microcosm of the growing cultural and religious diversity of the broader Irish population and Europe generally. The primary school is a crucial domain for inclusive religious education for a more plural, integrated and tolerant society. Such an education, when implemented, could transform individuals and communities in a life-giving way, leading them to live better lives, to create more inclusive societies and to build a more compassionate marketplace.

Catholic schools launched a new religious education curriculum in 2015, entitled *Catholic Preschool and Primary Religious Education Curriculum for Ireland*. The programme 'Grow in Love' is being developed based on this curriculum. It was rolled out for junior and senior infant classes in

September 2015 and will be fully implemented for all classes by 2018. What is innovative about this initiative is not only that this Catholic programme educates within its own faith tradition; it also educates in a specific way about other religious traditions and includes ethics and values that these traditions reflect in their lived practices and rituals. A drawback of this new and imaginative programme is that it does not officially allocate enough time to education about other selected religions and beliefs. Currently, the programme allows two weeks in the whole year to be allocated to learning about other religions and beliefs for senior classes in primary schools. The idea is to prepare primary children who will be transitioning into secondary education and who wish to study religion in general and world religions in particular. Essentially, the new Roman Catholic programme offers children the opportunity to be grounded in their own Catholic Christian tradition and to learn religious and spiritual literacy, which includes inter-religious literacy. This prepares them for opportunities for dialogue with other religious traditions and secular beliefs impacting on their lives.

## Connected to Traditions

Every human being needs a sense of life-giving connectedness in order to contribute to a meaningful and fruitful process of creating an inclusive society or community. Such a process can include participation in a particular faith community, or it can be about fostering a sense of spirituality in a so-called 'non-religious' or purely secular belief society. There needs to be recognition that there are diverse ways of living and thinking about humankind, its environment, and its meaning and purpose. Different traditions and belief systems exist in a plural society.

It can be claimed that every human person is an embodied spiritual person. It is often said that the human spirit is unquantifiable. This is experienced in sports, academics, film – in every human endeavour, the human spirit achieves new heights and potential. Therefore, it can be said that spirituality does not necessarily depend upon a particular organized religion.

A life-giving spirituality, in the broadest sense, is not dependent upon a specific traditional 'organized' religious worldview. However, it is helpful to have some form of actual or concrete expression that creates a structure in which our deepest desires can surface and be named and celebrated in a life-giving and meaningful way.

For Irish primary schools, a structured and organized religious world-view, such as that reflected for Catholics in the 'Grow in Love' programme and in the 'Follow Me' series of the Church of Ireland, can help shape a specific religious consciousness in order to allow engagement with other religious perspectives without diluting the particular religious identity of the young adherents. Educate Together schools have developed in Ireland since 1978 as an alternative to so-called 'religious' or confessional approaches to religious education. These schools are becoming popular in Ireland as an alternative choice to provide a secular education that encourages and develops the ethical dimension of every child. The universal spiritual nature of every child is nourished through learning about and celebrating different religions in the classroom. This is religious education which does not involve formation in a particular faith system or secular belief system. Though the children in these schools learn about different belief systems and religious traditions, they do not practise a specific religion within the school setting. Children are taught to appreciate the ethical dimensions of religions and belief systems. In this way, children learn from what religious traditions teach about the environment, justice, spirituality, respect, and so on.

Another developing type of primary school is the Community National School (CNS), the first of which were opened in 2008. Currently, there are eleven such schools, which are run by the Irish stage ETBs (Educational Training Boards). The schools have an educational programme entitled 'Goodness Me Goodness You', which supports the three dimensions of an inclusive and transformative religious education. These dimensions are: learning about a religion or belief; learning from a belief system (ethics dimension); and learning into a belief system (faith-formation dimension), for those for whom this is appropriate. In this type of school, faith forma-tion is a part of religious education for children, as well as learning about and from other religions and beliefs. (For a detailed overview of individual religious education programmes offered in various types of Irish primary schools, see the NCCA website.) In relation to the merits of learning into a belief system, John Keast suggests that 'learning about religion is insufficient in itself to produce the kind of respectful attitudes that community and school cohesion requires in a multi-faith society'.[2]

Religious practice may indeed happen after school time, at home or indeed within the faith community. Whatever parents choose for their children, I believe that it is important to have a specific formation in a particular life-giving religion or belief – such as Christianity, Islam, Judaism and Buddhism, for example – or indeed a secular belief system to give a tangible shape and identity to a particular spiritual vision. Such formation helps when it comes to dialogue with alternative religions and points of view. Without anchors, signposts and the wisdom of long-established traditions, spirituality is reduced to whimsical feelings and fantasies that could be harmful and life-restricting.

## Faith Formation Only in Schools?

The debate about religious education in Irish schools hinges on whether or not a particular faith formation within a specific religious tradition should occur in the school during school time. If faith formation happens outside of school hours, that may be appropriate and allows the school to spend more time on areas like maths, science, English, and so on. But then, why should the subject of religious education be taken out of the school? One could ask why not take other subjects out of the school, such as drama or PE, for instance, and have these subjects be taught after school hours. Perhaps parents could teach their children at home. Home schooling is becoming

---

2    See J. Keast, 'Use of "Distancing" and "Simulation"', in J. Keast, ed., *Religious Diversity and Intercultural Education: A Reference Book for Schools* (Strasbourg: Council of Europe publishing, 2007), 62.

popular for some parents interested in ensuring a holistic education for their children. With growing internet access and increasing numbers of parents wanting individual educational requirements (special needs) for their children, is the school itself necessary? Of course, the question can be asked: should schools be the only places where faith formation takes place? The answer is no. The parish or the community of believers should provide support for faith development and all stakeholders must see themselves as partners in the holistic education effort.

The question of a religious ethos surfaces for many parents. With the majority of Irish primary schools having a Roman Catholic ethos, how will that ethos or 'way of doing things' be sustained and fostered in a multidenominational and multicultural Ireland going forward? Religions are living traditions that need to be practised and lived to be understood as life-giving pathways for developing life-giving and authentic spirituality. If we believe in a holistic education for our children, then spirituality is a vital part of that vision and needs to find a place within every school, home and community.

The 2011 and the 2016 censuses illustrate the changing demography of Ireland. Such a changing demography impacts on all aspects of life, especially the school system. The primary school system is predominantly Christian, with over 90 per cent of primary schools under Catholic Church management. Any change in Ireland's school system will have to reflect that the majority of the Irish population is Roman Catholic: 84 per cent indicated on the 2011 census form that they are Catholic, an increase on the previous census, and 6 per cent of the total population in the Republic of Ireland indicated that they have no religion. In the 2016 census, there was a slight decrease, with 78 per cent claiming to be Roman Catholic, and 10 per cent of the total population indicated that they have no religion. While there is a majority of Roman Catholics in Ireland, there is also a significant increase in those who claim to have no religion. There has also been an increase in the presence of other religions. For example, there are over 60,000 Muslims currently living in Ireland. Religion and the diversity of religious traditions cannot be ignored in the Irish primary school system, no matter what type of patronage and ethos governs the school.

## The Turn to Religion

Religion has moved into a much more public space in western European societies recently and is enjoying greater visibility some of it for the wrong reasons. Consequently, there is debate about its practice and role in society. Religions and religious practice are part of living faith systems, not to be privatized and fossilized in a secular museum outside the school to be visited now and then. This is an important point when it comes to religious education in Irish schools, especially in primary school. Societies cannot ignore the religious issue in the world today. If they do, they do so at their peril. Think of 9/11 in America and numerous other terrorist attacks around the globe. The western world in particular may have thought religion was irrelevant prior to 9/11 as it pursued its secular agenda. However, western countries are now taking religion seriously, not just out of fear of terrorism, but because of the good influence that a religious perspective can have. This is why religion has become a significant contributor to the political, economic, and social policy debates taking place in the west. Courses in Islam became very popular after the attacks on the Twin Towers in New York. People are learning about religious fundamentalism, as well as studying about the meaning and purpose of religious pluralism. Think of countries where religion is at the heart of the nation state, particularly Middle Eastern countries, North African and some Oceanic countries. It can be said that the USA is a very religious country and is influenced predominantly by a form of Christian religion when it comes to domestic and foreign policy, despite the first amendment of its constitution, which contains a clear separation of religion and state. Societies, and particularly western liberal democracies, cannot afford to ignore the major political influence the religious dimension has on the globalized world. Therefore, citizens everywhere need to know about the religious politic in the global marketplace that all citizens of the world share. For Ireland, both confessional and non-confessional schools play a key part in fostering an informed religious consciousness. Hence, religious education within the Irish education system and other education systems is important and relevant, as it serves to inform all citizens of the role of religion(s) for the life-giving transformation of the world.

## Learning about and from Diverse Cultures and Religions

Understanding cultures and how they encounter themselves, the environment and religion is essential for peace, harmony and prosperity in every part of the world. All persons are situated in a historical, cultural context and are primarily shaped by its contours, conditioned by its inherent logic, and emotionally embedded in its assumptions. Cultures have religious/spiritual and secular dimensions that exert a significant influence on the overall dynamic of personal and communal formation. The profession of teaching in the human world meets differences of all kinds – cultural, religious, gender, sexual orientation, race, class, ethnicity, and so on. Each of these differences can be further differentiated as no two people within any of these ways of being in the world have the same precise viewpoint. Theologian Michael Paul Gallagher, citing cultural anthropologist Mary Douglas, observes that

> Differences between cultures are rooted in how people learn to perceive their social relationships with one another. In this regard four factors are mutually reinforcing: the acquired ways of perceiving one's place in society, the social context and its dominant patterns of interaction, individual behaviour choices, and the forms of religious vision typical of different cultures.[3]

For effective teaching and learning, attending to differences and perceiving how these unique qualities can enhance mutual respect, democratic participation and responsible citizenship is vital for the life of any society/community. A skilled teacher of religion will help a child/learner to not only affirm their sense of identity (who they are and how they belong); the

---

3    See M. P. Gallagher, *Clashing Symbols: An Introduction to Faith and Culture* (Mahwah, NJ/NY: Paulist Press, 1998), 25.

attuned teacher is also a resource and a support for the learner's capacity and potential to learn and to grow as a person. This happens because the teacher has the capacity to be present to the learner within his/her cultural and religious/spiritual dimension.

Effective teachers of religion and secular beliefs are acutely aware of cultural dimensions associated with learning, including the postmodern cultural dynamic of the deconstruction of 'grand narratives'. Postmodernism is a cultural perspective that influences and shapes the deconstruction of meta or grand narratives that have been in place as some kind of organizing ideology for how we should live and behave in the world. Well-known narratives, such as communism, capitalism, Nazism, fascism, democracy, secularism, and so on, are ideologies created to shape some kind of uniform consensus. Communism, Nazism, fascism, and others have already been deconstructed. Religious worldviews can be viewed as metanarratives for shaping people's outlook and spirituality. These religious narratives are frameworks for meaning and purpose for themselves, the world, and an ultimate reality. Theologian T. A. Veling writes extensively about this and posits that 'to enter the postmodern world is, in effect, to enter the interpretive discourse of our cultural, religious, and social frameworks'.[4]

Not only do differences and similarities emerge from within a specific faith/belief perspective; differences and similarities can also arise between and across diverse religious and cultural traditions. As people engage with each other in a multicultural and multidenominational society like Ireland today, they engage the worldviews and meaning-making dimensions that contrast with a previously embedded mono-cultural reality. Though a teacher might claim to be of 'no particular religious and cultural worldview', an extreme form of postmodernism would want us to believe that there is the obvious reality a personal and communal narrative – story, myth, legend, ritual, belief, and so on – to understand and make sense of the world. Because every person has his or her own narrative of identity, it is, therefore, not possible to have developed a worldview or meaning

---

4    See T. A. Veling, *Living in the Margins: Intentional Communities and the Art of Interpretation* (Oregon, USA: Wipf and Stock, 2002, 2nd edn), 32.

perspective from 'nowhere'. There is no neutral ground or neutral world-view from which to interpret the world around us.

Educators learn that a culture is the essential amniotic fluid for the life of every person in relationship with themselves, others, the environ-ment, and an ultimate reality. Every human being belongs to a particular cultural heritage and this inherited culture is the primary source people draw on for understanding themselves, others, creation and a transcendent reality. In addition, many find that a particular spiritual narrative is help-ful in defining who they are and how they belong in a particular culture. Emerging deep from within a culture and sometimes rooted in an organized religious structure, this spiritual outlook can be an agent of empowerment and transformation for people. In relation to difference and education, an important question is: how do we begin to reflect on our culture, religion and beliefs and their underlying assumptions? In order to answer this question, another concern arises: is it really possible to stand outside our own cultural, religious and non-religious narrative from time to time and explore our behaviour, analyse our thinking and feeling, and critique our attitudes towards others, the world, transcendence, and ourselves?

In response to these questions, I believe that when we engage with others from different cultures, religious worldviews, sexual orientations, genders, and so on, we then become conscious that we, too, belong to a particular cultural context. We become acutely aware that we are shaped by this milieu and some can have ambivalent feelings towards those who are not from the same cultural context. For teachers/educators, there is a challenge to engage the 'difference' of the other seriously and celebrate it in the classroom. There is always a danger that, consciously or uncon-sciously, an attempt will be made to make the other become 'the same' as the dominant culture.[5] In other words, the other could become essentially an image of my own culture or even over-identify with my sense of what it means to be Irish, for example. Sometimes we call this response 'cultural integration', whereby those we perceive as different think, feel, and behave

---

5    For more philosophical underpinning to how we should treat the other, see the writings of Emmanuel Levinas, particularly 'God and Philosophy', in *The Levinas Reader*, trans. S. Hand (Hoboken, NJ: Wiley-Blackwell publishers, 2001), 166ff.

like us politically, morally, religiously, socially, and economically. For example, the travellers in Ireland have resisted many attempts at 'integration' into the dominant and mainstream culture of Irish society. The travellers themselves perceive this attempt at integrating them into mainstream Irish society as an attempt to destroy their unique way of life. From the outside, it seems that conformity, uniformity, and sameness are the preferred option for any society to function well, to advance and to live in perpetual harmony. However, this is not always the case and such an assumption could be questioned. The imposing of a particular ideology without consent on various groups in order for them to conform to a specific vision of society causes unhelpful tension and conflict. A way forward might be to understand how every person is shaped and conditioned in a particular cultural perspective and then learn how various cultural groups can make a unique contribution to a diverse society, as opposed to insisting upon a linear, mono-cultural/mono-religious society. Learning about, from and within one's own particular narrative, culture and religious tradition is essential in the endeavour to know the other. Teaching children the art of respectful conversation is very significant.

## Conclusion

Theologian Roger Haight observes that

> Dialogue involves a give and take, a communication that requires not just testifying, announcing, and teaching but also listening, hearing, and learning. It presumes mutual recognition and at some level a sense of equality among the participants as a characteristic of the conversation.[6]

In relation to conversation and the principles of carrying out a fruitful and life-giving exchange, Haight further suggests that 'Dialogue also rules

6    R. Haight, *The Future of Christology* (New York and London: Continuum, 2005), 134.

out any proselytism or aggressive, conquering evangelisation'.[7] Dialogue/ conversation is the preferred option or strategy for an interculturation/ interculturalism that offers a process for critical reflection that leads towards life-giving transformative action and learning for an inclusive plural society.

Conversation is difficult. In view of that, some guidelines or princi-ples are suggested for conducting an intercultural conversation in the Irish primary classroom, keeping in mind that these principles do not make the process any easier:

1. Conviction within a tradition/narrative is necessary for a groundedness in a particular identity;
2. Mutual respect between individual persons and communities;
3. Trust, endurance, and integrity are invaluable in conversation designed to initiate life-giving transformation;
4. Listening to, and not just hearing, the other perspective is a skill that can enrich understanding and empathy;
5. Kenosis: Emptying out negative or destructive prejudices is a process which allows space to examine exclusivity and introduce inclusive conversation;
6. Understanding plurality and diversity is helpful for transcending ethnocentrism;
7. The managing of conflict appropriately and respectfully is necessary. Conflicts are inevitable between individuals, but they can be managed in ways that are conducive to respectful conversation and the genuine acceptance and appreciation of the gifts of the other, as well as one's own.

The transformation of society into a tolerant and democratic reality needs a transformative learning strategy, like the one outlined above, which enables learners to accept who they are and be comfortable with their own particular religious and cultural identities. The primary school is an important con-nection in this task, as already discussed. A transformative learning strategy within primary schools will go a long way in understanding pluralism and

---

7    Haight, *The Future of Christology*, 134.

the great need for civic inclusion and political and social representation in all aspects of Irish society and beyond. Religious education beyond faith formation within Irish primary schools can help learners understand, tolerate, accept and appreciate the other who comes from a different religious and secular belief system. Thus, a great service is provided for the pluralist democratic community in developing an inclusive and tolerant perspective change. Transformative learning of this nature ought to be a priority for all within the primary system and should not have to wait until a later educational stage.

# Bibliography

Aslan, E. et al. (eds), *Islam, Religions, and Pluralism in Europe* (Wiesbaden: Springer VS, 2016).

Catholic Schools Partnership, *Catholic Primary Schools in a Changing Ireland: Sharing Good Practice on Inclusion of All Pupils* (Maynooth: Columba Centre, 2015).

Coolahan, J. et al., *The Forum on Patronage and Pluralism in the Primary Sector: Report of the Forum's Advisory Group* (Dublin: Department of Education and Skills, 2012).

Gallagher, M. P., *Clashing Symbols: An Introduction to Faith and Culture* (Mahwah, NJ: Paulist Press, 1998).

Grenham, T., 'Discovering the Universal in the Particular: A Vision for Christian Mission Spirituality', *Missiology: An International Review* XL (1) (2012), 49–61.

Grenham, T., 'Pluralism in the Primary School: Engaging with and Learning about Cultures and Religions', in T. Grenham and P. Kieran (eds), *New Educational Horizons in Contemporary Ireland: Trends and Challenges* (Bern: Peter Lang, 2012), 255–275.

Grenham, T., *The Unknown God: Religious and Theological Interculturation* (Bern: Peter Lang, 2005).

Haight, R., *The Future of Christology* (New York and London: Continuum, 2005).

Hession, A., *Catholic Primary Religious Education in a Pluralist Environment* (Dublin: Veritas, 2015).

Hiebert, P. G., *Transforming Worldviews: An Anthropological Understanding of How People Change* (Michigan: Baker Academic, 2008).

Irish Episcopal Conference, *Catholic Preschool and Primary Religious Education Curriculum for Ireland* (Dublin: Veritas, 2015).

Keast, J., 'Use of "Distancing" and "Simulation"', in J. Keast (ed.), *Religious Diversity and Intercultural Education: A Reference Book for Schools* (Strasbourg: Council of Europe publishing, 2007), 61–65.

Lane, D., *Stepping Stones to Other Religions: A Christian Theology of Inter-Religious Dialogue* (Dublin: Veritas, 2011).

Levinas, E., 'God and Philosophy', in *The Levinas Reader*, trans. S. Hand (Hoboken, NJ: Wiley-Blackwell, 2001), 166–189.

NCCA, *Consultation Report* (Dublin: NCCA, 2017).

NCCA, *An Overview of Education about Religions and Beliefs (ERB) and Ethics Content in Patron's Programmes* (Dublin: NCCA, 2015).

Renehan, C., *Openness with Roots: Education in Religion in Irish Primary Schools* (Newcastle upon Tyne: Cambridge Scholars Publishing, 2014).

Tuohy, D., *Denominational Education and Politics: Ireland in a European Context* (Dublin: Veritas, 2013).

Veling, T. A., *Living in the Margins: Intentional Communities and the Art of Interpretation* (Oregon, USA: Wipf and Stock, 2002).

## 15   The Centrality of Adult Faith Development for the Future of the Catholic Church in Ireland

## Introduction

In light of the exceptional circumstances facing the Catholic Church in Ireland, it is no longer possible to assume that things can go on as before. The Church at present could be described as being under siege. There is a sense of paralysis, as revelations regarding abuse perpetrated in the past have left the hierarchy and other religious leaders coping with an unprecedented situation. Understandably, leaders are constantly focused on dealing with the latest crisis, and thus there is little focus on the long-term view, which requires critical reflective and actively involved Catholics.

This chapter proposes that although immediate issues cannot be ignored, the nurturing of ordinary Catholics in their faith is a pressing and urgent need. The Gospel imperative of living and preaching the good news remains a challenge, even as people struggle to come to terms with the horrendous crimes that have been laid at the Church's door. This chapter will examine religious education for adults, in particular those who are contributing to maintain and develop structures within parish communities in a voluntary capacity. The major hypothesis underpinning this discourse is that the faith development of adults is fundamental to a renewed hope and dedication among members of the Church community, and has the potential to enable growth in people's own lives, and in their understanding of their mission as baptized Christians. The Second Vatican Council was the catalyst for a seismic shift in the way lay people contribute to parish life; while this contribution is now accepted as standard, the necessary educational background required for such involvement has not been put in place, despite many Church documents stressing the importance of such education.[1] The *General Directory for Catechesis* names one of the particular tasks of adult catechesis as encouraging adults 'to assume responsibility of the Church's mission and to be able to give Christian witness in society'.[2]

This research is structured around two major issues undergirding education: the philosophical and psychological perspectives involved. First, it explores how philosophical questions influence and direct the kind of education that is, or could be, offered to, in particular, lay people who are involved in ministries in their local community. An examination of the terminology used to describe faith education within a Church context will help to illuminate the philosophical position from which this education is offered, and thus illustrate the importance of adult educational methodologies.

Secondly, research in the area of developmental psychology will be identified as a key influencing factor on education and, especially within this context, adult faith development. Emphasis will be placed on theories concerning the development of the self and faith development. This chapter will also ask how developmental theory can be of benefit in the light of the current crisis in the Irish Catholic Church, and thus provide some insight into the ways in which appropriate adult faith development can be offered to lay people in ministry and the parish generally.

## Philosophy and Theology in Adult Faith Development

Why education? This question, which is so fundamental to what happens in the educational process, is rarely asked, except by theorists in the sometimes rarefied atmosphere of educational institutions. However, if true

---

1    For example, Congregation for the Clergy, *General Directory for Catechesis* (Dublin: Veritas, 1998); International Council for Catechesis, *Adult Catechesis in the Christian Community: Some Principles and Guidelines* (Slough: St Paul, 1990); Irish Episcopal Conference, *Share the Good News*, 2010; John Paul II, *Catechesi Tradendae: Catechesis in Our Time* (Sydney: St Paul's, 1979). The two major documents from the Vatican on catechesis are: Congregation for the Clergy, *General Catechetical Directory*, and the earlier document of the same name from the Sacred Congregation for the Clergy, *General Catechetical Directory* (Sydney: E. J. Dwyer, 1972).

2    *GCD*, paragraph 175.

educators, including those in the Church, do not explore why they do what they do, then they are in danger of betraying the very purpose they seek to fulfil.[3] Faith education in parishes and dioceses, if it is to be effective, needs to move beyond training people to undertake a particular ministry, without providing them with a more fundamental understanding of the background to the ministry and the importance of undertaking this task on behalf of the community.

There are a variety of approaches to education and there are a variety of philosophical starting points and each may be appropriate within a given context.[4] One school of thought which can be easily identified in adult faith education is one which emphasizes faith education as being focused on intellectual understanding of the faith (liberal adult education, as defined by Elias and Merriam).[5] There is a primacy given to the intellectual element in assent to faith, since 'understanding comes by the power of the intellect

3    C. Silberman, *Crisis in the Classroom* (New York: Random House, 1970). Silberman
      explores this question in relation to school education, but it equally can be asked of
      education in any sphere.
4    J. L. Elias and S. B. Merriam, *Philosophical Foundations of Adult Education* (Malabar,
      FL: Krieger Publishing Company, 2005, 3rd edn). It is beyond the scope of this chapter
      to explore each of these schools of thought but even the titles help to illustrate the
      complexity of the starting point for the education of adults: liberal adult education;
      progressive adult education; behaviourist adult education; humanist adult education;
      radical and critical adult education; and analytic philosophy of adult education. Faith
      educators often began using other starting points.
5    J. Astley, *The Philosophy of Christian Religious Education, How Faith Grows: Faith
      Development and Christian Education* (London: National Society/Church House
      Publishing, 1994). Astley examines some of the particular concerns in the philosophy
      of education when religious or faith education is being discussed. Some educational-
      ists such as Hirst believe that any religious education, whose aim is to nurture people
      in the Christian community, is not education because 'the presentation of particu-
      lar commitments as if they were radically disputable on rational grounds is seen as
      anti-intellectual'. P. H. Hirst, 'Education, Catechesis and the Church School', *British
      Journal of Religious Education* 3 (3) (1981), 87. Hirst's assertion can be challenged in
      the context of children, of whom he writes here, but the education of adults normally
      includes mature people who are eager to challenge what they are presented by any
      Church teacher. A 'shared praxis' model of adult faith development, proposed below,
      is essential dialogical.

guided by revelation and the Church's teaching'.[6] As Aquinas wrote, 'Now the act of believing is an act of the intellect assenting to the divine truth at the command of the will moved by the grace of God'.[7]

This emphasis on reason as a central element of faith is particularly important for adult Christians, as they strive to answer the questions posed by living the Christian life. Within the Catholic Church, adults have become the focus of faith education in recent decades. Thus the *General Catechetical Directory* (1971) states that:

> Catechesis for adults, since it deals with persons who are capable of an adherence that is fully responsible, must be the chief form of catechesis. All other forms, which are indeed necessary, are in some way related to it.[8]

This statement marks a significant shift in direction for the Catholic Church post-Vatican II, from a predominantly child-centred education to a greater balance between the religious education of adults and the religious education of children.[9] (Prior to this period, the Church always had some adult education, but primarily focused on education for ordained ministry.) The Church has gradually come to recognize, along with society in general, that education is pivotal to the ongoing development of the individual and of the community. This trend is particularly discernible from the 1970s onwards.[10] Education became imperative in the years after Vatican II, as various council documents requiring change were issued, in turn, and clergy and laity alike endeavoured to both understand and implement them, with

6    T. H. Groome, *Christian Religious Education: Sharing Our Story and Vision* (San Francisco, CA: Jossey-Bass, 1999, 2nd edn), 58.

7    St Thomas Aquinas, *Summa Theologica*, Q. 6, Art. 2, trans. Fathers of the English Dominican Province, 3 vols, vol. 2 (New York: Joseph F. Wagner, 1949), 1201.

8    *GCD*, paragraph 20.

9    In the Vatican Council itself, the beginnings of an appreciation of the importance of religious education for adults can be identified. See *Gravissimum Educationis: Declaration on Christian Education*, articles 10–12, which stresses the importance of higher education for lay people.

10   The *GCD* statement does not mark the beginning of adult education in the Catholic Church, but from the early 1970s onwards, the average Catholic parish began to devote some of its energies to adults in a systematic way not seen before.

great attention given to knowledge of the Church's teaching as a means of bringing about greater adherence to practice of the faith.

*The General Catechetical Directory* issued a strong mandate for adult faith development in its 1971 statement, and in the 1970s and 1980s the catechesis of adults moved into the mainstream of the Catholic Church's educational endeavours. In 1999, the Council for Research and Development conducted a survey of the nature and extent of adult religious in Ireland. This research concluded that:

> Adult religious education in Ireland today is vibrant enough to profit from a degree of change. This is a vigorous, rapidly growing sector with roots all around the country.[11]

This conclusion was reached in 1999, but many of the post-Vatican II educational initiatives reviewed in that research are now defunct. The current situation of adult education faith development, while there has been expansion in some areas, would suggest that this conclusion did not bring about the change that had been envisaged, despite a number of very important developments. Notable among these developments was the establishment of the office of a resource person for the Council for Pastoral Renewal and Adult Faith Development at the Irish Catholic Bishops' Conference, and the publication of *Share the Good News: National Directory for Catechesis in Ireland*. In local parishes, however, there is a tendency to focus any educational efforts for adults on providing training for people to fill gaps in the ministries of the parishes, while there is little comprehensive faith education, with notable exceptions.

## Terminology and Adult Faith Development

In exploring a philosophy of faith education for adults, the language one uses is pivotal. In order to employ an inclusive understanding of what is involved in enabling the adult to come to an adult faith, the term 'adult

---

11    A. Hanley, 'Faith for Life: Adult Religious Education in Ireland: A Survey' (Council for Research and Development, 1999).

faith development' is used in *Share the Good News: National Directory for Catechesis in Ireland*:

> 'faith development' as an all-inclusive term, allows us to treat together, under one heading, when appropriate, all the necessary and nuanced meanings that terms such as initial proclamation, initiation and catechesis, for example, suggest but cannot individually contain. Those who are charged with faith development, therefore, within a particular Christian community whether at parish or inter-parish level, at deanery, diocesan, regional or national level, will need ... to be adequately educated and trained in discerning roles, what forms of faith development are necessary, appropriate and of value for particular individuals, groups and communities.[12]

This term draws attention to the fact that faith has to continue to grow and that adults need to constantly 'develop' their faith, as 'Adults cannot be content with primary school religious knowledge. Doubts and difficulties about faith nearly always come from misunderstanding or lack of adult knowledge about our religion.'[13] To help adults to have a robust faith to deal with the challenges of life, adult faith development needs to draw upon a wide range of sources, including the life experience of the adults in the group. Sources such as the human sciences, including psychology, sociology, anthropology and cultural studies enable the learner gain insights into what it means to be fully human.[14]

Pope Francis advocates this breadth of sources for evangelization (and by extension for adult faith development) when he writes,

> A theology – and not simply a pastoral theology – which in dialogue with other sciences and human experiences is most important for our discernment on how best to bring the Gospel message to different cultural contexts and groups.[15]

12   Irish Episcopal Conference, *Share the Good News*, paragraph 64.
13   Ibid. paragraph 68.
14   Adult education as a discipline strongly emphasizes the importance of recognizing the experience of adults as they come to education. This has been one of the fundamental tenets of the discipline, since the seminal work of people such as M. Shepherd Knowles, *The Modern Practice of Adult Education: From Pedagogy to Andragogy* (New York: Cambridge, 1980, revised and updated edn), and S. D. Brookfield, *Understanding and Facilitating Adult Learning: A Comprehensive Analysis of Principles and Effective Practice* (San Francisco, CA: Jossey-Bass, 1986).
15   *EG*, paragraph 133.

There are occasions when the use of the word 'catechesis' is entirely appropriate. Adults who decide to become members of the Catholic Church are initiated through a process known as the Rite of Christian Initiation of Adults (RCIA).[16] The intention is to socialize people into the tradition and rituals of the Catholic community. In this situation, it can be taken for granted that the adults involved are freely submitting themselves to becoming members of the Church. In the process known as the 'catechumenate', future Church members are given 'that specific formation by which the adult, converted to the faith, is brought to the confession of baptismal faith during the Easter Vigil'.[17]

In this chapter, the term 'adult faith development' is used to denote the education of adults within the local Catholic community, in preference to 'catechesis', 'religious education' or 'religious formation'. Adult faith development is chosen since it denotes a dynamic process which is reflective of the ongoing development which continues in adults throughout their lives. This choice supports the presumption that adults are not empty vessels to be filled, but active participants in any education experience. To be effective, the educational process should meet adults in their life situation and encourage reflection and action. As Groome asserts,

> Assuming that the whole Church teaches and learns together, then, graced by presence of the Holy Spirit, there are three sources of such teaching and learning (or what Raymond Brown calls 'organs of teaching and belief')[18] within the Christian Church. These are the teaching of the official Magisterium, the research of theologians and scripture scholars, and the discernment of the people (which has officially been called the *sensus fidelium*), or the sense of the people.[19]

An educational process, therefore, that encourages a conversation between all three sources of teaching is one that has the potential to be

---

16    The RCIA has a major educational focus within local communities, but as an initiatory rather than ongoing programme, it falls outside the scope of this research.

17    *GCD*, paragraph 256.

18    R. Brown, 'Bishops and Theologians: "Dispute" Surrounded by Fiction', *Origins* 7 (43) (1978), 675.

19    Groome, *Christian Religious Education*, 200.

truly 'developmental' of the life of faith of the Christian. This attitude understands adult education as allowing adults to reflect on and understand their own religious faith, so that they can freely choose to follow the Christian way of life within the Catholic community. An underlying assumption is that participation will be freely chosen. Vatican II affirmed the right of all people to religious freedom, holding that everyone 'has a duty, and therefore a right to seek the truth in matters religious', and 'as the truth is discovered, it is by personal assent that men [and woman] are to adhere to it'.[20] The term 'adult faith development' affirms this freely chosen environment.

The importance of freedom in adult faith development cannot be overestimated. Elizabeth Johnson explains the importance of freedom in the Christian belief system as follows:

> Humanly speaking, a genuine gift is given freely, out of love and not out of necessity; its reception is occasion for gratitude and joy. In the divine freedom to be present to all creatures, empowering them to birth and rebirth in the antagonistic structures of reality, the Spirit is intelligible as the first gift, freely given and giving.[21]

Johnson's summary of the importance of freedom in God's dealing with human beings is a challenge to all educators to educate in a way that it consistent with this ideal, empowering people 'to birth and rebirth in the antagonistic structures of reality'.

There is really no terminology that adequately describes the task of enabling Christian adults to explore their faith in a manner that is appropriate to their status as mature people. However, the discussion here is important because it helps to illustrate the complexity and importance of the task. And the term 'adult faith development' takes into consideration the content and processes consistent with a particular attitude to (or philosophy of) education.

---

20    *Dignitatis Humanae*, Declaration on Religious Liberty, paragraph 3.
21    E. A. Johnson, *She Who Is: The Mystery of God in a Feminist Theological Perspective* (New York: Crossroad, 1992), 143.

# The Role of Content in Adult Faith Development

In keeping with the heritage of Thomas Aquinas, one major focus of this new orientation of the faith development of adults is directed towards religious literacy, to ensure that Catholics have a comprehensive knowledge of the teaching of the Church. As Elias puts it,

> Religions place great emphasis on the truths and values contained in the writing of their traditions. Study of the Bible, commentaries on the Bible, classical writings of theologians, and contemporary efforts to relate religious traditions to present culture and experience form the basis of liberal religious education and are found in adult religious education.[22]

The *General Directory for Catechesis* made the following significant statement:

> Who has encountered Christ desires to know him as much as possible, as well as to know the plan of the Father which he revealed. Knowledge of the faith (*fides quae*) is required by adherence to the faith (*fides qua*). Even in the human order the love which one person has for another causes that person to wish to know the other all the more. Catechesis, must, therefore, lead to 'the gradual grasping of the whole truth about the divine plan', by introducing the disciples of Jesus to a knowledge of Tradition and of Scripture, which is '*the sublime science of Christ*'.[23]

The Catholic Church, from the 1980s onwards, has placed a particularly strong focus on religious orthodoxy: the *Catechism of the Catholic Church* was published in 1994 to counter a perceived lack of understanding of Church teachings. In the introduction, John Paul II declares the *Catechism* to be,

> a statement of the Church's faith and of catholic doctrine, attested to or illumined by Sacred Scripture, the Apostolic Tradition and the Church's Magisterium. I declare it

22    J. L. Elias, *The Foundations and Practice of Adult Religious Education* (Malabar, FL: Krieger, 1993, revised edn), 158.

23    *GCD*, paragraph 85.

to be a sure norm for teaching the faith and thus a valid and legitimate instrument for ecclesial communion.[24]

In the wake of the publication of the *Catechism*, a raft of programmes and written material was produced.[25] As Dolores Leckey writes,

> Laywomen and laymen need to know the current foundational, reliable teachings about their Church, and their role in it. They need to know the documents of the Second Vatican Council, the highest level of teaching authority in the Roman Catholic Church in our time, and to discover therein their rights, their responsibilities, their roles, as articulated in this great ecclesial event of the twentieth century.[26]

Knowledge of the tradition is and will remain of fundamental importance for Catholics, but a relationship with God and service to other human beings is inextricably bound up with this knowing.[27] A life-giving process for the education of adults is essential to impart the knowledge of the Christian tradition. Such a process of learning needs to be linked in a meaningful way to the lived experience of adults and needs to make sense of their lives in dialogue with the tenets of their faith.

24   *CCC*, paragraph 3.
25   The following is a brief list of some of these programmes: *The Companion to the Catechism of the Catholic Church: A Compendium of Texts Referred to in the Catechism of the Catholic Church* (San Francisco: Ignatius Press, 1994); P. Hebblethwaite, *What Are We to Teach? Foundations for Religious Teaching in the Light of the Catechism of the Catholic Church* (London: Bishops' Conference of England and Wales, 1994); K. M. Laughery, *Faith Alive: A Study Companion to the Catechism* (Liguori, MO: Liguori Publications, 1995); W. J. O'Malley, *The People's Catechism: Catholic Faith for Adults* (New York: Crossroad, 1995).
26   D. R. Leckey, *The Laity and Christian Education: Apostolicam Actuositatem, Gravissimum Educationis, Rediscovering Vatican II* (New York: Paulist, 2006), 96.
27   Authors such as Stephen R. Prothero, *Religious Literacy: What Every American Needs to Know – and Doesn't* (San Francisco: Harper, 2007, 1st edn), have explored the area of religious literacy. Determining what is essential for Catholics to know about their faith been a central issue in recent Church documents, with a concern that ignorance of Church teaching impacts on the adherence of Catholics to their faith.

## The Place of Process in the Education of Adults

However, the Church also recognized the importance of process, as well as content, in adult religious education. There is a growing understanding that the culture and experience of people is foundational to a growing adult faith. The 1990 document, *Adult Catechesis in the Christian Community: Some Principles and Guidelines*, states that

> The consciousness of just how complex the world is in which we live requires humility and realism on the part of pastoral workers and leads them to be ever attentive, in the proclamation of the Christian message, to the real conditions in which people live. This sensitivity helps to overcome the distance between Church and society, between faith and culture, which is an important issue in dealing with adults.[28]

This statement signals the move away from a philosophical position that understands education as the transmission of the Church's tradition in an unchanging world to people who are receptacles of this tradition. But it is important to acknowledge that Church documents reflect a number of philosophical or theoretical positions on faith development of adults. However, these documents do, at times, as illustrated by the quotation above, demonstrate elements reflective of a more progressive understanding of the requirements of adult faith development.[29] This progressive philosophy of education is based on the belief that the previous experience of the person plays a key role in their learning.[30] In this view, for education to be fruitful, there is need for

28    International Council for Catechesis, *Adult Catechesis in the Christian Community: Some Principles and Guidelines*, paragraph 3.
29    Progressive adult education 'emphasises such concepts as the relationship between education and society, experiences centred education, vocational education and democratic education'. Elias and Merriam, *Philosophical Foundations of Adult Education*, 10.
30    Pivotal figures in educational developments of the twentieth century, such as John Dewey, *Experience and Education* (New York: MacMillan, 1952); Knowles, *The Modern Practice of Adult Education: From Pedagogy to Andragogy*; and Paolo Freire, *Pedagogy of the Oppressed*, trans. M. Bergam Ramos (London: Penguin, 1972) have all contributed towards a recognition of the way that adults learn.

> Attention to environmental and social factors that shape individual growth ...: a focus
> on human growth through a range of human experiences ...: and attention to the
> possibilities of achieving social and political change though educational processes.[31]

Transformative education can only be capable of changing lives if the learning is integrated in such a way that it engages the imaginations of learners
in their own living environment and social reality. Having the empowerment to critically reflect upon the limitations of such a context can open
up the possibilities for socially and politically changing that environment
for the better of all. This is an important part of the process of evangelization and renewal.

## Evangelization and the Renewal of Humanity

Content and process are two ways that manifest the philosophical orientation in education, but the question of why is primary, and the one that gives
direction to all that happens in the educational arena. The Vatican II document on evangelization, *Evangelii Nuntiandi*, sums up the fundamental
thrust of educational endeavours within the Church as 'bringing the good
news into all the strata of society, and through its influence transforming
humanity from within and making it new'.[32] This broad vision of Church as
the agency for renewing humanity was a long way from the inward-looking
focus of the Catholic Church in the pre-Vatican II era.

The focus on the importance of adults in the Church was a sign of this
new outward-looking vision. *Evangelii Nuntiandi* states, 'for the Church,
the first means of evangelization is the witness of an authentically Christian
Life'. It goes on to say,

> Modern man [*sic*] listens more willingly to witnesses than it does to teachers and if
> he does listen to teachers it is because they are witnesses.[33]

---

31  Elias, *The Foundations and Practice of Adult Religious Education*, 164.
32  *EN*, paragraph 18.
33  *EN*, paragraph 41.

So the Catholic Church is challenging all its members to become people who proclaim the 'Good News' by their lives, and it seeks to resource them for this task by a rounded educational process. For those involved in lay ministry, this challenge is an imperative. Loretta Girzaitis summarizes some of the educational tasks that are necessary if the Church's aim of proclaiming the 'Good News' is to be carried out by adult Catholics. She says that adults need help

> (1) To discover and develop their potential as persons created according to the image of God; (2) to recognise the meaning of life and to respect it in all its dimensions; (3) to incorporate the message of Jesus into one's personal life; (4) to articulate and share the teachings of Jesus with others; (5) to understand and reflect the signs of the times so as to give direction to change in order to shape the future; (6) to provide opportunities for on-going learning at all periods of life; (7) to participate in and celebrate in the Church, the community of believers; (8) to aid committed Christians to serve the needy, the poor, the lonely, the outcast, the discriminated against, and the segregated.[34]

These tasks for the building-up of lay people within the Church largely omit the focus on content noted earlier, and deemed central by the hierarchy for adult faith development. The list demonstrates Girzaitis's own philosophical leaning towards a more humanistic theoretical approach, such as that advanced by the educator Thomas Groome.

## Groome's Shared Praxis Methodology

Thomas Groome has sought to resolve the sometimes opposing positions between focusing on the transmission of content and a more process-orientated education.[35] This methodology is described by Groome:

---

34  L. Girzaitis, *The Church as Reflecting Community: Models of Adult Religious Learning* (West Mystic, CN: Twenty-Third Publications, 1977).

35  T. Groome, 'Shared Praxis: A Possible Theory/Method of Religious Education', in J. Astley and L. Francis (eds), *Critical Perspectives on Christian Education* (Leominister: Gracewing, 1994), 218–237. T. H. Groome, *Sharing Faith: A Comprehensive Approach*

> The praxis way of knowing for Christian religious education ... involves a criti-
> cal reflection within a community context on lived experience. The reflection is
> informed by one's own past and future and by the Story and Vision of the Christian
> community.[36]

'*Praxis*' is a Greek word that has no exact English equivalent. It is used to designate a process designed to 'offset the dichotomy between theory and practice'. Groome's methodology was heavily influenced by Paolo Freire, who highlighted the importance of the education process as either liberating or enslaving the learner. If learners are not encouraged to bring their own life experience and knowledge into the learning situation, then they become passive recipients.

Freire believed that 'education must not allow people to settle for what *is* already, but lead them instead to build a better world'.[37] The importance of education as a liberating activity is fundamental to Freire's thinking, and while he would seem not to have used the phrase 'education is never neutral', it is found in Richard Shaull's foreword to *Pedagogy of the Oppressed*.[38] Freire's concept of education as essentially being about liberation of the mind is one that poses an immense challenge to the official Church. If educated lay people are not simply vessels for the reception of the Church's teaching, but people who will challenge that practice and teaching, then the potential for conflict is obvious.

The concept of education as liberating has enormous implications for Groome. Using insights from Freire and adult education theory, he designed his methodology in a way that enables learners both to participate in their own learning and also to imbibe and respect the tradition within

---

  *to Religious Education and Pastoral Ministry* (San Francisco: Harper, 1991); Groome,
  *Christian Religious Education*.

36   Groome, *Christian Religious Education*, 152.

37   Ibid. 9.

38   Shaull writes, 'There is no such thing as a neutral educational process. Education either
     functions as an instrument which is used to facilitate the integration of the younger
     generation into the logic of the present system and bring about conformity to it, or
     it becomes "the practice of freedom" by which men and women deal creatively with
     reality and discover how to participate in the transformation of the world.' Freire,
     *Pedagogy of the Oppressed*.

which they learn. *Praxis* methodology has strands that are recognizable from several different philosophical educational traditions, from liberal[39] to progressive/humanistic,[40] but is particularly appropriate in adult religious education, as it brings together the concerns of the learner as well as the concerns of the Church for religious literacy.

Groome's *praxis* methodology responds to the 'why' of Christian religious education:

> Religious education activity is a deliberate attending to the transcendent dimension of life by which a conscious relationship to an ultimate ground of being is promoted and enabled to come to expression.[41]

Groome here names the ultimate purpose of religious education, as he understands it, but the definition tends to camouflage his concern for the 'kingdom of God' in the here and now. Christian involvement in the world, as well as concern for the life hereafter, has always been a significant emphasis in Church life, but especially so since Vatican II. In particular, education for justice has become a prominent feature within the Catholic Church in the last forty years. The 1998 *General Directory for Catechesis* makes this point with clarity:

> Jesus, in announcing the Kingdom, proclaims the justice of God: he proclaims God's judgement and our responsibility. The proclamation of this judgement, with its power to form consciences, is a central element in the Gospel, and Good News for the world: for those who suffer the denial of justice and for those who struggle to re-instate it; for those who have known love and existence in solidarity, because penance and forgiveness are possible, since in the cross of Christ we all receive redemption from sin. The call to conversion and belief in the Gospel of the Kingdom – a kingdom of justice, love and peace, and in whose light we shall be judged – is fundamental for catechesis.[42]

---

39    As defined by Elias, 'The emphasis in this theory is upon liberal learning, the organisation of bodies or disciplines of knowledge, and the development of the rational powers of the mind.' Elias, *The Foundations and Practice of Adult Religious Education*, 157.

40    That is, student-centred learning that focuses on a student's own knowledge and experience.

41    Groome, *Christian Religious Education*, 22.

42    *GCD*, paragraph 102.

So the 'why' question of adult faith development needs a response that recognizes that all catechesis is fundamentally directed towards educating people in a way that encourages active involvement in transforming the world, and leads the Church towards a closer approximation of the reign of God.

Pope Francis, since his election in 2013, has again highlighted this demand for 'All Christians, their pastors included, to show concern for the building of a better world'.[43] The Catholic Church in Latin America, from which Francis comes, embraced a transformational approach to faith development which focused on the education of adults.

## Faith Development in the Latin American Church

The faith development of adults was a central focus of the Church in Latin America in the 1970s and 1980s. This focus incorporated what was designated as 'liberation theology', embracing a *praxis* methodology. Robert O'Gorman, who lived and worked in Mexico, has written of his experience and the potential for transformation of the educational process. He highlights a number of important differences between the Latin American experience of adult faith development and the experience of the Church in the west. First, he names the importance of the ultimate aim of adult faith development as the transformation of society and Church rather than a more inward-looking Church-only focus. He writes,[44]

> Its [adult faith development] aim is to evangelise – to recreate society according to the model of the reign of God. Evangelism, in its best meaning, is education for action, public action – the transformation of society.

43   In this quotation, as in others in this work, an ecumenical catechesis is implied.
44   R. T. O'Gorman, 'Latin American Theology and Education', in J. L. Seymour and D. E. Miller (eds), *Theological Approaches to Christian Education* (Nashville: Abingdon, 1990), 208.

A second point that O'Gorman makes in relation to the Latin American experience is the fundamental importance of education in the life of the Church:

> Education is central to the activity of the Church. It is not a by-product or only one of the many Church ministries. The goals and vision of education itself must become the goals and mission of the Church. In other words, education cannot be a program. The Church, at the national level, must deliberately attempt to translate the renewal of the Church and furthermore, contextualise this translation by incorporating the instrumentalities that arise from the people. We must take seriously the declaration 'we are the Church.'

O'Gorman thus firmly places education at the heart of the Church's endeavours. He demonstrates the influence that education can have on transforming the individual Christian, the ecclesial community and wider society. In many ways, O'Gorman articulates a way forward for education in a parish context, because it encapsulates the fundamental features of an education that prepares people for the task of public ministry within the Church and in society. O'Gorman uses the word 'education' for the task of enabling in the development of their faith. The use of 'education' rather than the more traditional 'catechism' suggests a different, more exploratory and adult approach to the task of introducing people to, or developing people in, the faith.

The following description of what is involved in adult faith development is taken from *Serving Life and Faith*, from the United States Bishops' Conference. It highlights the importance of adults becoming more fully human through the educational mission of the Church:

> Adult religious education programmes are intentional learning experiences that deepen, expand and make explicit the learning in faith that is, hopefully, already part of the participative life of the believing community. They are an essential expression of the Church's educational mission that enables adults to become more fully human, more faithful disciples of the Lord Jesus.[45]

---

45    United States Catholic Bishops' Conference, *Serving Life and Faith: Adult Religious Education and the American Catholic Community* (Washington, DC: Dept. of Education, US Catholic Conference, 1986).

The Christian community forms its members in many different ways, such as participation in the liturgy and in the life of the community, and in the example of the members of the community. But it is the 'intentional' efforts of the community to form its members through education that is the present concern.

The local parish is at the heart of much adult faith development in the Catholic Church today, as a grassroots movement led by pastoral assistants and volunteers, as well as by local clergy. A look at the typical Irish parish newsletter illustrates the range of adult education being offered at a local level. Many such programmes are for parents whose children are being prepared for the sacraments, as well as for adults preparing to enter the Church. Many parishes have a variety of small groups who gather for discussion, centred on Bible study or topics of interest to the specific group – bereavement, environment, peace, for example; the list is endless. Some dioceses sponsor programmes of renewal run at local level, which a wide range of people from different cultural and social backgrounds attend, with varying commitments to the life of the Church. All this activity forms part of the fabric of the local parish in the Catholic Church in Ireland today.

For each of these tasks, there is need for leaders and education of such lay leaders in these educational processes is of critical importance. One of the greatest sources of stress for the people chosen to lead such groups is their being open to the different perspectives of the people who attend. Elias stresses the importance of understanding the complexity of human behaviour:

> Though religious faiths provide for their members clear meaning making systems and coherent codes of values, there is much that remains unclear and unresolvable in religious faiths and ethical systems dependent upon them. Religious bodies that attempt to provide simple answers to all problems of meaning and behaviour do an injustice to the complexity of human life and provide false hope for their adherents.[46]

---

46   Elias, *The Foundations and Practice of Adult Religious Education*, 67.

The complexity of the task of bringing adults to a mature understanding leads to the proposal in this thesis that a process such as Groome's shared praxis model is appropriate. This enables adults to examine their faith (or lack of faith) in an environment open to their questions, while recognizing that the presentation of the Church's teaching is vital. The dialogue that ensues is an essential part in the process of maturing faith.

## Psychology and Adult Faith Development

The discipline of psychology provides another layer of insight for the educational task, by uncovering and clarifying some of the major life tasks and changes experienced by adults.[47] These insights can enable educators to understand adults in the group and provide educational experiences that have the potential to enable growth in faith. As Elias states,

> The journey of faith is a dimension of the human journey. Faith development and psychosocial development are not separate and opposed concepts. Also, they are not to be seen as identical. How faith is related to other dimensions of human life is a theological problem to which many solutions have been given. Attempts are made to build syntheses between faith and ordinary human life. A more appealing approach is to see the relationship between the two as a tension-bearing and paradoxical relationship. In this view, faith at times makes demands that go counter to what persons naturally desire. Another way to see the relationship is to see faith as a power that transforms or changes ordinary human life by accepting what is good in

47  The research and theories explored in this section are but a sample of particularly significant areas for the exploration of adult faith development. Other theorists of importance include Jean Piaget, *Science of Education and the Psychology of the Child* (New York: Viking, 1971); Lawrence Kohlberg, *The Psychology of Moral Development: The Nature and Validity of Moral Stages, Essays on Moral Development* (San Francisco: Harper and Row, 1984); Daniel J. Levinson, 'The Human Life Cycle: Eras and Development Periods', in *The Seasons of a Woman's Life* (New York: Ballantine Books, 1996).

it and bringing it to fuller development by adding the dimension of depth and the holy to what is considered to be common and ordinary.[48]

An understanding of these developments in psychology has great potential to enable the educator to design, plan and facilitate adult faith development programmes that are appropriate to the age and stage of the participants. The field of psychology is immense: just one area in developmental psychology is considered here, as illustrative of the potential psychology has to enhance adult faith development within the parish context. The chief proponents of development psychology in the area of faith is James Fowler and those who have built on his theory of faith development.

## James Fowler: Stages of Faith

James Fowler, building on the work of developmental theorists such as Piaget and Kohlberg, and using the analytic tools of constructive developmental theory, devised a theory of faith development. His theory is based on the premise that all people have a meaning-making system which can be characterized as 'faith'.[49] Faith in this sense is an integral set of personal beliefs, values and meanings that give coherence and direction to a person's life, and defines what constitutes 'ultimacy or transcendence for them'.[50]

Faith development is seen by Fowler as a gradual movement from ego-centric faith to self-transcending faith.[51] However, while Fowler is careful to define faith in a general way, his theory resonates with the overtones of

---

48   Elias, *The Foundations and Practice of Adult Religious Education*, 68.
49   Fowler acknowledges the work of Paul Tillich, Reinhold Niebuhr and in particular the thought of William Cantwell Smith as foundational to his understanding of human faith. Fowler, *Stages of Faith*, 9–15.
50   James Fowler, notes given at a seminar in Sydney in 1994.
51   Palmer Parker gives a helpful description of transcendence: 'We must resist the popular tendency to think of transcendence as an upward and outward escape from the realities of self and world. Instead, transcendence is a breaking-in, a literal in-spiration

religious faith, and his 'stages' describe one way of articulating the journey of faith. This project is concerned with the growth in development of adult faith, and so the stages outlined below describe the characteristics of stages three to five, as most adults in the community, according to Fowler, operate predominantly within these stages.

## Synthetic-Conventional Faith: Stage Three[52]

In this stage, believing adult members of a community have already been socialized beyond intuitive-projective faith and mythic literal faith ability to 'take perspective'[53] and so can integrate the stories of the community into a complete whole. There is an emerging need for greater belonging and a growing adherence to the story of the group with whom the person identifies. People are, at this stage, loyal and committed members of their chosen communities, religious or otherwise. Beliefs are acquired without reflection and are taken on an 'all or nothing' basis.[54] From the parish perspective, people in stage three are those most likely to be loyal, committed members who will contribute abundantly to the daily life of the community. However,

---

that allows us to regard ourselves and our world with more trust and hope than ever.' Cited in Fowler, *Stages of Faith*, 13.

52  This section explores only stages three to five of Fowler's theory, as these are the most commonly found in the adult population. Stages one and two (intuitive-projective and mythic-literal faith) are sometimes present in adults, and are a challenge to the adult educator, but beyond the scope of this research.

53  Fowler understands this as 'a proficiency for constructing the perspective of another' (*Stages of Faith*, 72). He uses the work of Selman in defining this concept. See R. L. Selman, 'The Developmental Conceptions of Interpersonal Relations', in *Harvard–Judge Baker Reasoning Project*, vols 1 and 2 (1974).

54  Fowler, *Stages of Faith*, article 3.

One decisive limit of the Synthetic-Conventional stage is its lack of *third-person per-spective taking*. This means that in its dependence upon significant others for confirmation and clarity about its identity and meaning to them, the self does not yet have a transcendental perspective from which it can see and evaluate self-other *relations*.[55]

In a time of rapid change, such as the Irish Catholic Church is experiencing today, faithful Catholics in stage three can find their faith severely tested. For some, the response to the radical discontinuity between what the Catholic Church officially espouses, and the way that authority figures have acted, may result in a rejection of the Church and their religious faith.

It is at this juncture that the value of faith development becomes most critical. Providing a forum that allows people to explore their own faith and their issues with the Church is urgent. Because of Fowler's focus on the *processes* of faith rather than the *content* of faith, learning at this stage can engage people in a personal journey which brings to the fore the contradictions and difficulties of living as a Catholic in the Ireland of today. Fowler himself suggests that educators need to 'avoid trying to provide comprehensive answers for questions [people are] not yet asking'.[56] However, once people do start to question, as many are in the present situation, there is a need to allow people to struggle with the difficult questions without providing them with ready-made answers. At this point, well-designed adult development programmes for lay people can be the setting for positive faith development rather than disillusionment and abandonment of a faith which has been central to people's lives.

Fowler writes that as people begin to doubt the creditability of the authority of groups or individuals they have long relied upon, they can turn to a 'nihilistic despair about a personal principle of ultimate being'.[57] For some, the process of rejecting the authority of the Church and its leaders may lead to adherence to other authorities, while for others there can be a new opening to reliance on one's own authority. This movement to reli-

---

55    J. W. Fowler, *Faithful Change: The Personal and Public Challenges of Postmodern Life* (Nashville: Abdingdon, 1996), 62.
56    J. W. Fowler, 'Faith and the Structuring of Meaning', in *Toward Moral and Religious Maturity*, ed. C. Brusselmans (Morristown NJ: Silver Burdett, 1980), 83.
57    Fowler, *Stages of Faith*, 173.

ance on one's own authority is characterized in developmental theory as 'stage change'.[58] For those in stage three, the transition to stage four can be traumatic, but, as noted above, the provision of structured educational experiences can help people navigate this new stage in their lives.

## Individuative-Reflective Faith: Stage Four

In stage four, there is an emergence of a capacity for self-reflection.[59] Meaning and belief are now chosen out of the many possibilities that have become evident. Self-chosen meaning is possible because of an emerging internalized self-authority.[60] There is a new autonomy which allows for the possibility of choice regardless of external pressures which may demand alternative choices. At this stage, the decision to belong to a group is made from a coherent worldview.

People in parish communities who are in stage four are now choosing to belong in the face of the contradictions within the faith community of which they are part. Parishioners in this stage can be a very important part of the community, since they can offer the critical voice that helps the community deal with the past. They can take on a 'new quality of responsibility' for themselves and others.[61] People in stage four who volunteer for ministry can be a major part of reconstructing a parish as it comes to terms with new realities. They will value education as a part of understanding the Church's history and tradition, but will not assimilate this new knowledge uncritically.

One characteristic of people in stage four can be an over-confidence in their own judgement. They will sometimes lack tolerance,

---

58　J. W. Fowler, *Becoming Adult, Becoming Christian: Adult Development and Christian Faith* (San Francisco: Harper, 1984), 57–8.

59　Fowler, *Stages of Faith*, 174–83.

60　Ibid. 179.

61　Fowler, *Faithful Change*, 63.

especially towards people who are not in their stage of development. For some,

> Disillusionment with one's compromises and recognition that life is more complex than stage four's logic of clear distinctions and abstract concepts can comprehend, press one towards a more dialectical and multileveled approach to life's truth.[62]

In education settings for people in lay ministry, there will be some at stage three and some at stage four, and tensions are an inevitable result. Those in stage four will sometimes be very dismissive of all those in Church authority, while people in stage three are very loyal to authority.[63] Leaders of a group have to be prepared to meet the challenge of these differences.

## Conjunctive Faith: Stage Five (The Inter-Individual Self)

In stage five, there emerges the possibility of embracing the polarities of life and there is, for the first time, recognition of the value of paradox. At stage five, there is an acceptance of the values and beliefs of others, with a true recognition of the possibility of multiple value systems which have their own validity. Fowler says of stage five:

> Conjunctive faith exhibits a combination of committed belief in and through particularities of a tradition, while insisting upon the humility that knows that the grasp of ultimate truth that any of the traditions can offer needs continual correction and

---

62  Fowler, *Stages of Faith*, 183. Kegan, another developmental theorist, suggests that only 3–10 per cent of any given population reach a stage beyond four (Kegan, *In Over Our Heads*, 91–6).

63  Young people in stage three may choose to reject some authorities, for example the authority of parents (which may include loyalty to Church authorities), while giving loyalty to their peers.

challenge. This is to help overcome blind spots (*blind sides*) as well as the tendencies to idolatry (the over identification of our symbolisations of transcending truth with the reality of truth), to which all our traditions are prone.[64]

Such people in Church communities, who continue to belong, can offer the community real leadership, as the tolerance they exhibit is reassuring to people in times of crisis. They themselves are unthreatened by the polarities within the community, and are able to hold the tensions in a way that encourages and reassures people within the community. Members of a community who are in stage five are capable of offering much needed critique to the Church community, without the stridency of those in stage four.

The value to Christian communities of people in stage five of faith development is paramount. If people at this stage are willing and prepared to lead educational processes within the community, they are able to hold together the multiple positions of people in the other stages without undermining participants' faith. In such education, people can be both comforted and challenged in their faith journey. For those who are in volunteer ministry, they can be led to a deeper understanding of the ministry they offer, and consequently become part of the transforming ministry of the Church community. Unfortunately, the number of people who reach this stage are very few.

## Fowler's Stages of Faith in Review

Fowler has another stage in his theoretical framework, which he calls 'universalising faith'.[65] He suggests that those people who are in the stage of conjunctive faith recognize the imperative of making all things new, but they have attachments and commitments that make it difficult to confront the systemic injustice that they recognize within their own communities.

---

64    Fowler, *Becoming Adult, Becoming Christian*, 65.
65    Fowler, *Stages of Faith*, 68.

Because of the inherent contradictions in stage five, Fowler postulates a further stage, which he understands as a moving beyond the

> finite centres of value and power that bid to offer us meaning and security. An identification with or participation in the Ultimate brings a transformation in which we begins to love and value from a centring location in the Ultimate.[66]

This stage is not one that Fowler actually confirmed through his research with people, and he demonstrates its existence through naming people whom he believes exemplify this stage, such as Gandhi, Martin Luther King and Mother Teresa.[67] It is difficult to find connections between this stage and lay volunteer ministers. Fowler's stage theory is a useful tool for developing programmes and for recognizing some of the tensions that emerge in educational gatherings.

Fowler's work is critiqued by a number of people. One of the concerns that arise is his very wide definition of faith to include all faith, not just religious faith. In fact, Fowler did his research primarily with people for whom religious faith was important, so his findings can be substantiated as applicable to people of religious faith. A further critique of Fowler's work is that for Christians who believe that faith is a gift, the idea of faith developing is unacceptable.[68] Fowler himself has made the point that he is theorizing about the structures of faith rather than the content of faith:[69] 'Faith is made up of the processes or operations of human believing, valuing, understanding and relating. These constitute *how* faith is held.'[70]

While, in common with all theories, there are areas in Fowler's work that can be and are critiqued, his 'stages of faith' have proven to be a useful

---

66   Fowler, 'Faith and the Structuring of Meaning', 31.
67   S. D. Parks, 'The North American Critique of James Fowler's Theory of Faith Development', in J. W. Fowler, K. E. Nipkow, and F. Schweitzer (eds), *Stages of Faith and Religious Development* (London: SCM, 1991).
68   See C. Ellis Nelson, 'Does Faith Develop? An Evaluation of Fowler's Position', in J. Astley and L. Francis (eds), *Christian Perspectives on Faith Development: A Reader* (Leominister: Gracewing, 1994).
69   J. W. Fowler, 'Faith and the Structuring of Meaning'.
70   J. Astley, *How Faith Grows: Faith Development and Christian Education* (London: National Society/Church House Publishing, 1991), 6.

tool for adult religious educators. This theory helps to shape educational opportunities in ways that recognize that people's faith evolves and the faith questions in any group vary considerably and need to be addressed with a real sensitivity to the different stages that people are at.

## Conclusion

This chapter has explored some key issues that should inform sound adult faith educational development in the parish context of the Irish Catholic Church. It has argued that theorists such as Groome, Elias and Fowler have much to contribute to understanding how adult faith development can become effective education. Groome's 'shared praxis' approach to adult faith development suggests an educative process that is grounded in both content and theory. Elias identifies the importance of a professional approach to the education of adults. And finally Fowler gives insight into the various stages of faith of people in any parish context and the ways in which this can inform the practice of the educator.

Adult faith development that is transformative needs to be under-pinned by the best theoretical frameworks available, which can form the essential building bricks for sound education practice. The local Church in Ireland is declining in numbers and the age profile is increasing. A small window of opportunity exists to bring new life to parishes and the Catholic Church in Ireland. The author is well aware of the challenges that such a comprehensive faith education programme presents, but the future of the Church depends on such an initiative.

## Bibliography

Aquinas, Saint Thomas, *Summa Theologica*, trans. Fathers of the English Dominican. Province. 3 vols, vol. 2 (New York: Joseph F. Wagner, 1949).

Astley, J., *How Faith Grows: Faith Development and Christian Education* (London: National Society/Church House Publishing, 1991).

Astley, J., *The Philosophy of Christian Religious Education* (Birmingham, AL: Religious Education Press, 1994).

Brookfield, S. D., *Understanding and Facilitating Adult Learning: A Comprehensive Analysis of Principles and Effective Practice* (San Francisco, CA: Jossey-Bass, 1986).

Brown, R., 'Bishops and Theologians: "Dispute" Surrounded by Fiction', *Origins* 7 (43) (1978), 673–82.

*The Companion to the Catechism of the Catholic Church: A Compendium of Texts Referred to in the Catechism of the Catholic Church* (San Francisco, CA: Ignatius Press, 1994).

Congregation for the Clergy, *General Directory for Catechesis* (Dublin: Veritas, 1998).

*Declaration on Christian Education: Gravissimum Educationis*, in A. Flannery (ed.), *Vatican Council II: The Basic Sixteen Documents* (Dublin: Dominican Publications, 1986).

*Declaration on Religious Liberty: Dignitatis Humanae*, in A. Flannery (ed.), *Vatican Council II: The Basic Sixteen Documents* (Dublin: Dominican Publications, 1996).

Elias, J. L., *The Foundations and Practice of Adult Religious Education* (Malabar, FL: Robert E. Krieger Publishing Company, 1993, revised edn).

Elias, J. L., and S. B. Merriam, *Philosophical Foundations of Adult Education* (Malabar, FL: Krieger Publishing Company, 2005, 3rd edn).

Fowler, J. W., *Becoming Adult, Becoming Christian: Adult Development and Christian Faith* (San Francisco, CA: Harper, 1984).

Fowler, J. W., *Faithful Change: The Personal and Public Challenges of Postmodern Life* (Nashville, TN: Abingdon Press, 1996).

Fowler, J. W., 'Faith and the Structuring of Meaning', in C. Brusselmans, J. A. O'Donohoe, J. W. Fowler, and A. Vergote (eds), *Toward Moral and Religious Maturity* (Morristown, NJ: Silver Burdett Co., 1980), 5–42.

Freire, P., *Pedagogy of the Oppressed*, trans. M. B. Ramos (London: Penguin, 1972).

Girzaitis, L., *The Church as Reflecting Community: Models of Adult Religious Learning* (West Mystic, CT: Twenty-Third Press, 1977).

Groome, T. H., *Christian Religious Education: Sharing Our Story and Vision* (San Francisco, CA: Jossey-Bass, 1999, originally published 1980, 2nd edn).

Hanley, Ann, *Faith for Life: Adult Religious Education in Ireland: A Survey*, Council for Research and Development, Irish Bishops' Conference, November 1999.

Groome, T. H., 'Shared Praxis: A Possible Theory/Method of Religious Education', in J. Astley and L. Francis (eds), *Critical Perspectives on Christian Education* (Leominister: Gracewing, 1994), 218–237.

Hebblethwaite, P., *What Are We to Teach? Foundations for Religious Teaching in the Light of the Catechism of the Catholic Church* (London: Bishops' Conference of England and Wales, 1994).

Hirst, P. H., 'Education, Catechesis and the Church School', *British Journal of Religious Education* 3 (3) (1981).

International Council for Catechesis, *Adult Catechesis in the Christian Community: Some Principles and Guidelines, Libreria Editrice Vaticana* (Slough, UK: St Paul Publications, 1990).

Irish Episcopal Conference, *Share the Good News: National Directory for Catechesis in Ireland* (Dublin: Veritas Publications, 2010).

John Paul II, *Catechesi tradendae: Catechesis in Our Time* (Sydney: St Paul's, 1979).

Johnson, E. A., *She Who Is: The Mystery of God in a Feminist Theological Perspective* (New York: Crossroad, 1992).

Kegan, R., *The Evolving Self* (Cambridge, MA: Harvard University Press, 1982).

Kegan, R., *In Over Our Heads: The Mental Demands of Modern Life* (Cambridge, MA: Harvard University Press, 1994).

Knowles, M. Shepherd, *The Modern Practice of Adult Education: From Pedagogy to Andragogy* (New York: Cambridge, 1980, revised and updated edn).

Kohlberg, L., 'The Psychology of Moral Development: The Nature and Validity of Moral Stages', *Essays on Moral Development volume 2* (San Francisco: Harper and Row, 1984, 1st edn).

Laughery, K. M., *Faith Alive: A Study Companion to the Catechism* (St Louis, MO: Liguori Publications, 1995).

Leckey, D. R., *The Laity and Christian Education: Apostolicam actuositatem, gravissimum educationis, Rediscovering Vatican II* (New York: Paulist Press, 2006).

Levinson, D. J., 'The Human Life Cycle: Eras and Development Periods', in *The Seasons of a Woman's Life* (New York: Ballantine Books, 1996).

Nelson, C. E., 'Does Faith Develop? An Evaluation of Fowler's Position', in J. Astley and L. Francis (eds), *Christian Perspectives on Faith Development: A Reader* (Leominister: Gracewing, 1994).

O'Gorman, R. T., 'Latin American Theology and Education', in J. L. Seymour and D. E. Miller (eds), *Theological Approaches to Christian Education* (Nashville, TN: Abingdon, 1990), 195–215.

Parks, S. D., 'The North American Critique of James Fowler's Theory of Faith Development', in J. W. Fowler, K. E. Nipkow, and F. Schweitzer (eds), *Stages of Faith and Religious Development* (London: SCM Press, 1991).

Piaget, J., *Science of Education and the Psychology of the Child* (New York: Viking Press, 1971).

Prothero, S. R., *Religious Literacy: What Every American Needs to Know – and Doesn't* (San Francisco, CA: Harper, 2007, 1st edn).

Sacred Congregation for the Clergy, *General Catechetical Directory* (Sydney: E. J. Dwyer, 1972).

Selman, R. L., 'The Developmental Conceptions of Interpersonal Relations', in *Harvard–Judge Baker Reasoning Project*, vols 1 and 2 (1974).

Silberman, C. E., *Crisis in the Classroom: The Remaking of American Education* (New York: Random House, 1970).

United States Catholic Conference, *Serving Life and Faith: Adult Religious Education and the American Catholic Community* (Washington, DC: Department of Education, US Catholic Conference, 1986).

# Notes on Contributors

CATHERINE BREATHNACH was the director of the innovative Adult Learning BA for Personal and Professional Development at All Hallows College, Dublin between 2014 and 2017. Previous roles included research fellow at the Centre for Nonprofit Management at the School of Business, Trinity College Dublin and director of Alumni development at University College Dublin. She has also worked in various capacities with the Department of Adult and Community Education and the Centre for Teaching and Learning at Maynooth University, RTE and the National Youth Council of Ireland. She was awarded a PhD by the National College of Ireland/HETAC. She holds a Master of Business Studies awarded by the Graduate School of Business UCD, and an MA in Adult and Community Education awarded by Maynooth University. Her primary degree was undertaken at UCD where she studied History and Politics. Her areas of research interest include adult and organizational learning, and the non-profit sector.

EUGENE CURRAN is a Vincentian priest and served in All Hallows College in a number of capacities. Born in Dublin in 1961, he has spent most of his ministry in education. His doctoral studies were in CTU Chicago and focused on developments in adult education and faith formation, drawing on the work of Bernard Lonergan and Maria Montessori. He started as a teacher of English and French in Dublin and moved from there to London. In All Hallows, he was head of the School of Adult and Community Learning and one of the team that introduced the ALBA programme; the BA for Personal and Professional Development (of which he is especially proud).

GRÁINNE DOHERTY is currently completing her doctoral studies at Roehampton University, London, while also working in pastoral development. Until its closure, she was a staff member of the Theology Department in All Hallows College, Dublin, lecturing there for fourteen years. Her special areas of research and teaching include feminist theology, sexuality and gender ethics, theologies and ethics of justice, leadership and power (primarily Catholic social teaching) and theology of ecology.

MARJORIE FITZPATRICK is a sociologist, living in Dublin. She was a member of the staff at All Hallows College, Dublin, since 1993 as lecturer and mentor of Research Methodology. She has qualifications in teaching at post-primary and third level: English, religion, theology, catechetics, human resource management and adult religious education. She is also a trained classical singer and member of choral societies. Dr Fitzpatrick received her PhD with specializations in the sociology of music and Eliasian sociology from University College Dublin (NUI). She has been engaged in research over several decades at university level. She was Director of Quality and Institutional Memory in All Hallows College.

THOMAS G. GRENHAM is currently Assistant Professor of Religious Education and Practical Theology in the School of Human Development, DCU Institute of Education, Dublin City University. He was formerly the Director of Undergraduate Programmes and Head of Theology at All Hallows College, Dublin City University, Dublin, Associate Dean for student affairs and head of the Department of Pastoral Theology at the Milltown Institute of Philosophy and Theology, Dublin, and a lecturer in Religious Education at Mary Immaculate College, Limerick. He served as a missionary for many years among the Turkana of Kenya (1985–95). He received a master's degree in pastoral ministry and an interdisciplinary PhD in religion and education from Boston College, Massachusetts, USA. His publications include *The Unknown God: Religious and Theological Interculturation* (2005), *Pastoral Ministry for Today: 'Who Do You Say That I Am?', Conference Papers 2008* (ed. 2009) and *New Educational Horizons in Contemporary Ireland: Trends and Challenges* (ed., with Patricia Kieran, 2012).

EILEEN HOULAHAN is a Holy Faith Sister. After sixteen years both in teaching and administration at primary-school level, Eileen trained as a spiritual director at the Jesuit Centre of Spirituality, Dublin, and completed further studies and an MA in spirituality at the Milltown Institute of Theology and Philosophy, a postgraduate certificate in spirituality at Boston College and a PhD in All Hallows College. She is involved in the ministry of spiritual direction and has worked for many years as a lecturer and as a director for both fulltime and part-time programmes in theology and spirituality at third level. She is currently the director and a presenter on the Pathways Adult Faith Programme for the Dublin Archdiocese in Clonliffe College. Her research interests are the implications of and the need for adult faith development for the future of the Catholic Church in Ireland.

SHEENA HYLAND is currently Assistant Professor of Teaching and Learning at the National College of Ireland, Dublin. She was formerly Assistant Professor of Educational Development at University College Dublin. For over ten years, she was a lecturer in philosophy at All Hallows College, where she was also Director of Teaching and Learning. She holds a PhD in philosophy from University College Dublin. Her current research focuses on issues in teaching and learning in higher education.

MARY IVERS was Director of Postgraduate Research and Head of the Department of Psychology at All Hallows College. A chartered health psychologist and professional personal coach, she has over eighteen years' experience teaching and supervising undergraduate and postgraduate students. She lectures in Health Psychology and Research Methods and is currently Research Laboratory Manager with the School of Psychology in UCD Dublin. Outside of academia she has a private personal coaching practice. Her key research and practice interests focus on marginalization, cancer survivorship, education and the development of agentic thinking.

GARY KEOGH is a lecturer in religions and theology at the University of Manchester and lead tutor in theology at Hibernia College, Dublin. He is the author of *Reading Richard Dawkins* (Fortress, 2014) and *The Evolution of Hope* (Peeters, 2015). He also writes and contributes regularly to media discussions on topics pertaining to education, religion and ethics for RTÉ radio and *The Journal.ie*.

CORA LAMBERT holds an MA in Holistic Development for Pastoral Ministry. She was Director of Community-Based Service Learning in All Hallows College. Her areas of academic interest include leadership, learning service learning and civic engagement.

SIOBHÁN LARKIN has been in involved in adult religious education for the past thirty years and has a particular interest in the patterns of faith development in adults. She holds a doctorate in ministry studies and a master's degree in ministry from the University of Divinity, Melbourne, and a master's degree in education from Boston College.

ANNE LOONEY has recently taken up the post of Executive Dean of Dublin City University's new Institute of Education. From 2001 until 2016 she was the CEO of the National Council for Curriculum and Assessment, the agency responsible for curriculum and assessment for early years, primary and post-primary education in Ireland. She held the position of interim CEO at the Higher Education Authority until March of this year. A former teacher, she completed her doctoral studies at the Institute of Education in University College London. In 2014/15, she was Professorial Research Fellow at the Learning Science Institute Australia, based at the Australian Catholic University in Brisbane. Her current research interests include assessment policy and practice, curriculum, teacher identity and professional standards for teachers and teaching. She has also published on religious, moral and civic education, and education policy. She has conducted reviews for the OECD on school quality and assessment systems. She is a member of the boards of Early Childhood Ireland, and the Ark Cultural Centre for Children. She tweets at @ annelooney.

DEE MCKIERNAN is a registered counselling psychologist (Reg. Psychol., PsSI) and clinical supervisor with the Psychological Society of Ireland. She runs a private practice in Oscailt Integrative Health Centre, Dublin 4, and lectures in TCD, DCU and UCD on various psychological topics. Research interests include psychological distress, chronic illness, psycho-oncology, clinical supervision and mindfulness-based interventions.

CIARÁN Ó MATHÚNA is the co-ordinator of the Professional Diploma in Education (Further Education) at Marino Institute of Education, Dublin, where he also lectures on the BSc in Education Studies, along with delivering and co-ordinating undergraduate research on the Bachelor of Education course. With particular interest in adult and further education, narrative research, adult learning, transformative education, and research methodologies, Ciarán has presented research papers at many conferences, including at UCD, Queen's University, Trinity College, Mater Dei, St Patrick's College, Dublin, Sligo IT and Limerick Education Centre. Ciarán's professional background is as a co-ordinator of adult and further education, having worked within the VEC/ETB, voluntary and private sector. Ciarán completed a master's degree in management in 2007. In 2008, Ciarán began his PhD research, which he completed in 2013. The focus of his research was on the transformative learning experiences of adult learners in higher education, for which he received the academic excellence award from All Hallows College. Ciarán is a member of the Further Education and Training Forum, representing Marino Institute of Education. He is also a member of the Institute of Guidance Counsellors of Ireland and the British Psychological Society.

ANDREW O'REGAN has over twenty-five years' experience of working, researching, teaching and governance in third-sector and non-profit organizations in Ireland. His research interests include non-profit management, civil society and voluntary action, and the relationship between individual identity and voluntary action. He was one of the establishing directors of the Centre for Non-Profit Management at the School of Business, Trinity College Dublin, and has lectured there, at All Hallows College, and at the Institute of Public Administration. With teaching interests in the areas of qualitative research methodologies, third-sector studies, leadership in organizations, and business and society, he has substantial experience of programme development in higher education. He has conducted research and consultancy for a range of Irish public and non-profit agencies and has served on public and private boards and policy committees. He received his PhD from the University of Dublin, Trinity College, for a dissertation on agency and the voluntary actor. He was Dean of Academic Affairs at All Hallows College, Dublin.

DENIS ROBINSON is a Spiritan priest and is currently the director of the Centre for Religious Education, director of the MA in Christian Leadership in Education, and director of the Adult Education Certificate in Spirituality and Human Development at Marino Institute of Education, Dublin. He lectures in the areas of prayer, the spirituality of leadership, school ethos and values, pastoral care, mystical theology, Christian anthropology, postmodern spirituality, and faith development and Christian praxis.

# Index